T0210862

Free Software, the Internet, and Global Communities of Resistance

This book explores software's pivotal role as the code that powers computers, mobile devices, the Internet, and social media. Creating conditions for the ongoing development and use of software, including the Internet as a communications infrastructure, is one of the most compelling issues of our time. Free software is based upon open-source code, developed in peer communities as well as corporate settings, challenging the dominance of proprietary software firms and promoting the digital commons. Drawing upon key cases and interviews with free software proponents based in Europe, Brazil, and the U.S., the book explores pathways toward creating the digital commons and examines contemporary political struggles over free software, privacy, and civil liberties on the Internet that are vital for the commons' continued development.

Sara Schoonmaker is Professor of Sociology at the University of Redlands, USA.

Routledge Studies in New Media and Cyberculture

For a full list of titles in this series, please visit www.routledge.com

Free Software, the Internet, and Global Communities of Resistance

Sara Schoonmaker

Routledge
Taylor & Francis Group

LONDON AND NEW YORK

First published 2018
by Routledge

2 Park Square, Milton Park, Abingdon, Oxfordshire OX14 4RN
52 Vanderbilt Avenue, New York, NY 10017

*Routledge is an imprint of the Taylor & Francis Group, an
informa business*

First issued in paperback 2019

Copyright © 2018 Taylor & Francis

The right of Sara Schoonmaker to be identified as author of this
work has been asserted by her in accordance with sections
77 and 78 of the Copyright, Designs and Patents Act 1988.

All rights reserved. No part of this book may be reprinted
or reproduced or utilised in any form or by any electronic,
mechanical, or other means, now known or hereafter invented,
including photocopying and recording, or in any information
storage or retrieval system, without permission in writing from
the publishers.

Notice:
Product or corporate names may be trademarks or registered
trademarks, and are used only for identification and explanation
without intent to infringe.

Library of Congress Cataloging-in-Publication Data
CIP data has been applied for.

ISBN: 978-1-138-94298-1 (hbk)
ISBN: 978-0-367-87464-3 (pbk)

Typeset in Sabon
by codeMantra

To Hazel, Susan, Avery – mother, sister, daughter

Contents

Acknowledgments

Writing this book has been a journey into the social worlds of diverse international communities. In many ways, the fieldwork for this project mirrored the communities themselves. I benefitted from the web of connections between community participants around the world, and from their generous ethic of sharing information, time, and work. I greatly appreciate all of the free software and net neutrality participants who shared their ideas and experiences with me, as well as their openness to putting me in touch with others in their communities that they thought could contribute to the project. Faculty Research Grants from the University of Redlands provided funds to support the research. The reviewers at Routledge offered invaluable feedback that allowed me to improve the manuscript.

Since I began the research for this project in 2006, many people have provided insights and support that helped me to develop the work. My colleagues and friends in the Sociology and Anthropology department and the Johnston Center for Integrative Studies at the University of Redlands provided fertile ground to push intellectual boundaries and develop my thinking. I benefitted from discussing draft chapters of the book with the perceptive students in my Spring 2017 Johnston seminar, that began as Consume the Local/Hack the Global and metamorphosed into Sustainable Alternatives to Capitalism. Choice interventions and camaraderie came from Victoria Bernal, Janet Boguslaw, Jon Cruz, Tess Cruz, Karen Derris, Lorenzo Garbo, Pierre-Amiel Giraud, Avery Gordon, Dorene Isenberg, Padma Kaimal, Sawa Kurotani, Sharon Lang, Penny McElroy, Jennifer Nelson, Laura Robinson, Bill Rocque, Andy Rotter, Christiana Soares de Freitas, Pat Wasielewski, and Tekle Woldemikael. During the final stretch of the writing process, Franco Gasperoni challenged me to rearticulate the transformative significance of free software as a new form of property.

At pivotal times and places, strategic emotional backing came from Jon Arellano-Jackson, Chris Beach, Porsha Beed, Steve Bromer, Krista Comer, Sanjay Carter-Rau, Nick Fisher, Barbie and Loring Fiske-Phillips, Debbie Gardner, Kaye Gates, Marilyn Golden, Sharon Graff, Lynn Hanna, Jim Hood, Aaron Johnson, Jill Kirchner-Rose, Nancy Lemon,

Barb Lord, Leela MadhavaRau, Heidi Malone, Joy Manesiotis, Andrés Mares-Muro, Ann Morrill, Milton Ospina, Jen Ramos, Karen Rose, Renée Rosen-Rager, Peter Schoonmaker, Casandra Smith, Caley Soury, Denise Spencer, Nick Swensen, Georgia and Rick Sforza, Sara Beth Terrell, and Gavin and Tricia Thrasher.

All along the way, my daughter Avery showered me with love and helped me to find clarity with her incisive artist's sensibility. Susan Schoonmaker extended sisterly solidarity and fond companionship, which was especially dear after the deaths of our parents, Ted and Hazel Schoonmaker. Ted and Hazel's loving commitment to community and justice are with me always and helped me to recognize the profound significance of building the commons. The progressive community at Redlands United Church of Christ was a continuing source of support, music, and welcome. My extended Osajima, Schoonmaker, and chosen families provided gatherings full of delightful food, chaos, and connection. My life partner and in-house editor, Keith Osajima, offered his brilliant mind, generous spirit, abiding love, and sense of adventure. Thanks, as always, for helping me to mix work so thoroughly with pleasure.

1 Hiding in Plain Sight

Software, Surveillance, and Capitalism in Everyday Life

Wherever you are in your daily travels, pause and take a look around. Even if you are trekking Africa's highest mountain, summiting Mount Kilimanjaro, it is likely that software is hiding in plain sight. You are probably equipped with state-of-the-art hiking gear, including a handheld Global Positioning System (GPS) unit that receives information from satellites and atomic clocks to find the location of the device and display it on a map. Your device locks onto several satellites, which can locate anyone on earth. It stores and locates waypoints to help you navigate the trail, or find your way back to camp. Your GPS unit offers a range of data, from maps to coordinates of elevation; latitude and longitude; temperature; distances and elevation; barometric pressure; sunrise, sunset, moonrise, and moonset; and logs of trip data for up to 48 hours. It allows you to send messages to similar devices, facilitating contact with other hikers if you get separated. At the end of the day, you may use the device for entertainment, playing geolocation games such as geocaching.

For those of us with more mundane pursuits, software is embedded in myriad activities. We are usually in range of cell phone towers emitting signals that smartphones can access. Indeed, for most of us, our smartphones are comparable to the hikers' handheld GPS systems. The phones themselves, as well as most of the apps, have GPS tracking to monitor where we are. They provide us with information about restaurants, ATM machines, gas stations, cultural attractions, and other sites along our path. Significantly, however, these phones simultaneously collect data about us. They collect data on where we go, what we spend our money on, what we look up on the Internet, the music we listen to, the people we text or email, and more. For users of social media, they document our posts, our photos, our likes, and other reactions to events and people. While hikers use handheld GPS devices to plot treks, consumers in towns and cities use smartphones to navigate our lives.

Wearable digital technologies such as smart watches and activity or fitness trackers collect data about our health and activity. These data document the number of steps we walk or run, our heart rate, sleep patterns, the steps we climb, and the calories we consume. Consumers employing such devices actively collect data about our physical activity, syncing the devices to our computers or smartphones to track long-term trends in our health metric data. In the process, Turkle (2015) views these consumers as developing an algorithmic or quantified self, treating bodies as computational objects, as sources of data. She urges us to reflect on the kinds of authority we give such technologies to shape our views of ourselves, our bodies, and our minds. For example, when we as consumers use such technologies, we may develop habitual ways of thinking about ourselves in terms of quantifiable units and achievements that can be scored. Such a process of quantifiable scoring implies that we can understand ourselves in those terms, tracking our progress over time.

Software is hiding in plain sight in cars. In 1977, General Motors (GM) introduced the first embedded software into its Oldsmobile Toronado model. By 1981, GM had integrated about 50,000 lines of software code to facilitate engine control in its diverse range of domestic passenger car models. It started a trend for other car manufacturers to follow. Since about 2000, software has powered new developments in cars, so that even basic models of cars include dozens of microprocessors and microcontrollers. Higher-end cars run on millions of lines of software code that monitor and control systems ranging from airbags to power trains (Madden 2015; Walls 2016).

Software is increasingly integrated into many objects in our homes, from microwaves to televisions, thermostats, "smart" toys, printers, and fax machines. Samsung markets the Family Hub smart refrigerator as a center of family life, allowing consumers to organize calendars, food shopping, watching movies, and listening to music. While such refrigerators are currently limited to the high end of the market, over the next decade, software will increasingly be integrated into a broader range of refrigerator models.

Smart speakers, or digital assistants, like Google Home and the Amazon Echo allow consumers to set alarms, stream music, podcasts, or audiobooks and access data on weather, traffic, and more. Amazon made the Echo widely available in the U.S. in 2015, expanding to Canada and the United Kingdom in 2016. The Echo can serve as a home automation hub, controlling several smart devices using the Alexa voice-controlled intelligent personal assistant service. Similar to the iPhone's Siri assistant, Microsoft's Cortana, and the "OK Google" voice recognition feature, the Echo is designed to respond to voice commands.

The prevalence of software in the above range of devices poses questions about privacy and surveillance. For example, since the Amazon Echo is continually listening and often recording, privacy advocates warn that it is vulnerable to surveillance. A company like Amazon could retain data recorded by all Echo users and potentially make that data available to other corporations or to government agencies such as law enforcement. Moreover, it is possible to gain remote access to a device like Echo to listen to private conversations. Similar to privacy concerns related to webcams on laptops, such devices are vulnerable to remote recording by criminals or domestic surveillance by government intelligence agencies.

Such privacy concerns arose in 2017, when Mattel began marketing Aristotle, a voice-activated baby monitor that serves as a digital nanny. Mattel provided information about the product for an online article in *CISION PR Newswire* (2017), describing Aristotle as "designed with a specific purpose and mission: to aid parents and use the most advanced AI [Artificial Intelligence]-driven technology to make it easier for them to protect, develop, and nurture the most important asset in their home – their children." Mattel developed the Aristotle platform by partnering with Microsoft to create an Artificial Intelligence (AI) system geared toward babies, as well as older children. The AI system integrates Microsoft Cognitive Services, as well as search capabilities through the Bing search engine. Aristotle includes a hub with a smart light system, including lights for reading and diaper changing, as well as a night light. Moreover, Aristotle includes multiple color lights "specifically designed as a dynamic feedback system tied to the AI" (*CISION PR Newswire* 2017). To develop this AI hub, Mattel partnered with Qualcomm Technologies. The corporate designers integrated a Wi-Fi camera with object recognition, so that Aristotle can turn on a lullaby and adjust the room's lighting if a baby starts to cry. These designers included features for toddlers and older children, so that Aristotle's lights turn color during interactive sessions. In these sessions, Aristotle asks the child questions; if the child answers correctly, the lights turn green. From Mattel's perspective, "Aristotle is designed to comfort, entertain, teach, and assist during each developmental state – evolving with a child as their needs change from infancy to adolescence" (*CISION PR Newswire* 2017).

Consumer advocacy groups such as the Campaign for a Commercial-Free Childhood (CCFC) (2017) critiqued the Aristotle platform as engaging in surveillance. They viewed the device as a potential threat to privacy, since it could collect and store data about children's activities. Since Aristotle is linked to other applications and online retailers, that data can be shared with corporations and used for targeted advertising to children and their families.

Indeed, from Aristotle to the Echo, from smartphones to cars, televisions, and numerous "smart" objects in our lives, software is hiding in plain sight. Its pervasive presence raises questions about who controls that software, as well as the massive amounts of data it is used to collect about us. Edward Snowden (2016) argues that many consumers are concerned about whether their devices are secure from potential intrusions on their privacy. At the same time, however, they may not consider potential problems with control over those devices. For example, iPhones are known for their reliability and security. Consumers may use them with a sense of confidence that Apple will protect their privacy and provide a reliable, secure device. Despite this security, however, Apple routinely pushes software updates that change the configuration of the phones. Snowden (2016) challenges us to consider whether a device is truly secure when we do not know what it is doing. If we lack the knowledge to understand how it is configured, or the option to make choices about that configuration, we lack control over it. We simply consume the device as a "black box," trusting the corporation to set it up for us.

Software thus raises questions about knowledge, power, and control. Many of those questions are linked to surveillance, since software enables the collection of data about our activities, our health, and our relationships. These data are vulnerable to surveillance, posing potential threats to civil liberties such as the right to privacy. Moreover, these data can be accessed by corporations to target us with advertising. Such data are central to marketing and profit-making in contemporary capitalism. As Columbia University law professor and privacy advocate Eben Moglen (2011) argues,

> Software is what the 21st century is made of. What steel was to the economy of the 20th century, what steel was to the power of the 20th century, what steel was to the politics of the 20th century, software is now. It is the crucial building block, the component out of which everything else is made, and, when I speak of everything else, I mean of course freedom, as well as tyranny, as well as business as usual, as well as spying on everybody for free all the time.

To understand the significance of software's pervasive presence in everyday life, we thus need to analyze software as central to processes of production, marketing, and other aspects of social, cultural, and political life in contemporary capitalism. As software hides in plain sight, processes of surveillance and capitalist production are even more deeply hidden. Exploring the connections between software, surveillance, and capitalism is key to grasping contemporary relations of power, as well as strategies for resistance and transformation.

Informational Capitalism and Globalization

Contemporary examples of the ubiquity of software in daily life are an acceleration and intensification of the dynamics of capitalist development that scholars have analyzed for many years. We can understand the current significance of software more fully when we place it in the context of these historical dynamics. World systems theorists chronicle the development of capitalism over a span of 500 years, through cycles of expansion of world trade and production, as well as crises of overaccumulation and competition (Wallerstein 1974, 1999; Arrighi 1999). Marx and Engels highlight the nature of capitalism as a global system, where the process of colonial expansion laid the foundation for the development of a world market. In the *Communist Manifesto,* they argue that

> The market has given an immense development to commerce, to navigation, to communication by land. This development has, in its turn, reacted on the extension of industry; and in proportion as industry, commerce, navigation, railways extended, in the same proportion the bourgeoisie developed, increased its capital, and pushed into the background every class handed down from the Middle Ages.
> (Accessed June 1, 2017, www.marxists.org/archive/marx/ works/1848/communist-manifesto/ch01.htm#007)

Capitalism is fraught with contradictions, rooted in the dynamics of the profit motive that push capital to constantly seek new markets and ways to exploit human and natural resources.

Communications and transport played a key role in facilitating capitalism's historical development as a global system. Since the mid-nineteenth century, capitalist enterprises operating in different parts of the world exchanged information through communications systems, from the telegraph to the telephone and eventually the Internet (Hirst and Thompson 1999). As Murdock (2014, 138) argues, "[c]apitalism has always relied on advanced communications systems to track, collate, and co-ordinate the dispersed production and consumption activities it sets in motion." In the chapter on capital in the *Grundrisse Notebook V,* Marx (1973) discusses how communications and transportation systems facilitate processes of capital circulation and play a key role in capitalism's global dynamic. He argues that

> while capital must on one side strive to tear down every spatial barrier to intercourse, and conquer the whole earth for its market, it strives on the other side to annihilate this space with time, i.e. to reduce to a minimum the time spent in motion from one place to another.
>
> (Marx 1973, 539)

This dynamic accelerates as capital develops on a global scale. According to Marx, as capital increasingly expands into the international market, "which forms the spatial orbit of its circulation, the more does it strive simultaneously for an even greater extension of the market and for greater annihilation of space by time" (Marx 1973, 539).

Capital thus pursues the construction of communications and transportation systems to create the conditions for commodities to circulate on the market. Building upon this analysis, we can understand struggles by corporations to annihilate space with time by promoting state-of-the-art means to communicate about their operations, as well as to transport commodities. Such innovations facilitate what Harvey (1999, 118) calls "successive waves of time-space compression." The importance of communications and transportation thus extends from early sea routes and highways to contemporary struggles to establish the political conditions to access the Internet.

Indeed, since the 1970s, the convergence of telecommunications and computing made digital technologies increasingly central to economic, political, social, and cultural life. This convergence eventually made it possible for the Internet to become a vehicle for both communications and the transport of digital commodities, as consumers downloaded music and other products and services in digital form (Schoonmaker 1993, 1994, 2002). Corporations, governments, producers, and consumers rely on access to electronic information to conduct their major activities. To grasp this increasing centrality of information to capitalism on a global scale, Castells (1996) refers to it as global informational capitalism. Fuchs (2016, 2) highlights informational capitalism as one of capitalism's multiple dimensions, arguing that "[c]ontemporary capitalism is an informational capitalism just like it is a finance capitalism, imperialist capitalism, crisis capitalism, hyper-industrial capitalism (the importance of fossil fuels and the mobility industries), etc." Fuchs (2014) notes that information technologies, science, theoretical knowledge, and knowledge labor constitute key productive forces of informational capitalism. As Sassen (2005, 54) argues, information superhighways bring "higher levels of control and concentration in the global market."

Informational capitalism is thus one of capitalism's multiple dimensions. It is constructed through processes of struggle, within the broader context of neoliberal globalization as the current dominant form of capitalism. As Fuchs (2014, 44) argues, neoliberalism is a "mode of existence" or "regime" of global capitalism. Since the U.S. government has strongly promoted this neoliberal regime, it is also known as the "Washington Consensus" (Langman 2012). Harvey (2005, 2) traces the rise of neoliberalism since the late 1970s, as a system "characterized by strong private property rights, free markets, and free trade." Neoliberal globalization, or what McMichael (2000, 2017) calls the globalization project, thus has a number of key characteristics. Economically, interests of transnational corporations take priority over those of smaller, local firms. Politically, trade agreements or other legal conditions often support the proprietary interests of transnational firms or governments in the global North rather than small producers or grassroots groups, particularly in the global South. Culturally, values of sharing and community access tend to be subordinated to values prioritizing high levels of commodity consumption.

Equally important, neoliberalism is constructed through discourse, or narratives of power and knowledge. Building on Foucault (1978), I employ a poststructuralist perspective that power and knowledge are inextricably linked through discourse. In discourse, social actors draw upon cultural values and language that resonate with particular ways of understanding the social world. Through discourse, they articulate their positions on the key issues at stake (Foucault 1978; Escobar 1995; Schoonmaker 2002). For example, the discourse of neoliberalism is rooted in the assumption that free trade is the most rational approach to structuring global markets, largely because it protects the proprietary interests of corporations in maximizing their profits. Proponents of this discourse depict any state attempts to regulate markets through protections for local industries, workers, or environmental health as barriers to trade that undermine global economic growth. Over the years, such proponents have included the World Bank, the International Monetary Fund, and U.S. presidents such as Ronald Reagan, George H.W. Bush, Bill Clinton, George W. Bush, and Barack Obama. Support for the neoliberal discourse is sometimes partial and complicated; such was the case with President Obama's advocacy for the neoliberal Trans-Pacific Partnership (TPP) global trade agreement and simultaneous support for some protections for the environment and local industry.

Escobar (1995) highlights the importance of understanding the economy as a discourse imbued with cultural values and meanings. People both respond to and are shaped by these cultural meanings as they participate in processes of socialization and enculturation. Escobar (1995) thus views the economy as a cultural production, through which we become particular kinds of people who value practices like economic productivity and success, as well as engaging in those practices through work and consumption. A poststructuralist perspective thus allows us to understand economic and political structures as constructed through discourse as forms of knowledge and understanding, as well as through material practices. In the next chapter, I discuss the key role of the proprietary, freedom, and sovereignty discourses in the development of the digital commons. Indeed, the proprietary discourse is closely linked to the neoliberal discourse, since both are rooted in values of protecting corporate proprietary interests by boosting profits and expanding into new markets.

Global Communities of Resistance

Due to their centrality to informational capitalism and neoliberal globalization, software and the Internet have become key terrains of struggle over the past decades. Free software and net neutrality advocates work simultaneously to create alternatives to informational capitalism and neoliberal globalization. They forge alternatives rooted in the freedom to share and collaborate, as well as respect for sovereignty and civil liberties like the rights to free speech and privacy. Like other projects seeking to develop alternative forms of globalization from below, they mobilize participants to resist neoliberal globalization (Della Porto, Andretta, and Mosca 2006; Langman 2012). In the process, free software and net neutrality advocates develop communities that involve what Sassen (2005, 54) calls "distributive outcomes – greater participation of local organizations in global networks."

These communities resonate with Portes' (2000, 254) conception of globalization from below, where common people respond to neoliberalism by "creat[ing] communities that sit astride political borders and that, in a very real sense, are 'neither here nor there' but in both places simultaneously." While some movements promoting globalization from below focus on environmental justice, or the rights of the poor, workers, women, immigrants, or indigenous people, free software and net neutrality advocates struggle to promote the development of free software and conditions for equal access to the Internet. They thus focus on questions central to informational capitalism.

Portes (2000) highlights the power of such diverse transnational efforts to develop alternative forms of globalization from below. He argues that

> [m]ultinational elites and national governments may believe that the process of transnationalization is still too feeble to pose any significant challenge to the status quo. In reality, the tiger may have already left the cage, and there would be little point in closing it after him.
>
> (Portes 2000, 266)

Throughout this book, I explore a range of ways that free software and net neutrality communities engage in local actions linked to global projects, thus developing alternative forms of globalization from below. They are examples of "tigers" that have created global communities of resistance. These communities challenge neoliberalism and informational capitalism with vibrant forms of peer-produced software, free culture, and other contributions to the digital commons. Like other projects seeking to develop alternative forms of globalization from below, they mobilize participants to "redress their grievances and foster more democratic, participatory, humanistic, egalitarian, ecologically sound alternatives" to neoliberalism (Langman 2012, 865).

The Argument

In the following pages, I examine the ways that global free software and net neutrality communities of resistance challenge neoliberalism and informational capitalism. These challenges are rooted in a common goal of developing a digital commons, where all participants can access, use, modify, and share software and the Internet. In the next chapter, I highlight the meaning and significance of the commons, as well as the methods used in this study. I analyze the development of the digital commons, based on two sets of struggles. First, free software advocates in the U.S. created free software as an alternative form of property distinct from private property. Second, researchers in Brazil advocated opening up access to emerging global computer networks. These two groups did not know each other or coordinate their activities; however, they laid the foundations for the development of the digital commons. Indeed, the digital commons are based upon free software and an open, decentralized Internet. Proponents of the digital commons continued to develop it after 2001, by forming Creative Commons and Wikipedia.

As participants in diverse free software projects collaborate to produce the software, they develop global communities. In Chapter 3, I analyze the possibilities and challenges involved with developing free software communities by comparing the Debian and Drupal projects. Both projects involve participants from around the world who coordinate their work over the Internet. They engage in myriad activities, from coding the software itself to writing documentation and translating programs into different languages to make them accessible to wider groups of people. Both projects involve a mix of forms of software production, combining work by unpaid peer producers with work by paid developers. The key difference between the projects is the nature of the software that they produce. Debian software allows developers to include proprietary elements that restrict users' freedoms. Drupal software is free software, contributing to the digital commons by allowing users freedom to access, modify, and share the software without restrictions. Moreover, Drupal project participants made conscious efforts to expand their project beyond North America and Europe into the global South. In the process, they forged a global community that implicitly resisted neoliberalism and informational capitalism. They did not explicitly organize political resistance; however, by building free software and extending their global community, they created an alternative form of globalization from below.

Free software communities thus play key roles in developing the digital commons. In Chapter 4, I explore the ways that communities work to organize themselves to protect the freedoms of their participants. I focus on the case of LibreOffice and The Document Foundation, whose participants created the project by splitting off from the OpenOffice. org community. They were concerned about increasing corporate influence over OpenOffice.org that could undermine the freedom to access, modify, and share the software. They created an innovative new organizational structure to support these freedoms and to work for values of digital inclusion central to the digital commons. In the process, they also constituted an implicit global community of resistance to neoliberalism.

Free software itself, as well as the community organizations required to produce it, thus contribute to developing the digital commons. Because software is central to production in informational capitalism, however, conditions for software use and production become sites for political struggles. Corporations and governments often promote the interests of proprietary software, thus undermining free software. In response to these threats, free software activists mobilize to protect and defend the conditions to produce free software. In Chapter 5, I highlight the efforts by free software activists in France to organize such political action, building alliances with free software activists in other parts of Europe as well as the U.S. In the process, these activists forged a free software global community of resistance with an explicitly political focus.

As noted above, the Internet is an equally important foundation of the digital commons as free software. Moreover, both software and the Internet are key productive forces for informational capitalism. As in the case of software, corporations and governments often promote proprietary interests in accessing the Internet. In response, net neutrality activists struggle to shape the political conditions for Internet access. They fight to protect the Internet as an open, decentralized system that all users are free to access on an equal basis. In the process, they struggle against corporate and government practices that prioritize profit and collect data about consumers and citizens. They view many of these practices as forms of surveillance that threaten civil liberties and democratic institutions. In response to these threats, net neutrality activists employ strategies to gain greater control over the existing telecommunications infrastructure. They seek to evade practices of surveillance, as well as to devise alternative telecommunications infrastructures of their own. In the process, they create explicit global communities of resistance to defend the Internet as a basis for the digital commons.

In the following chapters, I thus explore key dynamics of struggle over neoliberalism and informational capitalism. I highlight examples of key projects and activist strategies that contribute to the development and defense of the digital commons. These projects are beautifully varied, created by participants in many countries around the world. They are diverse and global. They are not intended to be exhaustive, however; there are a multitude of other such projects around the world. Over time, such projects change, as advocates of free software and net neutrality continue to design inventive ways to build, share, and transform software and the Internet. As danah boyd (2014, 27) notes in her study of teen use of social media, these technological platforms are "moving landscape[s]." Like social media, particular free software projects or activist strategies will change over time; however, "the core principles and practices...are likely to persist" (boyd 2014, 27). Indeed, in the case of implicit and explicit free software and net neutrality global communities of resistance, they are likely to persist because they target core dynamics of neoliberalism and informational capitalism. Until those systems are radically transformed, such communities are likely to continue to create imaginative ways to contribute to developing the digital commons.

2 Coding the Digital Commons
Foundations in Free Software and the Emerging Internet

Over the past decades, the commons have become a central terrain of struggle over the politics of globalization. Indeed, efforts to protect and create diverse forms of the commons challenge the dominant form of neoliberal globalization that seeks to open markets around the world to global capital. The underlying dynamic of neoliberal globalization involves privatizing property in myriad forms, from centuries-old biological resources like seeds to digital music files downloaded from the Internet. Corporations and governments construct a proprietary discourse that defines legal conditions to protect the interests of private property; these conditions include copyright and other forms of intellectual property law, international trade agreements, and development policies.

Voicing a key unifying theme for diverse efforts to develop alternatives to neoliberal globalization, Vandana Shiva (2001) emphasizes the importance of the commons, and of biodiversity in particular, as a community-owned and managed resource central to the lives of indigenous people. As a medicinal and agricultural resource, biodiversity is threatened by "biopiracy...the use of intellectual property systems to legitimize the exclusive ownership and control over biological resources and biological products and processes that have been used over centuries in non-industrialized cultures" (Shiva 2001, 49). Refusing to acknowledge the indigenous knowledge and centuries of innovative practice involved with collective use of plants for medicinal and nutritional purposes, patents impose a legal system that benefits corporations by granting them the rights to manufacture and market what are advertised as new "inventions."

Shiva's (2001) writing and activism are part of a larger body of work on the commons that have the potential to challenge the proprietary discourse and neoliberal globalization. For Bollier (2008, 9), the commons have emerged as a "parallel social order," an alternative to state or private property where people create a new model of social organization that coexists with dominant models and, over time, could possibly replace them. There are diverse forms of the commons, ranging from those based on public ownership and protection of natural resources to knowledge commons based on principles of open access to information. Amidst their diversity, these forms of the commons share a commitment to collaborative work, shared stewardship and ownership of resources essential to society as a whole. Hess and Ostrom (2006, 3) understand the commons as a "complex ecosystem... a resource shared by a group of people that is subject to social dilemmas." Benkler (2013a, 1533) builds upon their work, arguing that this resource "can occur at a wide range of scales and, critically, raises challenges of use, governance and sustainability that can be viewed as social dilemmas." These struggles over who has access to the commons, and under what conditions, are central to the contemporary politics of globalization.

Like the commons themselves, struggles to create and protect them take myriad forms. While Shiva (2001) organizes to defend age-old commons against biopiracy, Bollier (2008) urges commoners to wage such struggles by inventing and defending alternatives to proprietary social forms within the structure of the old. Bollier's (2008) strategy makes sense in many cases and indeed seems almost inevitable, considering the extent to which a mix of commons and proprietary forms are ingrained in our everyday lives. As Benkler (2013a) notes, the sidewalks, roads, water, sewer, and electricity that we use each day are forms of the commons, governed by legal arrangements where providers are required to offer similar terms of service to all paying customers. Utility companies, for example, do not generally offer higher quality service to customers who pay higher fees, while requiring those paying lower fees to endure brownouts. Use of these forms of the commons, however, is shaped by proprietary systems, and particularly by the inequalities of access to quality resources within those systems. In principle, roads and sidewalks are commons governed by legal arrangements that apply to all users; however, in practice, low-income neighborhoods tend to have more potholes and cracked sidewalks. Nevertheless, as Benkler (2013a, 1538) states, "[i]n personal and commercial life, property is ubiquitous and highly visible to us. What is less visible is that this property system is suspended in commons that undergird and are interpolated throughout the proprietary system elements." The inequalities endemic to proprietary systems thus do not negate the pervasive presence of the commons, although they may make it difficult to notice the contours of the commons that form such an integral part of social life.

Boyle (2008) makes a similar argument with respect to the public domain, which includes all material not covered by intellectual property rights. Material in the public domain thus includes whole works; however, more nuanced understandings of the public domain include what Boyle (2008, 38) describes as "reserved spaces of freedom inside intellectual property." Such spaces include rights to fair use and limits on ownership of standard themes for all works that are protected under copyright law. Similar to Benkler's (2013a) image of the commons as permeating the system of private property, Boyle (2008) offers a view of the public domain as constituted by a system of private plots with public roads running through them. The public domain is free of property rights, allowing consumers to make whatever use of that material that they wish. It is complex and variegated, however, since it exists alongside and within the interstices of the proprietary system of intellectual property.

Since the 1970s, struggles over the commons have taken distinct forms in the context of global informational capitalism, where corporations, governments, and other social actors rely on access to electronic information to engage in economic, political, social, and cultural activities. As will be discussed throughout this book, these actors struggle to create and defend conditions for access to informational productive forces such as computer networks, software, and industries linked to digital technologies. Since software is the underlying commonality to all of these struggles, ranging from conditions for access to the Internet to software licensing and more, I refer to them as "software politics." Understanding software politics involves identifying the complex political and economic interests involved with software and digital technologies, as well as the discourses those interests employ to engage in particular strategies (Schoonmaker 2009; Schoonmaker and Giraud 2014).

In this chapter, I explore the nature of the digital commons as a new form of globality that poses an alternative to both neoliberal globalization and informational capitalism. I focus on two examples of localized struggles that contributed to the development of the digital commons in the 1970s and 1980s. I then consider Creative Commons and Wikipedia as two later projects where participants expanded and strengthened the digital commons after 2001.

First, in the early 1980s, free software advocates elaborated what I call a "freedom discourse," articulating the principles of freedom to access and share information as a common good rather than as private property. By codifying free software according to those principles under U.S. copyright law, these advocates created an alternative form of property that challenged the private property form.

They legally protected the freedom to code and share software, laying the foundation of the free software community, as well as the digital commons.

Second, in the late 1970s, governments from the global South articulated a sovereignty discourse to voice concerns about the conditions for exchanging flows of data through computer networks. The Brazilian government played a key role in putting this discourse into practice through its policy on transborder data flows. Over the next decade, concerns with sovereignty shifted to emphasize the importance of freedom to connect to computer networks located abroad, as computer communications became increasingly central to the work of Brazilian researchers as well as to corporate and government operations. There was thus a convergence between the freedom discourse of free software proponents in the U.S. and Brazilian advocates of the freedom to access the emerging Internet.

These struggles during the 1970s and the 1980s transformed legal arrangements and laid the foundation for the development of the digital commons, including digital technologies, software, and the Internet, in the decades to come. At different times and in different parts of the world, these actors applied the freedom discourse to create free software as a new form of property and to open up access to computer networks. In the process, they made vital contributions to the development of the digital commons in contemporary conditions of informational capitalism. Decades later, in the early 2000s, advocates for the digital commons created Creative Commons and Wikipedia. By developing these projects, they expanded and strengthened the digital commons in the fields of art, creative works, and shared encyclopedic knowledge.

Global Free Software and Net Neutrality Communities: Perspectives and Methods

In his study of free software communities, Kelty (2008) crafts a theory of free software participants as a "recursive public" vital for the development of the Internet as well as free software itself. He defines the recursive public as "*a public that is vitally concerned with the material and practical maintenance and modification of the technical, legal, practical and conceptual means of its own existence as a public*" (Kelty 2008, 3, emphasis in original). As a recursive public, free software participants thus struggle to conserve, reinforce, and spread the software through which they communicate, collaborate, and coordinate. They defend legal principles vital to the processes of coding and sharing free software, including a free and open Internet. These "militants of code," as Couture and Proulx (2008) call them, view software code as a common good rather than as merchandise to be appropriated by corporations. They open new spaces of collective action, employing modes of participation where developers and users cooperate to create software as a collective good. Such spaces of action constitute forms of social innovation that can potentially empower citizens to engage in software politics. Complex intersections between local and global interests and actions were thus involved with the creation of such publics. As Söderberg (2008) argues, free software has the potential to contribute to restructuring capitalism by resisting corporate control over communications and information technology and the labor involved with producing it.

In this book, I explore the contributions of free software and net neutrality advocates to developing the digital commons as an alternative to neoliberalism and informational capitalism. I view free software and net neutrality communities as prime examples of what Sassen (2005, 54) calls "elementary forms of transboundary public spheres or forms of globality centered in multiple localized types of struggles and agency." Indeed, hackers in the U.S. and proponents of opening up computer networks in Brazil were probably unaware of each other as they engaged in their distinct local struggles in the 1970s and 1980s. Over time, however, these struggles contributed to the development of global communities of free software and net neutrality advocates. These communities were committed to the principles of freedom to access and share information as a common good rather than as private property. In interviews, at conferences, and in other venues such as wikis and online discussion forums, free software and net neutrality advocates often refer to themselves as part of global communities. Much of their daily work involves collaborating with people from different countries on common projects. The global nature of these communities is a vital part of their recursivity in Kelty's (2008) sense. Without local struggles that are also unified within global projects, free software and net neutrality communities would not exist.

To study these global communities, I employed a qualitative methodology that combined participant observation with interviewing. I conducted semi-structured, in-depth interviews with 40 participants. These included free software proponents, activists, developers, and business executives with diverse relationships to free software communities. Many of these participants raised concerns about net neutrality, which became more of a focus during the latter part of the research when I also interviewed net neutrality activists. I selected and recruited participants after engaging in participant observation at free software community events, such as the Ubuntu download party in Paris in 2009; the Open World Forum in Paris in 2010, 2011, and 2014; the Southern California Linux Expo in Los Angeles in 2011; The Document Foundation meeting in Berlin in 2012; and the *Forúm Internacional do Software Livre,* or International Free Software Forum, in Porto Alegre, Brazil in 2014. In 2010 and 2011, I was invited to attend a three-day corporate meeting of a free software services company that I refer to with the pseudonym of Digitech. I conducted participant observation at these meetings, which were attended by the corporate headquarters staff and the managers from Europe, the Middle East, and Africa. I interviewed 20 of these participants, 8 in person at the corporate meetings, and the rest over Skype.

These observations and interviews provided data about the perspectives and experiences of participants in a wide range of free software projects. I asked participants about their organization or community's major accomplishments, challenges, and goals. Depending upon their organizational or community involvement, I also asked about their participation in processes of developing free software systems, communities, or markets, as well as activism to promote or defend free software. Finally, I asked participants about their work history and the reasons why they chose to work in the free software field. I used a snowball sampling method to generate other participants in the study. I elicited recommendations for other interview participants, including recommendations for other free software or net neutrality projects or organizations that the participants viewed as particularly important. I gave interview participants a choice about whether they would be represented by a pseudonym to protect confidentiality.

These recommendations were invaluable in providing further interview participants. Moreover, they provided me with a picture of which free software and net neutrality communities the participants viewed as especially significant. As the research unfolded, I chose to focus on particular free software and net neutrality projects. These projects exemplified key struggles to develop global communities of resistance to neoliberalism and informational capitalism. With such a diverse range of projects from which to choose, it was important to narrow down the research to explore the dynamics of developing these communities, and their significance for the digital commons, in more depth. Furthermore, as I continued with the research, the connections between free software and net neutrality became increasingly clear. A number of free software advocates discussed the importance of net neutrality for their work, even though their own primary personal involvement was in free software communities.

For example, when I engaged in participant observation at the 15th International Free Software Forum (FISL15) in Brazil in early May 2014, many free software advocates were engaging in intense discussions about net neutrality. Indeed, the conference theme was the relationship of democracy to the politics of security and privacy. Just two weeks earlier, Brazilian President Dilma Rousseff had signed the *Marco Civil da Internet* into law. Presenters at the opening session of FISL15, including Governor Tarso Genro of Rio Grande do Sul, highlighted the importance of the Marco Civil as an Internet bill of rights. Ricardo Fritsch, the general coordinator of the Free Software Association (ASL) as well as the FISL15 conference organizer, emphasized the links between net neutrality and free software. He noted that the Marco Civil had been created through a collaborative process similar to the process of coding free software (accessed August 1, 2017, www.rs.gov.br/conteudo/196527/ governador-defende-software-livre-na-abertura-oficial-do-fisl-15).

Collaboration on the Marco Civil had been underway for years; however, it accelerated after Edward Snowden's 2013 revelations about surveillance by the U.S. National Security Agency (NSA). As I recorded in my field notes, from these Brazilian perspectives, "Snowden did us a big favor, since we know we are being spied on, especially if we are using proprietary software." The Marco Civil thus offered an example for the world to follow. It provided a civil rights framework for the Internet, a legal foundation from which to fight for Internet transparency and openness. My observations at this conference, as well as interviews done with some of the participants there, shifted my perspective to focus more clearly on the connections between free software and net neutrality.

An observation during my fieldwork in Paris in October 2010 offered an equally telling picture of the importance of net neutrality for free software communities. I had done interviews with several French free software activists, who were working extremely hard as they struggled to combine their activism with paid jobs. They were in the process of moving to a new office space; this move added to the stress and potential burnout, since their current space had been disrupted. We did our interviews in cafes, since there was no "official" space available. In my field notes, I reflected on the importance of space and place for these activists. I observed that many of the free software advocates I had interviewed did not have regular office spaces from which to conduct their work. Moreover, they did not work with each other regularly in the same physical space. I wrote,

> While neoliberal globalization is coordinated/administered from more official corporate, government or multilateral organizational spaces, globalization from below bubbles up in the flexible, somewhat chaotic and random spaces that community members find to meet…as well, of course, as the Internet, which seems like the most stable, reliable and globally accessible space of all.

In the context of dispersed or chaotic work spaces in their physical locations, free software activists thus depended on the Internet as a secure, trustworthy space to engage with each other and coordinate their efforts.

The interviews and observations thus provided the foundation for the study, which I then developed by focusing on the particular global projects highlighted in the following chapters. Interviews generally lasted between 45 and 90 minutes; they were tape-recorded and transcribed. Since I speak French, Spanish, and Portuguese, I offered interviewees the option of doing the interview in those languages or in English. I wanted to make it as easy as possible for participants to fully express their ideas. One interviewee chose Spanish, seven chose French, and twenty-nine chose English. At times, we used English to clarify ideas during the interviews in other languages.

In addition to this primary data, I drew upon secondary data about free software firms, communities and activist groups available online; I also researched net neutrality communities and activist groups. Engaging in what Landzelius (2006, 2) called "grounding cyberspace," I examined detailed activities of net neutrality communities and free software communities and firms; this included exchanges between free software community participants as they deliberated questions such as how to expand their communities further into the global South. Similar to Bernal's (2014, 6) anthropological study of websites developed by Eritreans in diaspora, I view the websites of free software and net neutrality communities as "cultural products" of those communities, "not simply a technology they use." Since the communities I studied were largely focused on creating software and web content management systems, these sites were central to their work. Like Bernal (2014, 22), "I do not approach cyberspace as a virtual realm apart from other realities. To the contrary, in order to make sense of online activities I place them in [a] wider context." This wider context includes broader struggles to create free software community organizations, as well as free software itself. Moreover, this context includes struggles to defend free software and net neutrality from corporate and government efforts to promote proprietary interests.

Indeed, these websites were spaces where free software and net neutrality participants from around the world could meet to share information, pose questions, and attempt to solve collective problems. They were critical sites where these geographically dispersed advocates met to generate information about their perspectives and struggles. Cyberspace was thus one of the main research sites for this project. I engaged in what Varisco (2002) called "participant webservation." Similar to Bernal's (2014, 26) approach to studying websites designed by Eritreans in diaspora, this kind of method allowed me to observe free software and net neutrality advocates "engaged in articulating their views and identifying the issues that are significant to them without any prompting from a researcher." I interpreted those online interactions by employing the knowledge I gleaned from interview data, participant observation at conferences and community events, and reading secondary literature.

In many ways, my method of studying global free software and net neutrality communities of resistance mirrored the organization of the communities themselves. Due to the international nature of these communities, studying them required that I interview people who lived in different countries and collaborated with each other over the Internet. As will be discussed further in the next chapter, free software proponents often coordinate their work online while residing in different countries. They gather at conferences to engage in face-to-face work and develop their relationships; however, in their day-to-day work, they often do not see each other in person. As I reflected in my field notes toward the beginning of the research in September 2010:

> My method is to meet people at conferences, make contact with them and then follow up with interviews. My interviewing process is thus similar to the participants' pattern of interaction with each other, since we meet in person at the conference and then continue our interaction by communicating at a distance after the conference is over.

The interview participants reflect the international nature of global free software and net neutrality communities of resistance. I identify the participants by the countries in which they live long term and do their work, rather than by their countries of birth or citizenship (although in many cases, these are the same). Their national location shapes the economic, political, social, and cultural contexts in which they develop perspectives and experiences, informing their work and their connections to the global communities. Thirteen interview participants were based in France, four in the Netherlands, four in Canada, three in Germany, three in Nigeria, two in the U.S., two in Tunisia, three in Brazil, two in the United Kingdom, one in Spain, one in Portugal, one in Belgium, and one in Switzerland. I interviewed some people more than once over a period of months or years between 2009 and 2016; I interviewed one key informant thirteen times, and others two or three times. The following analysis is thus rooted in qualitative interview data gleaned from participants in the global free software and net neutrality communities, working in diverse projects, peer communities, and corporate settings around the world.

Software as Code for the Digital Commons: Changing Market Conditions and the Creation of Free Software

Programmers developed free software in response to changing political, technological, and economic conditions in the computer market, which had key implications for informational capitalism. In the early days of computing in the 1960s, a distinct software market did not exist, and there was no need to legally define such a thing as free software. The computer business primarily involved selling mainframe computers to corporate customers like banks and insurance companies. Those major corporate customers relied on computers to process large amounts of data. Computer manufacturers like IBM, Rand, Burroughs, and Data General each configured the interaction between hardware and software systems in different ways. Programmers designed software programs to run on particular machines, and those programs were not compatible with each other. Computer manufacturers thus did not seek to control their software, since it would not be usable on each other's systems. Software was often not even compatible with machines of different series made by the same firm.

Computer scientists working for IBM made a major technological breakthrough in 1964. They developed the System/360 computer architecture that made it possible to run the same software on successive series of IBM machines. IBM promoted this advance in interoperability by giving away its operating system, making the source code available to all users who requested it, and encouraging users to copy or make changes to it to suit their needs. IBM did not refer to this as a free software business model; however, its mode of operations fit the spirit of that model as it was developed in later decades. In 1966, the vice president of IBM promoted what amounted to a free software approach in his effort to develop political conditions favoring the spread of this new software program. As a member of the President's Commission on the Patent System, he argued that software should not be governed by patents (Drahos and Braithwaite 2002; Schoonmaker 2007). In the process, he promoted the creation of market conditions conducive to free software, while opposing a proprietary model.

In the market conditions of the 1960s, programmers thus had free access to the source codes of software programs. They could make any changes they saw fit to improve the programs or adapt them to their needs. Computer manufacturers like IBM "encouraged their customers to form free software sharing organizations…helping to create a bigger community of software developers…that would in a few decades give (not sell) the world the Internet" (Drahos and Braithwaite 2002, 170). As Lessig (2004) pointed out, those programmers enjoyed the kinds of academic freedoms shared by scholars in university settings today, where people critique and build upon each other's work to contribute to the development of knowledge in the field. At MIT's Artificial Intelligence Laboratory, programmers first began to identify themselves as "hackers" and to develop a hacker culture that prized programming skills and the collaborative work required to write the code for increasingly complex software. As Steinmetz (2016, 221) argues, this positive hacker identity, rooted in a culture of sharing information to solve collective problems, contradicts the dominant "construction of the hacker as a criminal other." In Lessig's (2006, 8) words, "[o]ur government has already criminalized the core ethic of this movement, transforming the meaning of *hacker* into something quite alien to its original sense." According to this dominant construction, hackers are commonly perceived negatively, as people who break into others' computer systems. By contrast, Steinmetz (2016, 83) argues, "the more a person develops and expresses skill, the closer they move toward the subcultural ideal of 'hacker'." Hackers approach challenges scientifically and systematically, concentrating intensively on their work to forge creative solutions. I employ this conception of hackers throughout this book, when referring to hacker culture and activity.

Hacker influence spread exponentially after 1969 in the wake of another technological breakthrough. The U.S. Department of Defense (DOD) developed the ARPANET, the first transcontinental, high-speed computer network. Originally planned as an experiment in digital communications, the ARPANET was managed by the DOD's Advanced Research Projects Agency. When it was first developed, the ARPANET linked computers at four universities in California and Utah. It was an ambitious idea, because each university would be required to share its computer with the others. These machines were highly valued and extensively used. For example, the minicomputer that sent the first message over the ARPANET weighed 900 pounds and cost $80,000 ($500,000 in 2012 dollars). It was called an interface message processor (IMP); it operated through packet switching, where data were transmitted in small packets between computers, rather than through a continuous stream. The first IMP was installed at UCLA. It linked the computer science department's mainframe computer to phone lines that AT&T had modified to provide always-on connections to the computers and IMPs at the other universities (Blum 2012).

Over time, the ARPANET expanded to connect hundreds of defense contractors, universities, and research laboratories. By 1973, the ARPANET added its first international connection via a satellite link to University College London. Computer networks were generally sponsored by governments in different countries, however, rather than operating internationally on a regular basis. The U.S. government owned the ARPANET in the 1970s; it connected researchers in the defense field within the military or at universities that received government funding (Blum 2012). As Raymond (1999, 20) argued, the ARPANET "enabled researchers everywhere to exchange information with unprecedented speed and flexibility, giving a huge boost to collaborative work and tremendously increasing both the pace and intensity of technological advance." It embodied the utopian potential for globalization from below, while simultaneously providing the communications infrastructure to facilitate corporate activities on a global scale (Schoonmaker 2007).

The hackers were key actors in this process of transformation, since they were uniquely positioned to continue to foment and build upon the technological changes underlying software and emerging digital communications. Raymond (1999, 20) noted that the ARPANET's "electronic highways brought together hackers all over the U.S. in a crucial mass; instead of remaining in isolated small groups each developing their own ephemeral local cultures, they discovered (or reinvented) themselves as a networked tribe." During this period, hackers invented the Unix operating system and the C computer language. They designed them to be simple, flexible, and as portable as possible, so "[h]ackers could carry around software toolkits between different machines, rather than having to re-invent the equivalents of fire and the wheel every time" (Raymond 1999, 23). By 1980, the use of C and Unix spread from AT&T to various universities and other research facilities (Raymond 1999).

Software Politics: Proprietary Software as a Terrain of Struggle

During the 1970s, hackers thus honed both their technical skills and their ethic of collaboration as part of the process of developing the ARPANET, C, and Unix. Indeed, these technological developments contributed to the emergence of hackers as a recursive public (Kelty 2008), providing enhanced opportunities for communication and broadening access to software programs. By the late 1970s, however, conditions in the computer and software markets changed markedly. Demand for software soared and a range of computer manufacturers produced hardware compatible with IBM systems. IBM responded to these developments by shifting its software business model from the open source to the proprietary. It began attaching copyright notices to its software starting in 1978. In 1983, IBM stopped providing access to the source code for its software, as well as limiting the transfer of other technical information. As Drahos and Braithwaite (2002, 171) argue, "[h]aving set the industry standard through its dominance, IBM now wanted to use copyright to exclude others from competing under the standard."

With the technological development of software programs that could be imported between computing systems, a market incentive was created to hide the source codes of programs and copyright them. New struggles arose. Corporations strove to maximize opportunities to profit from software as a commodity; at the same time, they opposed and sought to transform previously accepted practices of developing software within a shared community. IBM led the fight to extend copyright law to software during the 1980s; it was eventually joined by other companies, including Microsoft. Corporate interests thus coalesced around the proprietary business model for the software sector, using intellectual property laws to protect their investments in software programs as lucrative new sources of revenue (Drahos and Braithwaite 2002; Lessig 2004; Schoonmaker 2007).

Hence, hackers and corporations engaged in a complex process of software politics. They simultaneously created and responded to key technological developments in software, communications, and information technology as vital informational productive forces of information capitalism. IBM's early strategy promoted the development of the free software model for software; however, over the years, corporations strove to create conditions for a proprietary model. This proprietary model required the construction of political and economic conditions in the software market that defined software as intellectual property and allowed firms maximum leeway to buy and sell that property. At the same time, however, solidifying the proprietary software model threatened the freedoms that the hackers had previously enjoyed. As Lessig (2004, 280) observed, "[t]he world of free software had been erased by a change in the economics of computing."

The construction of a proprietary software market thus had broad social implications that were felt most immediately by the hackers themselves, radically altering the conditions under which they did their programming work. The hackers responded by seeking to create a new set of conditions to support the practice of the hacker ethic that viewed software as a collective resource. This was the beginning of the struggle to create a digital form of the commons that would be shared with others who could both benefit from it and contribute to its further development. In 1984, Richard Stallman, a hacker at MIT's Artificial Intelligence Laboratory, initiated a project to create a free software system compatible with Unix. He called it the GNU Project, which stands for Gnu's Not Unix. He wrote *The GNU Manifesto* to explain the nature of this project and its underlying goals. He stated,

> I consider that the golden rule requires that if I like a program I must share it with other people who like it. Software sellers want to divide the users and conquer them, making each user agree not to share with others. I refuse to break solidarity with other users in this way. I cannot in good conscience sign a nondisclosure agreement or a software license agreement.
>
> (Gay 2002, 32)

Through the Manifesto, Stallman began to articulate the freedom discourse and its underlying values of sharing and solidarity among users. His commitment to the development of free software as a community resource led him to resign his job at MIT's Artificial Intelligence Lab so that his employer would have no legal excuse "to prevent me from giving GNU away" (Gay 2002, 32). Stallman organized a community of programmers to contribute to the development of GNU by writing compatible replacements for single Unix utilities that could then be combined into the larger GNU system. He envisioned this process as benefiting all computer users, since all the programming talent would be applied to "advancing the state of the art" rather than duplicating their efforts by programming separate proprietary systems (Gay 2002, 34).

A key part of the process of organizing the community of programmers was continuing to articulate the freedom discourse, which defined free software in terms of the freedoms it embodied. When Stallman founded the Free Software Foundation (FSF) in 1985, he institutionalized the freedom discourse as part of the FSF's mission. The FSF's web page states that it is "dedicated to promoting computer users' right to use, study, copy, modify, and redistribute computer programs.... The FSF also helps to spread awareness of the ethical and political issues of freedom in the use of software." The freedom discourse thus clearly defined four types of freedom for software users, central to protecting the liberty of those users within communities. These included the freedom to run the program for any purpose, to study the program and adapt it to the user's particular needs, to redistribute copies of the software "so you can help your neighbor" (Gay 2002, 41), and the freedom to make improvements in the program and release them for the benefit of the entire software community. The four freedoms require access to the source code so that users can make changes to the program. They are the guiding principles of what Stallman calls a "software-sharing community" (Gay 2002, 15), where the hackers who write code share software like cooks share recipes. In a frequently quoted 1996 essay entitled "The Free Software Definition," Stallman encouraged participants in this community to understand that the freedom involved with free software "is a matter of liberty, not price. To understand the concept, you should think of 'free' as in 'free speech,' not as in 'free beer'" (Gay 2002, 41).

Such statements were part of a process of developing a culture of freedom within a growing number of software-sharing communities, rooted in a common understanding of the importance of the four freedoms to the activities and existence of those communities. They were part of the cultural articulation of the freedom discourse, emphasizing the distinctive emphasis on freedom of speech and its importance to hackers who equated the freedom to write and share code with the freedom to publicly state their ideas.

These early free software advocates did not explicitly state that they sought to develop a digital commons; however, their work resonated with Benkler's (2013a) concept of the commons discussed above. Indeed, to create a digital commons, these early advocates faced "challenges of use, governance and sustainability that can be viewed as social dilemmas" (Benkler 2013a, 1533). Equally important, these efforts by the early free software proponents challenged corporate control in informational capitalism. By supporting community access and control over software, free software advocates staked their claim to vital informational productive forces essential for informational capitalism to thrive.

Copyleft: Legal Action to Construct Free Software and the Digital Commons

Stallman and other free software proponents engaged these challenges in 1989. They understood the importance of protecting the four freedoms in the legal sphere, as well as articulating the value of those freedoms within their shared cultural lives. Stallman pursued legal action to promote political and economic conditions for the continued development and use of free software. He used copyright law to create a legal construct to ensure that the four freedoms would be protected by copyrighting the GNU General Public License (GNU GPL).

The GNU GPL provided the code for the digital commons by establishing the legal terms to define and protect free software. All software under the GNU GPL was copyrighted under U.S. copyright law. At the same time, however, the license undermined the usual proprietary restrictions of copyright law through what Stallman (Gay 2002, 20) called the "method...[of] copyleft," providing all users with legal permission to change, copy, and distribute the software. Copyleft required that software licensed under the GNU GPL include the source code so that any future user would be able to modify the program. Through what Coleman (2004, 515) called a "clever legal hack," copyleft thus used the legal protection established by copyright law to subvert the fundamental logic of that law, requiring users to participate in the fundamental freedoms to access source code, make changes to the program, and allow others to do the same. The Preamble of this license addressed software users, stating that the license was

> intended to guarantee your freedom to share and change free software – to make sure the software is free for all its users.... that you have the freedom to distribute copies of free software (and charge for this service if you wish), that you receive source code or can get it if you want it, that you can change the software or use pieces of it in new free programs; and that you know you can do these things.
>
> (Gay 2002, 195)

The founder of one of the leading open-source software firms, Red Hat Software, described the GPL as "the most effective license for ensuring that this forced cooperation among the various team members continues to occur regardless of the competitive environment at the time" (Young 1999, 121).

This "forced cooperation" was central to Boyle's (2008) distinction between the public domain and the commons, and provided the cornerstone for the development of the digital commons. As discussed above, Boyle (2008) viewed the public domain as all material not covered by intellectual property rights. This domain ranged from complete works to parts of proprietary works designated as free for the public to access, based on provisions of copyright law such as rights of fair use. In contrast to the public domain, Boyle (2008, 39) defined the commons as a "resource over which some group has access and use rights" under certain conditions. He argued that a true commons allowed access by the whole society. Nonetheless, Boyle (2008) highlighted free software as an example of the commons rooted in a set of restrictions on who has access. The GNU GPL required users making changes to the code to leave that code open for others to make further changes. It constituted the code for the digital commons, because it designated specific conditions for users to participate in coding and sharing free software as a commons. Those users were not free to be unfree. In a somewhat paradoxical twist, the freedom to participate in free software as a commons was rooted in these restrictive conditions. The digital commons of free software were thus grounded in the copyleft license. Property rights, defined within U.S. copyright law, were the legal basis of this form of the commons.

Boyle (2008, xiv) described both the commons and the public domain as "property's outside." He argued that this "outside" was "harder to grasp than its inside" (Boyle 2008, xiv); in the case of ideas and information, it was critical to have as much material as possible in the public domain where it could be shared without being limited by private intellectual property rights. Paradoxically, the digital commons depended on the legal restrictions of copyleft to protect the freedoms of software users from encroachment by private property rights. To grasp the digital commons as "property's outside" (Boyle 2008), we need to understand its complex, *symbiotic* relationship to the "inside" of copyright law. To code the digital commons, Stallman employed the "inside" of copyright law to create the GNU GPL, allowing access to free software by anyone who agreed to support continued openness of the code.

Through the GNU GPL, Stallman thus created free software as a distinct form of "property's outside" (Boyle 2008). In the process, he institutionalized the freedom discourse within U.S. copyright law. He legally established free software as a new form of property based on complex forms of community ownership, rather than strictly proprietary ownership. This act protected the freedom for software developers to create this new form of property, as well as the four freedoms of software users to run, adapt, redistribute, and release the code as they saw fit. As Doueihi (2008) noted, coding is a scholarly, discursive practice formulated within particular legal conditions. By creating the GNU GPL, Stallman demonstrated insight into U.S. copyright law as having the legal power to enable or constrain the future development of free software. He transformed the legal conditions for software development by making it institutionally possible for the free software model to coexist with the proprietary model.

Certainly, the importance of discourse was magnified because the compilation of code, a veritable "scholarly practice" (Doueihi 2008), was in itself discursive, taking place within a legal context which can be framed as a discourse negotiated and constructed through writing. The formalization of free software, through licensing, was thus constructed within a particular context of knowledge and power. Software developers understood that their work required a degree of discursive mastery of the legal regime that regulated their practices.

Hackers thus combined discursive, legal practices with the technical compilation of code to construct free software as the code for the digital commons. Through their technical practices, hackers contributed to the ongoing development of the software itself; they created the code for running a range of programs to power computers, the ARPANET, and eventually the Internet. In the context of the above changes in the computer and software markets, however, the creation of free software required political action to legally constitute free software through the GNU GPL and copyleft. These actions created the legal basis for the digital commons. Hackers' political struggles to legally constitute free software thus also required constructing the freedom discourse to articulate and institutionalize the underlying values involved with free software. They employed the freedom discourse to challenge corporate efforts to exert proprietary control over software. In the process, they strengthened conditions for users and producers to control software as a central part of the productive forces of informational capitalism.

These struggles supported the growth of diverse free software communities. As will be discussed further in the next chapter, free software communities constituted social worlds of peer production and collaboration that contributed to the ongoing development of the software, as well as cultures of sharing infused with the freedom discourse. They integrated social and ethical elements that Stallman (Gay 2002, 22) called "a social advantage, allowing users to cooperate, and an ethical advantage, respecting the user's freedom." Free software originally arose from and was shaped by the U.S. cultural context emphasizing these values of individual choice and creativity.

Due to this emphasis on individualism, Coombe and Herman (2004, 569) viewed free software communities as part of a "digital counterculture." This counterculture tended to emphasize the rights and activities of "individuals – independent authors and cultural creators projected (but never acknowledged) as privileged Americans with indisputable First Amendment freedoms" (Coombe and Herman 2004, 569–70). In a similar vein, Chan (2004) depicted Stallman as critiquing Latin American government policies promoting the use of free software as part of broader strategies to foster national sovereignty in the information technology field. She quoted his statement describing such laws as

> not the kind of help we most ask for from governments...What we ask is that they not interfere with us with things like the Digital Millennium Copyright Act, with software patents, with prohibitions on reverse engineering that enable companies like Microsoft to make proprietary data formats and prohibit our work.
>
> (Chan 2004, 543)

She thus underscored Stallman's emphasis on the freedoms of individual users and creators as distinct from Latin American concerns with promoting national sovereignty through the development of digital culture and literacy.

These authors rightly noted the emphasis on individualism by Stallman and the FSF. They failed to acknowledge, however, Stallman's emphasis on the importance of freedom to society as a whole. Indeed, in his 1994 essay, "Why Software Should Not Have Owners," Stallman (Gay 2002, 47–48) grounded his entire concept of free software in a theory of society as needing

> information that is truly available to its citizens – for example, programs that people can read, fix, adapt and improve, not just operate...Society also needs freedom. When a program has an owner,

> the users lose freedom to control part of their own lives. And above all society needs to encourage the spirit of voluntary cooperation in its citizens.

Stallman thus understood individual freedom within a social context, as part of a broader societal value that promoted cooperation among citizens in producing and using information. The importance of free software was integrally linked to social processes of learning, of exchanging, and of creating information in digital form that was such a vital part of contemporary social life. This emphasis on developing the societal context to support conditions for freedom was a vital underlying value for the freedom discourse.

Free software thus played a pivotal role as the code for the digital commons, as U.S. free software advocates created an alternative form of property through copyleft. Nonetheless, these advocates' work laid only a partial foundation for the digital commons. Viewed from a global perspective, it was necessary to take global inequalities explicitly into account to develop the digital commons. Most countries in the global South lacked access to the technologies, skills, and industries to produce computers and software. Over time, access to the Internet became crucial for the continued construction of both free software and the digital commons. In the 1980s, when Stallman legally defined free software through copyleft, the Internet was just beginning to emerge. Free software proponents in the U.S. had not yet focused much attention on the importance of freedom of access to computer networks. By contrast, in the late 1970s, governments in the global South were acutely aware that access to computer networks was vital to the economic, political, and cultural conditions in their countries. They understood their lack of such access as shaped within the context of global inequalities. The Brazilian government was in a position to address these concerns. Hence, struggles in the global South, and particularly in Brazil, made indispensable contributions to the development of the digital commons that complemented work by free software advocates in the U.S.

Computer Networks and the Digital Commons: Struggles for Sovereignty and Access in the Global South

In the late 1970s, Latin American and African countries confronted global inequalities in the context of informational capitalism. They identified a new form of information dependency in the information technology sector, rooted in their lack of development of informational productive forces such as computer and software industries, as well as the scientific and technological resources to support the ongoing growth of those industries. They raised particular concerns that sensitive data about their economies and their citizens were being stored and processed in computers located outside of their national territories. They viewed these data as a resource with economic and social values whose unequal distribution was perpetuating global power inequalities. Transborder data flows were a major means of perpetuating these inequalities; such flows involved the storage, processing, and exchange of data between computers located in different countries (Murphy 1986; Organization for Economic Cooperation and Development 1979; Wigand, Shipley and Shipley 1984; Schoonmaker 2002).

Latin American and African government representatives voiced these perspectives in a series of international conferences, as well as in the call for a New International Information Order. In the process, they articulated what I call the sovereignty discourse that emphasized the need for governments in the global South to address conditions of global inequality in the information and communication technology field. This discourse was rooted in underlying cultural values of national sovereignty as a guide for national governments to implement development strategies. Hence, government action was viewed as a valid, and even necessary, vehicle to promote conditions of scientific and technological developments in the face of the economic and political powers of corporations and governments based in the global North (Schoonmaker 2002).

Representatives from the global South began to articulate the sovereignty discourse at meetings sponsored by the Intergovernmental Bureau for Informatics (IBI). IBI represented 37 member countries from the global South as well as France, Italy, and Spain. In 1978, IBI collaborated with the United Nations Educational, Scientific and Cultural Organization (UNESCO) to sponsor the first Intergovernmental Conference on Strategies and Policies for Informatics (SPIN I). At this conference, 78 national delegations focused on issues concerning data processing and computers. In the context of these broader concerns about the computer sector, these delegates approved a recommendation to develop international agreements on the rights of states with respect to transborder data flows. SPIN I was the first forum where representatives from the global South analyzed transborder data flows as an issue that required international coordination and negotiation. They framed this issue within the larger sovereignty discourse, highlighting the dangers for a new form of dependence to emerge, based upon the lack of informational productive forces such as the technologies, skills, and industries involved with computers. They continued to raise these questions about transborder data flows and sovereignty at regional IBI conferences in Latin America and Africa in 1979 (Sauvant 1984, 19–20; Intergovernmental Bureau for Informatics 1982, 14; Schoonmaker 2002).

At those conferences, participants passed resolutions that delineated the sovereignty discourse more fully. In the area of transborder data flows, this discourse was rooted in three fundamental concerns about how the flows could increase prospects for information dependency.

First, such dependency was based upon the unequal global distribution of data and the means to process them. Processing certain data abroad was perceived as potentially damaging to the interests of countries in the global South, since it reinforced the unequal distribution of informational productive forces, which they referred to as information resources. The resolutions encouraged governments to promote domestic control over information resources by retaining certain data within the country rather than allowing it to be stored and processed abroad. Second, information dependency posed threats to privacy as a right of national citizens. The technological means to compute, store, and process unprecedented quantities of data about individuals was viewed as warranting official supervision and the establishment of conditions for data access and dissemination. The resolutions recommended that governments implement policies to promote local control over the use of information resources, under specific guidelines that limited the dissemination of information about individuals. Finally, the resolutions encouraged governments in the global South to coordinate their legal approaches to regulating transborder data flows. In the context of an international policy environment devoid of an overarching legal framework governing transborder data flows, governments in the global South might address common concerns about information dependency by facilitating regional exchange of data and mutual access to data networks. Such a coordinated, cooperative approach would facilitate access to regional information resources. It would involve standardizing data transfer protocols as well as facilities for processing data (United Nations Centre on Transnational Corporations 1982, 114–16).

Through this process of discussion, governments from the global South thus articulated a sovereignty discourse that highlighted the importance of developing national strategies to promote the development of computer and software industries and to regulate transborder data flows. In the context of informational capitalism, these strategies constituted efforts to control access to vital informational productive forces. The majority of these governments, however, did not have the economic or political resources to implement such strategies (Schoonmaker 2002; United Nations Center on Transnational Corporations 1982). Their ability to apply the sovereignty discourse to concrete government actions was severely limited.

The Brazilian government was one of the few governments in the global South that had the institutional resources to act upon the sovereignty discourse by implementing development strategies in the computer sector. Brazil's substantial internal market for computers, and particularly its large numbers of potential corporate and government consumers were key conditions that made such strategies possible. The Brazilian government began promoting the development of computer manufacturing and software industries in 1976, when the informatics policy established the "market reserve" to protect the Brazilian market as part of the national patrimony. This policy viewed the national market as a public good to be "reserved" from foreign domination to foster the development of local industries, technologies, employment, and scientific knowledge in computer manufacturing and software. In 1984, the National Informatics Law extended the market reserve for eight more years, as well as prohibiting foreign investment in the mini and personal computer markets, limiting imports and the acquisition of foreign technologies (Adler, 1987; Evans, 1986). This law was designed to grow local firms by protecting them from foreign competition for a specific period of time. Its goal was to foster technological autonomy and to resist information dependency in this cutting edge sector of the global economy. In 1985, this strategy sparked conflicts with the Reagan administration on the grounds that it placed "unfair" limits on trade and investment by U.S.-based corporations. A number of studies explored the significance of the Brazilian informatics case for understanding conditions for state strategies to pursue information technology development in the global South (Tigre 1983; Adler 1987; Evans 1986, 1989; Schoonmaker 2002).

Little scholarly attention has been paid, however, to a critical component of the Brazilian informatics policy that focused on transborder data flows. This policy was important for three main reasons. First, it aimed to combat information dependency. It resonated with the three above concerns shared by representatives from the global South, voiced through the sovereignty discourse. It thus constituted a key case of that discourse being put into practice in the late 1970s and early 1980s. Second, the sovereignty discourse from that period provides a valuable historical perspective on contemporary Internet politics in the context of informational capitalism. Indeed, over three decades later, this discourse has striking similarities to contemporary struggles over privacy and civil liberties on the Internet. In 2013, the Brazilian government's response to Edward Snowden's revelations about bulk surveillance by the U.S. NSA resonated with earlier goals of the Brazilian transborder data flow policy. At both points in time, the Brazilian government emphasized the importance of protecting citizens' privacy, linking that privacy to broader questions of national sovereignty. Finally, these struggles over the Brazilian transborder data flow policy contributed to broader political and discursive conditions for accessing computer networks. Concerns about sovereignty shifted to emphasize the importance of freedom to connect to computer networks located abroad, as computer communications became increasingly central to the work of Brazilian researchers as well as to corporate and government operations. There was thus a convergence between the freedom discourse of free software proponents in the U.S. and Brazilian advocates of the freedom to access the emerging Internet. It became essential to access computer networks to further develop the digital commons.

Changing Conditions for International Computer Networks: The Emerging Internet

Prior to 1978, international data communications were carried out through telegraph channels that did not allow for computer communications. It was not yet possible to engage in transnational data communication through voice channels. In 1978, a Brazilian airline corporation learned about a telecommunications link that would connect it to an airline data service in the U.S. This service consisted of a database and data processing facilities that provided international information on airline tickets and reservations. It would allow the Brazilian airline to offer more efficient and comprehensive international services, since it could schedule international flights based on detailed, up-to-the-minute information about reservation availability and ticket prices. The Brazilian airline wanted to access those services. Several affiliates of foreign transnationals doing business in Brazil also expressed interest in taking advantage of similar economic benefits by establishing telecommunications systems for transborder data flows (United Nations Centre on Transnational Corporations 1983)

In May 1978, in the context of broader discussions in the global South about transborder data flows and sovereignty, the Brazilian government responded to this emerging corporate interest in accessing data services abroad. It became the first government in the global South to implement a policy requiring state approval for establishing the telecommunications links used to transmit transborder data flows. The content and context for the Brazilian policy was eventually outlined in a study on "Transborder Data Flows and Brazil," prepared by the Brazilian Special Secretariat of Informatics in conjunction with the Brazilian Ministry of Communications, and published by the United Nations Centre on Transnational Corporations. The study highlighted the importance of transborder data flows in the context of global power inequalities:

> Since information resources are crucial to decision-making and can be important sources of economic and political power, their location and use are of great significance. Brazil views the increased availability of information as an opportunity to reduce inequalities of power and to bridge gaps that exist between countries. Transborder data flows via transnational computer-communication systems play a particular role in this process by contributing to the transfer of information resources such as computer hardware, software, data bases and information jobs.
>
> (United Nations Centre on Transnational
> Corporations 1983, 183)

Consistent with the sovereignty discourse, the report thus presented regulating transborder data flows as a vital way to combat information dependency. Brazilian policy makers designed the transborder data flow strategy to create conditions for the flows to emanate to Brazil from other countries, rather than simply transmitting data out of Brazil for storage and processing in other parts of the world.

Brazilian concerns over transborder flows highlight the crucial changes wrought by the development of the Internet. In the late 1970s, establishing communication between computers was still an experimental idea that involved many unknown factors and complex technical problems to be solved. As discussed above, the first effort to create an interconnected network between computers was the ARPANET project, launched in 1969 and expanding over time to link a growing number of computers in the network.

By the early 1980s, a range of computer networks had developed; however, they were completely separate and disconnected from each other. As Blum (2012, 53) described the situation in the U.S., "[w]hile stretching nationwide and occasionally across the ocean, they operated in effect as private highways overlaid on the public telephone system." For example, major computer companies and government agencies had established their own independent computer networks. IBM, XEROX, and Digital Equipment Corporation had their own private networks, as did researchers in the fields of high-energy physics and space physics. There were a few European networks, as well as some regional academic networks (Blum 2012).

Computer networks were comprised of computers and telecommunications channels that transmitted and received data. The telecommunications channels were often referred to as computer communication or transborder data links; they were the part of the computer network that linked computers in different geographical locations. Transborder data flows were sent through links that could transmit computer-readable or digital signals internationally; usually these were undersea cables or satellites. A user could have more than one link in its computer network; however, it was most common to have only one link. Each system was thus comprised of a set of links; each link was privately owned by one user or leased by the user from the public telecommunications network (Schoonmaker 1990).

In a real sense, the Internet as we know it was born on New Year's Day 1983, when programmers employed new communications protocols that radically transformed computer communications. The Transmission Control Protocol/Internet Protocol (TCP/IP) allowed the previously disconnected networks to connect to each other and interact, while simultaneously maintaining their autonomy. Each of the networks connected through the telephone system. Blum (2012, 54) described it well: "The ARPANET was no longer a walled garden with an official government directory of participants, but rather had become just one network among many, linked together into an 'Internetwork'." Hackers were centrally involved in mainstreaming the Internet, by starting businesses as Internet Service Providers to sell or give away access to the growing range of consumers who wanted it (Raymond 1999).

The TCP/IP protocol ushered in a different standard for the industry, creating new possibilities for interconnections between networks. These communications protocols were the technical foundation for the decentralized, distributed structure of the Internet. The Internet's founders designed a protocol to connect disparate existing networks through telephone wires. They made use of the current decentralized system to overlay computer networks upon it. The Internet's decentralized design thus constituted a practical response to the constraints of the preexisting structure of the telephone system; it was not intentionally designed from scratch based on a philosophy that valued decentralized systems. Over time, the decentralized, autonomous structure of the Internet was reinforced as burgeoning numbers of actors set up their own networks. The number of computer networks increased dramatically from 15 in 1982 to over 400 in 1986 and over 35,000 in 2011. During this period, the number of computers connected to those networks soared from 2,000 in 1985 to 30,000 in 1987 and 159,000 in 1989; by 2011, there were two billion Internet users accessing the network through a growing range of mobile as well as desktop devices (Blum 2012).

Corporations continued to develop the Internet in the late 1980s, building long distance and local networks that operated using telephone lines with specialized equipment installed at each end of the network. By the early 1990s, firms such as MCI, PSI, UUNet, MFS, and Sprint began the process of installing their own fiber-optic networks. By the mid-1990s, Internet expansion continued with the construction of broadband networks (Blum 2012).

In Brazil, a range of academic researchers participated in this trend toward greater network connectivity. They worked extensively to develop the first Brazilian academic computer networks, to communicate both within the country and internationally. Carvalho's (2006) study of the development of the Internet in Brazil detailed this process. Beginning in 1981, researchers based at universities in Rio coordinated their efforts. By 1982, they developed the REDPUC project, which was one of the first networks in the world with the capability of transmitting at 10 megabits per second (Mbps). The researchers collaborated with the University of São Paulo; Telebrás, the state-owned telecommunications company; and Embratel, another major telecomunications company based in Rio. Through these collaborative efforts, they introduced hundreds of people to computer networks through specialized courses offered at the Catholic University of Rio de Janeiro (PUC/RJ). Emphasizing the emergence of a network of users who contributed to its operation, REDPUC's initial motto was "'REDPUC is made by Us'" (Carvalho 2006, 75, my translation). Over the next several years, researchers continued to develop the network to integrate voice and text services; by 1985, they developed a new motto that alluded to this expanded integration of the network's users, stating that "'REDPUC is made by Us...and You'" (Carvalho 2006, 75, my translation).

Despite the success in developing REDPUC, there were no national, or even regional, academic computer networks in Brazil until the period between 1988 and 1990. At that time, academic researchers and government officials in the science, technology, and telecommunications sectors negotiated access to BITNET hosts in the U.S. Some sought approval to establish a connection with UCLA, while others requested a dedicated international line to access BITNET through a connection to the University of Maryland. Such connections offered the possibility for these researchers to significantly expand their work (Carvalho 2006).

From the Sovereignty Discourse to the Freedom/Sovereignty Discourse: Developing the Digital Commons

This process of negotiating new terms for connectivity to international computer networks challenged the sovereignty discourse on transborder data flows. Indeed, the university researchers' requests conflicted with the emphasis on developing local data processing and storage facilities to guard against dependency on foreign ones. By contrast, these researchers sought to open up computer networks, not just within Brazil but with the emerging networks based in the U.S. and Europe. They viewed greater integration with international computer networks as key to developing their scientific work through engaging with researchers around the world and exchanging data as freely as possible. The researchers' efforts to participate in international computer networks required government officials to weigh the merits of the sovereignty discourse on transborder data flows against the expanding opportunities for scientific and technological engagement offered by the new international computer networks.

In April 1988, Brazilian researchers from the National Laboratory of Computer Networks (LARC) and the National Laboratory of Scientific Data Processing (LNCC) met with government officials from Embratel and the Special Secretariat of Informatics (SEI), the government agency in charge of implementing the informatics policy. At that meeting, the officials agreed that from then on, all university requests for individual links to academic networks outside Brazil would be automatically approved. By September of that year, Brazilian researchers gained access to BITNET. As Carvalho (2006, 84, my translation) argued, the decision to allow access "was a victory for LNCC and for the academic community as a whole.... [T]his decision reinforced the interests of other institutions that sought their own international connections."

In fact, this decision was part of a broader transition in Brazilian strategy that involved opening up the computer and software sectors to foreign interests. As mentioned above, trade conflicts arose with the U.S. government over the Brazilian informatics policy in 1985. Starting in 1990, the Brazilian government dismantled the policy under a complex combination of national and international pressures. It shifted to a neoliberal regime that opened Brazilian markets more fully to global capital. This new policy approach was rooted in the neoliberal discourse that viewed government policies as impediments to free trade. From the neoliberal perspective, such policies needed to be eradicated to allow the underlying economic logic of the market to promote global economic growth (Evans 1989; Schoonmaker 2002).

As discussed in the last chapter, the neoliberal discourse emphasized the freedom of corporations to expand into markets throughout the world under terms that were most profitable to them. It became the dominant discourse of globalization in the 1980s, as a range of governments and international institutions implemented this approach. In the process, government, corporate, and other institutional actors redefined development as a global project administered by international institutions, rather than a national project administered by governments (McMichael 2000, 2017).

The Brazilian researchers' requests to connect to international computer networks fit with this emphasis on opening the national market to foreign investment and influence. The researchers were focused on sharing ideas and data about their scientific work, however, rather than on opening the market to global capital. They sought to expand possibilities for researchers, universities, or scientific communities to engage with each other, rather than for corporations to enter new markets. It is thus important to note that the motivation for their challenge to the sovereignty discourse was not fundamentally a neoliberal one. Like Stallman and other proponents of free software discussed above, these researchers were primarily interested in sharing information and ideas with others in their fields. They resisted legal restrictions that limited their opportunities for engaging in collaboration with their colleagues. Furthermore, the Brazilian researchers recognized the importance of information and communications technology as a key vehicle that created the sociotechnical basis for such sharing to occur. Despite these differences between the researchers' motivations and the neoliberal agenda, their efforts to gain access to international computer networks coincided with the neoliberal shift toward opening markets to global capital.

At the same time, however, opening access to international computer networks laid the foundation for a vital second set of conditions for developing the digital commons. By challenging the underlying principles of the sovereignty discourse and applying key principles of the freedom discourse to the critical field of computer communications, the Brazilian researchers sought to define the technical, political, and discursive terms for access to computer networks. Rather than advocating the freedom to share and modify software code, as Stallman and other free software proponents had done, these researchers advocated the freedom to connect to computer networks located abroad.

Their efforts aligned with the emerging recursive public of free software. Researchers in Brazil were committed to opening up access to computer networks so that they could communicate with colleagues in other parts of the world. They shared this commitment to ensuring freedom of communication with hackers and researchers in other countries who were constructing computer networks and seeking to establish international contacts through their institutions. Hence, during the late 1980s and early 1990s, this range of actions by emerging recursive publics in different parts of the world created conditions for increasing access to global computer networks. The emergence of these networks, and their eventual connection to the Internet as a network of networks, was equally as important for developing the digital commons as the legal definition of free software through copyleft.

The Internet's central role in creating the digital commons has become increasingly evident over time. Since the 1990s, a variety of groups have contributed to the ongoing process of creating the political and discursive conditions to exchange flows of data through computer networks. They have continued to develop and apply the freedom discourse to advocate protection of human rights online, including civil liberties like free speech and the right to privacy. Such liberties require that the Internet be protected as an open, neutral, and decentralized network. Struggles to maintain and defend an open, decentralized Internet will be explored in detail in Chapter 6 on Internet Politics. These struggles build upon the earlier efforts of governments from the global South to create conditions to employ communications and information technologies in the context of global inequalities. While the technological context has changed substantially with the development of the Internet, as well as computers and software in multiple desktop and mobile platforms, some of the themes articulated in the sovereignty discourse from the 1970s continue to resonate in the twenty-first century. Indeed, contemporary Internet politics can be grasped more fully by placing them in the historical context of those early struggles over sovereignty.

For example, in her statement to the United Nations General Assembly in September 2013, Brazilian President Dilma Rousseff articulated concerns about national sovereignty that echoed parts of the earlier Brazilian policy on transborder data flows. President Rousseff was responding to Edward Snowden's revelations about the U.S. NSA's bulk surveillance of data, which she described as "a situation of grave violation of human rights and of civil liberties; of invasion and capture of confidential information concerning corporate activities, and especially of disrespect of national sovereignty" (Rousseff 2013, 2). President Rousseff thus viewed violations of sovereignty, human rights, and civil liberties as interconnected. She did not separate the violation of individual rights from the sovereign rights of Brazil as a nation. She drew on underlying values of sovereignty that aligned with the earlier sovereignty discourse, particularly with respect to the need for governments to protect their citizens' rights to privacy in a context where digital technologies made it possible to store large amounts of data about those citizens.

This emphasis on sovereignty thus differed from the freedom discourse, with its focus on the rights of individuals and the value of freedom to society. Like the earlier sovereignty discourse on transborder data flows, President Rousseff's remarks delineated the interests of individuals within a broader context of their citizenship in a nation from the global South. She emphasized the importance of that citizenship not just in any nation, but in a nation with a particular history and position in the global economy. She stated, "[a]s many other Latin Americans, I fought against authoritarianism and censorship, and I cannot but defend, in an uncompromising fashion, the right to privacy of individuals and the sovereignty of my country" (Rousseff 2013, 1–2).

Furthermore, there were significant differences between President Rousseff's statement and the earlier sovereignty discourse. As will be explored further in Chapter 6, the Brazilian government's major concern was to "adopt legislation, technologies and mechanisms to protect us from the illegal interception of communications and data" (Rousseff 2013, 2). President Rousseff thus viewed threats to sovereignty in terms of data being intercepted through spying activities such as those conducted by the NSA. She advocated neutrality of the Internet to ensure that data communications would both be protected from surveillance and allowed to move freely. Like the earlier advocates of the sovereignty discourse, she viewed access to data as connected to economic and political power. She did not, however, view the unequal global distribution of data as a problem that needed to be resolved by retaining data within the country rather than processing it abroad. Instead, she targeted the illegal interception of data, and restrictions on the ability to exchange data freely over the Internet, as the key threats to sovereignty. Sovereignty concerns had shifted focus from equalizing the global distribution of databases and processing facilities to equalizing conditions for access to communications networks.

President Rousseff, like other contemporary advocates of network neutrality, thus strove to establish the terms for free and unfettered access to the Internet for all users. By framing the freedom to exchange data without surveillance as a matter of national sovereignty, human rights, and civil liberties, President Rousseff rearticulated the freedom discourse with an emphasis on national sovereignty. As will be explored further in Chapter 6, a number of key actors in Brazil and the U.S. articulated such a discourse beginning in 1996. These actors expanded the freedom discourse beyond its original focus on individual rights and societal value, to conceive of freedom within a context of relationships between states in the global economy. To capture the significance of this discursive shift in focus, I call this the freedom/sovereignty discourse. Such a focus was particularly fitting to establish the terms to access the Internet for global communications, which occur largely between institutional actors like corporations and governments, as well as individual users. As will be detailed in Chapter 6, Rousseff and other contemporary advocates of network neutrality employed the freedom/sovereignty discourse to defend individual civil liberties, including the right to privacy, in the context of surveillance by governments and corporations and enduring inequalities between the global North and South.

Expanding the Digital Commons: Creative Work and Shared Encyclopedic Knowledge

Contemporary efforts to defend and expand the digital commons thus build upon the work of free software advocates in the U.S. and proponents of connecting to global communications systems in Brazil. Indeed, these earlier recursive publics laid critical foundations for the digital commons in the late 1980s and early 1990s. Toward the turn of the twenty-first century, however, advocates of free culture extended this work in a more intentionally global direction. They responded to changes in cultural production made possible by the rise of the Internet, which "unleashed an extraordinary possibility for many to participate in the process of building and cultivating a culture that reaches far beyond local boundaries" (Lessig 2004, 9). As Lessig (2004) argued, these changes unraveled the line between free, noncommercial culture and commercial culture. In the past, when people shared stories, music, tapes, and reenactments of scenes from plays or television with their friends, these activities were informal and free of regulation. New possibilities to share such forms of culture over the Internet, with diverse groups of people around the world, threatened corporations in industries such as music and film. As will be discussed further in Chapters 5 and 6, these firms fought protracted legal battles to protect their proprietary interests from what they depicted as piracy and threats to the rule of law.

In the context of these corporate efforts to promote their proprietary interests, advocates of free culture sought to protect the rights of cultural creators and users. In this respect, they acted to maintain their own conditions of existence as recursive publics (Kelty 2008). Beyond these efforts, however, they initiated projects to create legal and political conditions to share and remix each other's work. In the process, they built global communities that contributed to the development of the digital commons. For example, in 2001, free culture advocates launched two critical projects that expanded the digital commons in important ways. Lawrence Lessig and his colleagues applied the freedom discourse to diverse forms of cultural works, providing the producers of cultural content with alternatives to the proprietary form through what they called the Creative Commons (Lessig 2004). Moreover, Jimmy Wales and Larry Sanger cofounded Wikipedia as a free online encyclopedia, created through an ongoing collaborative process by the people who use it (Schweik and English 2012; Lih 2009).

Creative Commons and Wikipedia are open-content projects that provide public access to a digital product, such as text, music, photos, video, or encyclopedic content, without charging a fee (Schweik and English 2012). In the case of Creative Commons, the project also provides public access to a range of licenses for creative works, as well as information about the legal implications of those licenses. As in the case of free software projects, open-content project participants engage in collaborative communities and do much of their work over the Internet. These communities may involve a combination of peer producers and paid employees; however, they primarily rely on volunteer peer participants. By exploring key features of these two projects, I will highlight their differences from free software as well as the analytical value of conceptualizing these projects as part of the digital commons.

Creative Commons

In 2001, Lawrence Lessig, Hal Abelson, and Eric Eldred founded Creative Commons as a nonprofit organization, with support from the Center of the Study of the Public Domain at Duke Law School. Inspired in part by the GNU GPL, the Creative Commons community developed a range of licenses for producers of cultural content to choose from, all legally constituted under U.S. copyright law. In the process, Creative Commons enabled writers, musicians, and other artists to become digital entrepreneurs. These producers could choose multiple ways to protect rights of ownership over their creative works, as well as options to allow different degrees of sharing and remixing by others. The Creative Commons website offered resources explaining the key features of each license.

Creative Commons was rooted in the principles of the freedom discourse. As Lessig (2004, 282, emphasis in original) described, the goal of the project was

> to build a layer of *reasonable* copyright on top of the extremes that now reign. It does this by making it easy for people to build upon other people's work, by making it simple for creators to express the freedom for others to take and build upon their work.

Creative Commons participants thus focused on creating a legal structure of licenses to enable people who were both producing and consuming cultural products to expand the public domain. Artists and writers, for example, could define the legal terms under which their work could be accessed and shared, so that participants in the community could build upon each other's work. They employed the freedom discourse and applied it to the fields of creative works, emphasizing the value of freely accessing and sharing cultural content. They incorporated flexibility and freedom of choice into the licenses, so that producers of cultural content might decide on a range of ways to share their work. Overall, however, their goal was to "help build the public domain and, by their work, demonstrate the importance of the public domain to other creativity" (Lessig 2004, 284).

Participants in the Creative Commons created an international community, with local affiliates around the world collaborating in a common global project. As will be discussed further in Chapter 6, Brazilian free culture advocates worked to develop one of the early Creative Commons affiliates beginning in 2003. The Creative Commons team tracks the expansion of Creative Commons affiliates around the world, listing those affiliates in a page on Affiliate Locales on their website (accessed June 3, 2017, https://wiki.creativecommons.org/wiki/Category:CC_Affiliate_Locale). By 2017, free culture proponents established over 100 Creative Commons affiliates in over 91 jurisdictions, including a range of Latin American, European, Middle Eastern, African, and Asian countries, as well as the U.S. (accessed June 3, 2017, https://stateof.creativecommons.org/).

Language diversity is a key feature of the global Creative Commons community, revealing the ways that participants in language communities around the world collaborated with each other to develop a common global project. Over the years since 2001, translators worked to make Creative Commons licenses available in a diverse range of languages, including Dutch, Finnish, French, Italian, Japanese, Korean, Lithuanian, Malay, Polish, Serbian, Swedish, and Taiwanese Mandarin (accessed June 4, 2017, https://wiki.creativecommons.org/wiki/Category:CC0_Translations). In 2016 and 2017, over a dozen participants from nine Arab countries collaborated on the Arabic translation. They considered feedback from lawyers, license users, linguists, librarians, translators, and cultural experts. This skilled group of participants crafted a translation to significantly expand the accessibility of Creative Commons licenses. Since Arabic is the sixth most spoken language in the world, making these licenses available to Arabic speakers extends the reach of the global community. Also in 2016, a Croation language translation team consulted with intellectual property lawyers, professional translators, and participants in the Wikipedia community. They created a translation that they expect will expand the use of Creative Commons licenses by speakers of Croatian and other affiliated Southeastern European languages. In this Southeastern European region, producers and consumers of free culture, as well as participants in the Wikipedia community and online news sites, employ Creative Commons licenses (accessed June 4, 2017, https://creativecommons.org/2017/02/23/arabic-croatian-translations/).

One way to understand the extent of the global Creative Commons community is to examine the extent to which cultural creators employ Creative Commons to license their work. For example, according to Creative Commons' 2016 *State of the Commons* report, there were 1.2 billion works licensed under Creative Commons in 2016. The report highlights the expansion of the commons over the last decade. The number of works licensed under Creative Commons grew from 140 million in 2006 to 400 million in 2010, 882 million in 2014, and 1.1 billion in 2015.

Key examples of these works offer a picture of the diverse nature of Creative Commons as a global community. Participants in a wide range of commons projects employ Creative Commons licenses. First, the New York Metropolitan Museum of Art licensed 375,000 digital works with Creative Commons licenses and released them into the public domain. Second, 30 organizations in different parts of Africa collaborated on the African Storybook Initiative. They created 730 children's storybooks and 2,754 translations or adaptations of children's books in 94 African languages. Each month, an average of 4,800 people visited the project's website; these visitors downloaded over 636,000 storybooks over a two-year period. Third, New Zealand's official geological hazard site, GeoNet, provides citizens with data that enables faster responses to earthquakes, tsunamis, and volcanic activity. GeoNet offers data in real time that are licensed under Creative Commons in an open format. These data have been accessed and shared to support research on how to respond to disasters (accessed June 4, 2017, https://stateof.creativecommons.org/).

Finally, Creative Commons expanded through the work of Dr. Amin Azzam. Dr. Azzam designed a course for fourth-year medical students at UC Berkeley and UC San Francisco where they edited and improved 42 Wikipedia articles on health-related topics. He initiated this project to address a contradiction in medical students' use of Wikipedia. Certainly, the majority of medical students use Wikipedia as one of their sources of information for their work. Medical schools, however, generally do not teach the students how to edit Wikipedia articles or use Wikipedia from a critical perspective. Dr. Azzam used open educational practices to train students to contribute to Wikipedia, thus encouraging them to contribute to the commons. During the two months that the students were editing the articles as part of their class work, Wikipedia users viewed these articles 1.1 million times. In 2016, Wikipedia users viewed this group of articles 22 million times (accessed June 4, 2017, https://stateof.creativecommons.org/). When Dr. Azzam and his colleagues studied the students' learning process and their responses to the course, they found that students "felt they improved their articles, enjoyed giving back 'specifically to Wikipedia,' and broadened their sense of physician responsibilities in the socially networked information era" (Azzam et al. 2017, 194).

There are key connections between Creative Commons and Wikipedia as open-content commons projects. Certainly, Wikipedia cofounders Jimmy Wales and Larry Sanger viewed decisions about licensing as fundamental to constructing the Wikipedia project. As part of the process of deciding how to license Wikipedia content, they consulted with Richard Stallman. From the FSF's perspective grounded in the freedom discourse, Stallman advocated the GNU Free Documentation License (GFDL) to protect the freedoms of content producers and users (Lih 2009). According to the Wikipedia web pages on the GFDL and copyrights, as well as the FSF web page on the GFDL, FSF programmers designed this license to complement the GNU GPL. They developed the GFDL to cover manuals, textbooks, and other documents, rather than software. It protected the users' freedom to copy, modify, and redistribute the content. Equally important, the GFDL allowed authors and publishers to be publicly acknowledged for the work they had done, and to distinguish their work from other contributors (accessed June 5, 2017, www.gnu.org/licenses/fdl-1.3.en.html; https://en.wikipedia.org/wiki/Wikipedia:Text_of_the_GNU_Free_Documentation_License; https://en.wikipedia.org/wiki/Wikipedia:Copyrights#Contributors.27_rights_and_obligations).

Wales and Sanger chose to pursue a co-licensing strategy that integrated the work of the FSF with the emerging work of Creative Commons. As a result, most of the text and many of the images in Wikipedia are co-licensed under the GFDL and Creative Commons Attribution-ShareAlike 3.0 Unported License (CC BY-SA). The Creative Commons web page describing this license notes that users are free to make changes, copy, and redistribute the content as long as they give credit to the previous authors; usually, such credit involves including a link to the license and identifying what changes they made to the content. Both the GFDL and the Creative Commons license are based on the principles of copyleft, where users are legally bound to redistribute their work under the same license as the original work. As discussed above, such continuity of licensing protects the freedoms of sharing and redistribution for future users and is the foundation of the code for the digital commons (accessed June 5, 2017, https://creativecommons.org/licenses/by-sa/3.0/us/).

Copyleft principles, rooted in the freedom discourse that prioritizes the freedoms of users to share information as a common good, thus provide a similar institutional structure for Wikipedia, Creative Commons, and free software communities. Indeed, copyleft licenses provide common legal protections for these communities as distinct commons projects. The key differences between Wikipedia, Creative Commons, and free software arise from the nature of the projects of creating software compared to creating an online encyclopedia or other forms of free culture. As discussed above, Creative Commons community participants focused primarily on creating legal conditions for cultural creators and consumers to contribute to expanding the public domain. They engaged in this process in a wide range of ways, from licensing their works under Creative Commons to participating in translation projects to extend the availability of those licenses to diverse language communities around the world. In the process, these community participants created and expanded Creative Commons as a global community.

Wikipedia

In a similar vein, Wikipedia community participants from diverse countries, speaking a wide range of languages, engaged in local community activities that contributed to a broader global project. Known as Wikipedians, they developed and employed a sociotechnical system to structure their collaborative work. This system was distinct from Creative Commons, which relied on developing licenses for creative works and making them available in a range of languages.

Wikipedia is a sociotechnical system based on a free software application called MediaWiki. MediaWiki is designed to make it easy for users to make contributions through their web browser. Users can add text or images to a web page, as well as adding and editing text and images that other users have already contributed (Schweik and English 2012; Lih 2009). After developing the Wikipedia project for three years, Wikipedia participants launched WikiMedia Commons in 2004. They employed the same wiki-technology as Wikipedia to allow for collaborative editing. According to the WikiMedia Commons homepage, its participants collect media files, with 1 million files uploaded by 2006 and almost 31 million by 2016. It is a freely accessible database, licensed under the Creative Commons Attribution/Share-Alike License (accessed January 15, 2017, https://commons.wikimedia.org/wiki/Commons:Welcome). WikiMedia Commons provides a key resource for developing Wikipedia, since it stores different versions of the content of Wikipedia articles. This feature makes it easier for Wikipedia moderators to keep track of changes to the pages and to restore previous versions if they decide that a user's edits are not acceptable. Each Wikipedia article has an Edit History page, documenting the details of all of the changes that have been made over time (Lih 2009; Schweik and English 2012).

Wikipedians engaged in the open-content process to create an international encyclopedia and simultaneously constitute themselves as a global community. Similar to free software, participants in local communities collaborated with each other in a larger global project. The nature of the encyclopedic project, however, pushed the global nature of the endeavor forward in distinct ways. Wikipedians speaking similar languages collaborated across national boundaries to create Wikipedia editions for their common languages; this was comparable to the Creative Commons translation teams discussed above. According to the Wikipedia page on the size of Wikipedia, Wikipedians write in over 200 languages, with over 80 percent of Wikipedia written in languages other than English. Within the context of this global linguistic diversity, there are over 5.1 million articles in the English Wikipedia (Fichman and Hara 2014; accessed January 20, 2017, https://en.wikipedia.org/wiki/Wikipedia:Size_of_Wikipedia#Size_of_the_English_Wikipedia_database). Certainly, the global nature of the Wikipedia project is evident in this diversity of languages.

In order to collaborate in writing the encyclopedia, Wikipedia editors needed guidelines for writing the articles as well as for engaging with each other. The particular nature of the encyclopedic project required collaborators to come to a common understanding about how to present their ideas, and about how to engage in decision-making about the content they created together. This project differed from the process of writing code, where programmers collaborated to find ways to make a program work. The programming process was more focused on technical questions, whereas Wikipedians needed to find ways to communicate ideas about myriad topics that could involve conflicting perspectives and interpretations. Furthermore, the encyclopedia project differed from the Creative Commons project, which was more focused on enabling individual creators and consumers of free culture to contribute to the public domain. Creative Commons was a collective project; however, its collective nature was more grounded in providing a platform to present and access free culture. The creators and users of free culture engaged in these practices either as individuals or groups who collaborated on a particular cultural product. Nonetheless, these Creative Commons projects did not generally require collaborators to come to a common understanding on as broad a range of questions as Wikipedia.

Due to the particular challenges involved with collaborating to write an encyclopedia, Wikipedia cofounders Sanger and Wales emphasized the importance of the participation of a community of editors who treated each other with civility and respect. The Wikipedia community developed and practiced the principle of writing from a neutral point of view (NPOV). The Wikipedia website explains this principle as "striv[ing] for articles that document and explain major points of view, giving due weight with respect to their prominence in an impartial tone. We avoid advocacy and we characterize information and issues rather than debate them" (accessed January 25, 2017, https://en.wikipedia.org/wiki/Wikipedia:Five_pillars). Writing from a NPOV is particularly challenging when there are a range of distinct, and perhaps conflicting, perspectives involved on a topic. In such cases, the Wikipedia web page characterizes the role of the editors as "describ[ing] multiple points of view, presenting each accurately and in context rather than as 'the truth' or 'the best view'" (accessed January 25, 2017, https://en.wikipedia.org/wiki/Wikipedia:Five_ pillars). Editors thus strive for impartiality, representing all of the points of view according to underlying principles of verifiable accuracy. Such accuracy requires editors to cite reliable, authoritative sources and to avoid including their personal opinions or experiences.

From the beginning of the Wikipedia commons project, Sanger encouraged what he called "bold" participation. He declared, "'Wikis don't work if people aren't bold'" (quoted in Lih 2009, 91). Indeed, "Be bold" became an editing guideline for the English Wikipedia, with its own web page, stating

> [t]he Wikipedia community encourages users to **be bold when updating the encyclopedia.** Wikis like ours develop faster when everybody helps to fix problems, correct grammar, add facts, make sure wording is accurate, etc. We would like *everyone* to be bold and help make Wikipedia a better encyclopedia.
> (Accessed January 23, 2017, https://en.wikipedia.org/wiki/ Wikipedia:Be_bold, emphasis in original)

From a sociological perspective, Sanger and others in the Wikipedia community explicitly promoted boldness as a social norm, as part of creating a culture of participation that encouraged Wikipedians to share their ideas fully without holding back. The Wikipedia:BeBold web page had its own acronym, WP:BOLD, as well as detailed instructions for how the community encouraged participants to respond when their views conflicted with others. In bold, large type, it states

> **Don't be upset if your bold edits get reverted....** Instead of getting upset, read WP:Assume good faith and WP:Civility, and be bold again.... Think about it this way: if you don't find one of your edits being reverted now and then, perhaps you're not being bold enough.
> (Accessed January 25, 2017, https://en.wikipedia.org/wiki/ Wikipedia:Be_bold)

Boldness is a complex social norm in Wikipedia, however, with nuanced guideline for behavior. After encouraging Wikipedians to be bold, the Be bold web page then includes an extended caveat. It states "[t]hough the boldness of contributors like you is one of Wikipedia's greatest assets, it is important that you take care of the common good and not edit disruptively or recklessly" (accessed February 1, 2017, https://en.wikipedia. org/wiki/Wikipedia:Be_bold). When editors are contemplating work on controversial articles with contentious editing histories, this web page instructs them to proceed with extra care. In many cases, the text as you find it has come into being after long and arduous negotiations between Wikipedians of diverse backgrounds and points of view. A careless edit to such an article might stir up a latent conflict, and other users who are involved in the page may become defensive.

(Accessed February 1, 2017, https://en.wikipedia.org/wiki/
Wikipedia:Be_bold)

The web page encourages prospective editors to read the article carefully, as well as to review the comments on the talk page where previous editors have discussed their distinct approaches to the article. Once prospective editors understand the history of contention over an article, they are in a better position to use their best judgment when considering what it means to take a bold approach to editing.

Furthermore, the Be bold web page encourages prospective editors to take extra care when considering edits to Good Articles or Featured Articles. The definitions of these articles offer additional insights into the ways that Wikipedia is governed, since there are clear processes for nominating, reviewing, and reassessing Good Articles. For example, the Wikipedia page on Good Articles describes these processes as "intentionally straightforward" (accessed January 15, 2017, https://en.wikipedia.org/wiki/Wikipedia:Good_articles). All editors who read or work on an article that they consider to be high quality may nominate that article for consideration to be designated as a Good Article. Once an article is nominated, an impartial reviewer reads the article to determine whether it fits the criteria. For example, Good Articles should be satisfactory overall; they should be reasonably well written, with clear organization and language. They need to provide sources, including citations when appropriate, to document the factual accuracy and verifiability of the information. As discussed above, such articles should be written from a NPOV, representing relevant viewpoints without bias. Good Articles generally include broad consideration of a topic, and when possible may include images with appropriate copyright licenses. They are stable over time, revealing that there are not contentious discussions on the talk pages where editors are disagreeing about the way that the article should be written. As the Good Articles page notes, "Good articles do not have to be as comprehensive as featured articles, but they should not omit any major facets of the topic" (accessed January 15, 2017, https://en.wikipedia.org/wiki/Wikipedia:Good_articles).

By contrast, the Wikipedia page comparing criteria for Good and Featured Articles notes that Featured Articles "must be *our very best work*…[with] a professional standard of writing that is *engaging, even brilliant*" (accessed January 15, 2017, https://en.wikipedia.org/wiki/Wikipedia:Compare_criteria_Good_v._Featured_article, emphasis in original). Featured Articles are of a high, reliable quality that meets a professional standard, including elegant prose; observance of all of Wikipedia's guidelines for style, citations, and factual accuracy; comprehensiveness of coverage, so that no major facts or details are excluded; neutrality of viewpoints; and use of images with appropriate copyrights and fair use rationales.

Processes for review of articles to determine whether they meet standards for Good or Featured Articles provide ways for Wikipedians to participate in the development of this open-content commons project. Through such processes, participants contribute to defining and monitoring the quality of the project. Editors who begin "stub" articles from scratch have guidelines available so that they can develop pieces that are more comprehensive, better written, and documented by a wider range of research that supports their claims to factual accuracy. According to the Wikipedia page on Good Articles, 23,899 articles out of the total 5,124,272 articles on Wikipedia were classified as Good in 2016; this is about 1 in 215 articles. It is much more difficult for articles to be classified as Featured; 4,744, or about 1 in 1,090, were categorized as such in 2016. Considering both Good and Featured Articles, there are 31,605 articles, about 1 in 163 of the total articles on Wikipedia, that fit into one of these categories (Accessed January 21, 2017, https://en.wikipedia.org/wiki/Wikipedia:Good_articles).

These norms for writing high-quality articles offer guidelines for editors around the world to contribute to the project. To understand the process of contributing to Wikipedia, however, it is important to consider that some key contributors are bots, not humans. As Fichman and Hara (2014, 1) emphasize, Wikipedia is a "sociotechnical system...of interactions between people and technology, dependent on both humans and machines." On the technical side, the wiki system makes it possible for multiple users to collaborate on documents. A range of volunteers, users, and administrators employ these technological systems; in the process, they both create and operate within a set of policies that structure their interactions (Fichman and Hara 2014).

Bots make vital contributions to constructing knowledge in this system. Livingstone (2014, 10) builds upon Latour and Callon's actor-network theory to conceptualize bots as "immaterial editors"; even though they are originally coded by programmers, bots are "more than just tools, but truly autonomous or semiautonomous agents in a system." By examining the actors within the network of Wikipedia, Livingstone (2014) reveals how robots and humans interact and contribute to the Wikipedia community in similar ways. For example, bots and humans both interact with the Wikipedia site from user accounts. As of March 2013, 273 language versions of Wikipedia, about 96 percent of all communities, included at least one bot.

Wikipedia communities create policies about what bots are allowed to do. Bot policies generally include a definition of bots, guidelines for the kinds of work that bots may and may not perform, as well as specifications for bot editing speed. For example, many communities bar bots from work such as creating new articles; however, the Dutch and Arabic language communities view this work as beneficial (Livingstone 2014).

Bots perform a range of kinds of work that is vital for the development and maintenance of Wikipedia. Bots engage extensively in editing, performing almost 25 percent of this work in the range of language versions of Wikipedia. The amount of bot editing work varies, depending upon the size of the community and the availability of people to engage in it. In some communities with smaller numbers of human participants, bots do between 50 percent and 75 percent of the editing (Livingstone 2014). Equally important, bots maintain links between articles in one language to the range of versions of that article in different languages. Due to the centrality of links to wikis, where users can follow associations between different pages, the work of maintaining these links is a key part of the process of building the Wikipedia community. Maintaining these interlanguage links takes a great deal of time, and has been a key area where bots can free up human participants to engage in other aspects of the project.

Bot contributions have become increasingly important in a context where the Wikimedia Foundation suggested that the number of human participants in the community may be declining. According to the Wikipedia page on the size of Wikipedia, since 2006, there has been a slow, steady decline in the number of new articles created each month. At the same time, Wikipedia participants have contributed a relatively consistent amount of text to Wikipedia articles each year, indicating that they are focusing more on adding new content to existing articles than to creating new articles (accessed October 15, 2016, https://en.wikipedia.org/wiki/Wikipedia:Size_of_Wikipedia#Size_of_the_English_Wikipedia_database). Bots engage in a substantial amount of this editing. For example, sieBot performed almost 10 million edits in 260 different Wikipedia language versions; in a similar vein, EmausBot and Luckas-bot each performed over 13 million edits (Livingstone 2014).

Despite the importance of bot editors to the Wikipedia project, the role of bot editors is changing in the wake of the 2012 launch of Wikidata. Wikidata is a collaborative, secondary database supporting the Wikimedia Foundation's range of interconnected projects, including Wikipedia and the WikiMedia Commons. According to Wikidata's homepage, the data are licensed and published under Creative Commons Public Domain Dedication 1.0, which makes it possible to legally reuse the data in a wide range of different scenarios. Similar to free software and other Wikimedia projects, users can copy, modify, and distribute the data without asking for permission. Permission is granted by the license itself, which ensures the open, commons nature of the project. Wikidata records sources for the data, allowing users to verify its validity more easily. It is designed to support Wikipedia by providing a central repository for the interwiki language links described above, and thus making it easier to maintain them. A key feature of Wikidata is that the data are fully multilingual, so that if a user enters the data in one language, they are immediately available in all of the other languages. Users can thus readily edit the data in any language, promoting a global, multilingual process of content creation and access. Both humans and bots enter data in Wikidata (accessed October 20, 2016, www.wikidata. org/wiki/Wikidata:Introduction). As Livingstone (2014) notes, with a central repository of language links available, local Wikipedia communities will probably shift their reliance to that main source and decrease their reliance on the interwiki bots.

Wikidata facilitates Wikipedia's continued expansion as a global community, allowing editors from around the world to contribute in their own languages and simultaneously make that content available in other languages. As Wikipedia integrates the Wikidata platform to facilitate interactions between humans and technology, this sociotechnical system will continue to provide an environment for local participants to contribute to the global project of producing and sharing encyclopedic knowledge.

Conclusion: Recursive Publics and Digital Commons

From the late 1960s to the late 1980s, through a combination of efforts by actors around the world, two key sets of conditions were created to develop the digital commons. Many of the participants in this process did not know each other or consciously coordinate their work. Nonetheless, these researchers, hackers, and other free software proponents shared a commitment to promoting the freedom to access and share information as a common good rather than as private property. They articulated this commitment through the freedom discourse. Their common commitment provided a foundation for them to act as disparate recursive publics concerned with establishing the technical, political, and discursive conditions for their existence (Kelty 2008). In distinct ways, they all contributed to the initial development of the digital commons as an alternative to proprietary control over software and computer networks. As Bollier (2008) advocated, they engaged in struggles to create the commons as an alternative to existing forms of state and private property. They acted within the structure of the old proprietary and state systems to resist the current forms of software and computer networks available within those systems. In the process, they invented new forms of software and terms for access to computer networks consistent with their visions of freedom.

As discussed above, creating conditions to access global computer networks, and eventually the Internet as a network of networks, was vital for the development of the digital commons. The Brazilian government played a key role in this process; it implemented the sovereignty discourse articulated by a range of governments in the global South, through its policy on transborder data flows. By the late 1980s, Brazilian researchers pressed for access to global computer networks, leading the government to rearticulate the sovereignty discourse in terms that fit with the freedom discourse. These actions took place in the context of the rise of neoliberalism as the dominant form of globalization, where Brazil and other nations around the world opened their markets to global capital. Changes in Brazilian communications policy aligned with the neoliberal emphasis on increasing openness to global forces. Simultaneously, however, these changes resonated with the freedom discourse of free software proponents in the U.S. Indeed, both the U.S. and Brazilian efforts emphasized the importance of the freedom to share information and knowledge with colleagues around the world. President Rousseff rearticulated the concerns for Internet freedom as linked to sovereignty and global inequality in 2013, building on earlier efforts to transform the freedom discourse into a freedom/sovereignty discourse. This range of efforts contributed to the struggle to create a digital commons within existing proprietary and state systems.

The creation of conditions for free access to computer networks converged with efforts by hackers in the U.S. to code the digital commons. The nature of software technology, and in particular, the ability for hackers to transform programs if they have access to the source code, presented powerful technical possibilities to use software as a code for the digital commons. As discussed above, Stallman and the FSF dedicated themselves to developing a software-sharing community where hackers freely built upon each other's work. Since software licensed under the GNU GPL was not combined with proprietary elements, hackers had total freedom of access to its source code. The constitution of copyleft under U.S. copyright law ensured that the code remained unfettered by proprietary restrictions and that hackers guaranteed similar freedoms to future users of their work.

Stallman and the FSF thus invented a creative alternative to the neoliberal logic of opening markets and maximizing profits. Their work was rooted in the concept of creating and preserving a software-sharing community as an alternative to the rising dominance of proprietary software. They used the market and intellectual property law to devise software systems geared to coding a digital commons. Free software could be commodified in the sense that hackers could sell the versions they created on the market. By requiring hackers to make source code available to all users, however, the FSF contributed to the rise of the digital commons. It resisted the proprietary form of software that denied users the freedom to run, adapt, redistribute, and rerelease their work.

After 2001, Creative Commons and Wikipedia participants continued to build on these earlier strategies to develop the digital commons.

They expanded the digital commons by creating alternatives to proprietary cultural forms. Creative Commons advocates opened up opportunities for artists, writers, and other producers of cultural content to license their works and share them with others in a range of ways. Wikipedia participants collaborated to write and edit an encyclopedia that offers its users access to a community-produced resource on a growing array of topics.

Since the 1970s, a diverse range of proponents have thus contributed to the development of the digital commons. Over time, they acted less like recursive publics working to maintain the technical, legal, practical, and conceptual conditions for their own existence (Kelty 2008). They shifted their focus and engaged in a process of developing a diverse range of global communities. Amidst their diversity, these global communities shared fundamental common features. Local participants across the globe collaborated on common projects, from software development to free culture licenses and a global encyclopedia.

In the next chapter, I explore how free software communities developed globally, by drawing upon and extending the FSF's earlier work in myriad ways. I examine how conditions of free software production affect the development of the digital commons, highlighting cases of production in peer communities as well as a range of corporate settings. These cases illuminate the emergence of free software as a global community, engaged in the ongoing development of the digital commons. Certainly, the digital commons remain rooted in free software and free access to computer networks as alternatives to proprietary systems. Free software community participants continue to articulate the freedom discourse, based upon principles of freedom to access and share information as a common good rather than as private property. In the process, they resist what Coleman (2004, 509) calls the "neoliberal drive to make property out of everything." By creating global communities of resistance to neoliberalism, these free software advocates go beyond Kelty's (2008) sense of working as recursive publics. Indeed, in the process of forging these communities of resistance, they constitute alternative forms of globalization from below.

3 From Markets to Commons

Free Software as Catalyst for Change

In the context of informational capitalism, free software plays a pivotal role as what Kelty (2008, 2) calls a "reorientation of power and knowledge." Since software is integrated into the practices of corporations, governments, and other institutional and individual users, the nature of the software affects a wide range of economic, political, social, and cultural activities. As discussed in the last chapter, peer producers of free software developed a new form of community-based property. Insightfully employing U.S. copyright law for their own purposes, Richard Stallman and the Free Software Foundation (FSF) crafted the GNU General Public License (GNU GPL). In the process, they created a new form of property that legally protects users' freedoms through copyleft. These freedoms, multiplied among all current and potential future users of free software, provide a key foundation for the digital commons as a "complex ecosystem" (Hess and Ostrom 2006, 3) that emerges within the existing proprietary structures of capitalism. By constituting the free software property form, free software advocates thus intervened decisively in the intellectual property system, as well as in the broader structures of economic and political power and knowledge within informational capitalism.

Free software originates in, and continues to rely upon, what Benkler (2006) terms processes of peer production. Benkler (2006) identifies two key characteristics of peer production. First, individual producers choose to engage in production, rather than being compelled to do so. They thus engage in what Terranova (2013) calls "free labor," which is given voluntarily by the worker, as well as being unpaid. Second, Benkler (2006) theorizes peer production as occurring outside of a traditional organizational hierarchy. As will be discussed in this and the following chapter, free software communities have designed a range of peer governance structures that create opportunities to participate not only in creating the software, but in constituting and running the broader software projects and the communities themselves.

The deeper transformative potential of free software, however, lies beyond these qualities of peer production noted by Benkler (2006). In order to grasp the ways that free software contributes to the development of the digital commons, we must consider the implications of free software as a new form of property, as well as the conditions of its production. As a new form of property, free software acts as a catalyst for change in the market, shifting the economic and political conditions of capitalist production. I thus refer to free software as a catalytic form of property, distinct from proprietary software with closed source code. When the source code is open, users can modify and share the software; this disrupts the power of proprietary software companies to control software's production and sale. As Bauwens (2009, 122) argues, peer producers use this new form of property to "make sure that the commonly created value indeed stays 'common'." As discussed in the last chapter, free software thus constitutes a distinct form of "property's outside" (Boyle 2008, xiv), which is constituted in relationship to proprietary practices and forms through copyright law. Similar to other forms of commons, the digital commons emerge within and are interspersed throughout proprietary capitalist practices (Bollier 2008; Benkler 2013a).

As a catalytic form of property, free software may be created by developers working for free in a peer community or for pay in a market-based firm; it may be marketed for profit or given away. The nature of the production or marketing process itself does not alter the nature of free software as community-based property. This is where my perspective diverges from Benkler (2006), who emphasizes the importance of the peer production process as the major difference from the market-based, proprietary model. From my perspective, *it is the nature of free software as a new form of **property** that distinguishes it most decisively from proprietary software with closed source code, not the process through which it is produced.* Since copyleft licensing ensures that the source code remains open, this new, catalytic form of property can spread through markets and transform capitalist practices. In the process, commons-based practices emerge. These processes of change have the potential to spread quickly, due to the centrality of software to economic, political, social, and cultural practices in informational capitalism.

Of equal importance, proprietary strategies also shape and are shaped by the production and distribution of free software. Corporate interests in profit-making lie at the heart of struggles to undermine free software. Simultaneously, and perhaps paradoxically, proprietary strategies also seek to take advantage of business opportunities involved with free software. Bauwens (2009, 121) conceptualizes this as the "hyperproductive" nature of peer production, "forcing for-profit entities to adapt to its characteristics, thereby further integrating it into the existing political economy, but not without the transformative effects of its market transcending aspects." Peer production thus constitutes a force to be reckoned with in the market, as firms develop proprietary strategies to respond to the challenges and opportunities it creates. In the process, peer production transforms market dynamics. For Bauwens (2009, 122), peer production becomes "transcendent" when it "has sufficient post-capitalist aspects that can strengthen autonomous production communities in building an alternative logic of life and production that may, under certain conditions, overtake the current system."

In this chapter, I examine two cases of software production to grasp the conditions under which software might contribute to the development of the digital commons and alternative forms of globalization from below. Both cases are examples of the development of free software as a global community, constituted by local struggles that are simultaneously unified in global projects.

The first case is Debian, an open-source operating system built by a community of about 1,000 peer producers. Debian provides the code base for Canonical, a market-based firm, to create and market its own version of the operating system, called Ubuntu. Ubuntu is thus produced through an intriguing combination of market-based and peer production that both embodies and transforms capitalist practices. Debian is a global software project, with most of its participants located in the U.S., Europe, and Canada.

The second case is Drupal, a web content management system (CMS) widely used by universities and governments, including the U.S. government. Drupal is developed by a community of at least 17,000 developers, through the combined activities of unpaid producers in the peer community and paid coders at Acquia, a market-based firm. Drupal had been based primarily in Europe and the U.S.; however, communities in Latin America and India have organized themselves extensively. Beginning in 2013, the leadership at the Drupal Association (DA) worked with community participants to organize a third annual conference to take place in the global South. This was part of a strategy to promote the growth of those Drupal communities, and thus develop and extend it as a global community.

For each case, I explore two related sets of questions.

First, I consider the characteristics of software production, community organization, and property identified above. I explore whether the project involves the voluntary participation of peer producers, and whether those producers participate in a community that designs its own participatory governance processes. In addition to these key qualities of peer production, I explore the community's global organization. As discussed in the last chapter, the emergence of free software as a global community provides an organizational basis for it to contribute to alternative forms of globalization from below. Finally, I explore the licensing involved with the software, to assess whether it constitutes a catalytic property form that ensures that the software will retain its community-based character.

Second, I consider the relationship between the software project and the market. This includes the project's relationship with proprietary strategies. For example, participants in the software project may have developed their own proprietary strategies to make a living in the market. On the other hand, for-profit firms may have developed proprietary strategies to respond to or interact with the project. I highlight the examples of IBM and Google to explore the implications of such proprietary strategies for developing the digital commons. For example, IBM invested extensively in the development of Debian and other open-source systems to offer a wider range of options to its clients. Google developed Android as an open-source project to attract corporate partners that manufactured mobile devices and offered telecommunications services. It used open source as a gateway to attract users to its search engine, providing a customer base for advertising revenues and proprietary applications.

Debian as a Peer Producer Community

The Debian Project is an example of a free software community organized around the voluntary participation of peer producers. Debian is a computer operating system that manages computer hardware and software resources, similar to Microsoft Windows or macOS. Its very origins are rooted in the fundamental free software values of user freedom and collaboration among contributors to a common project. It was founded in 1993 by Ian Murdock, who was inspired by the development process implemented with the Linux kernel, where Linus Torvalds coordinated the contributions from a wide range of volunteer developers. In fact, Debian was one of the earliest operating systems based on the Linux kernel.

When he created Debian, Murdock wrote and released "The Debian Manifesto" to explain the rationale behind the project. He described Debian GNU/Linux, or simply Debian, as "a brand-new kind of Linux distribution," involving open and transparent collaboration between teams of people interested in developing particular components of the system. This modular approach to software development was an innovation on the model previously used in Linux, since it went beyond having individuals contribute and then having Torvalds as the leader of the project who integrated those contributions. With Debian, Murdock's modular approach put greater emphasis on organizing teams of developers, facilitating a process for developers with particular skills and expertise to join together to solve problems (accessed June 4, 2015. https:// debian. org/doc/manuals/project-history/ap-manifesto.en.html).

In 2004, Murdock gave a talk about this history of creating the project at the Debian Conference in Brazil. Afterward, he reflected on his experience at the conference in a blog post, stating,

Many people have thanked me for starting Debian, that they wouldn't be here without me, and I'd like to share the answer I've given many times this week for everyone to read: I wouldn't be here without you either. That's what it's all about, and we must never forget that.

> (Accessed July 6, 2015. http://ianmurdock.com/ debian/awakenings/comment-page-1/)

Murdock thus highlighted the importance of community participation and collaboration that fueled the project from its inception. Moreover, in a statement that highlights Debian's development in a range of different countries, he reflected on the significance of the global nature of the Debian community. Noting that people from 28 countries gathered for the conference in Brazil, he stated, "A new culture has emerged while no one was looking that truly transcends nationality or religion. We all speak different languages, but in many ways we speak the same language too" (accessed July 6, 2015. http://ianmurdock.com/debian/awakenings/comment-page-1/).

Over the years, Debian has grown to be one of the largest and most widely used free software projects, with over a thousand volunteers collaborating around the world to develop and maintain it. These volunteers engage in many different kinds of work. Generally, they work with source programs written by coders. The volunteers then configure, compile, and pack those programs, so that the programs are ready for users to install or update (Robles, Dueñas and González-Barahona 2007). Once each year, the developers elect a Project Leader, who appoints delegates to carry out specialized tasks and make decisions based on their technical knowledge as well as a group consensus process. If developers disagree with the Project Leader's performance, the community is organized to allow for the leader's recall or a reversal of the leader's decision.

Debian as a Global Community

The Debian Project is a prime example of free software as a global community. To date, it has been developed primarily in Europe and North America. As is the case with all free software peer communities, it is a bit difficult to estimate its exact size. Nonetheless, a range of data are available that give some sense of the extent of the community, as well as its global character. For example, a 2004 case study of the Debian Project revealed that there were 417 Debian developers in Europe and 364 in the U.S. and Canada (González-Barahona and Robles 2006). According to another study, the total number of Debian developers grew from 216 in 1998 to 859 in 2002 and about 1,237 in 2004. In 2004, these developers were part of a broader Debian community of about 1,300 volunteers working on a range of tasks around the world (Robles,

González-Barahona and Michlmayr 2005). According to more recent data on the Debian website, there were about 1,000 Debian developers in 2015 (accessed July 10, 2015. https://nm.debian.org/public/people/dd_u). Similarly, on July 30, 2017, the Debian Project's LinkedIn page stated that "Debian is produced by more than a thousand active developers spread around the world who volunteer in their spare time" (https://linkedin.com/company/debian). Given this range of data, it appears that since the early 2000s, the Debian community has had 1,000 or more developers collaborating in a peer community.

Debian is organized globally, where contributors from a range of countries work together on a regular basis. They engage in their common project primarily by communicating over Internet Relay Chat (IRC) and an array of electronic mailing lists. Teams of people from around the world collaborate on projects and often work together over long periods of time before they meet in person. Debian is available in 70 languages and supports a wide range of computer platforms (DebConf14 Portland: Final Report, 44. Accessed July 3, 2015 at http://media.debconf.org/reports/).

Given this international, geographically dispersed structure, it is vital for Debian community participants to have opportunities to come together and see each other face to face. Toward that end, since 2001, the Debian community has held an annual Debian Conference, which they refer to as DebConf. The conference provides an important venue for participants in the community to meet in person to work intensively on projects, as well as to listen to speakers and to strategize about next steps in the project's development. The conferences usually last about 10 days, allowing time for extended periods of collective work and play. As Coleman (2013) argues, such conferences are highly significant events for hackers, solidifying a sense of group solidarity and connection with the community. Given Debian's modular structure, it is particularly useful for co-participants on projects, who work together over the Internet on a daily basis, to have the chance to meet in person. Coleman (2013, 48) views these events as "rituals of confirmation, liberation, celebration, and especially reenchantment, where the quotidian affairs of life, work, labor and social interactions are ritualized, and thus experienced on fundamentally different terms."

This interpretation of the significance of DebConf for Debian community members was supported by one of the participants in DebConf14, which was held in Portland, Oregon in 2014. This participant described why it was important to him to attend:

> Debian is a bit like a huge telecommuting organization and it's my opinion that any such organization should try and ensure its members actually spend some time together on a regular basis. It improves the ability to work remotely an amazing lot if you can

actually put a face to the entity you're emailing/IRCing and have some sort of idea where they're coming from because you've spent some time with them, whether that's in talks or over dinner or just casual hallway chats.

> (DebConf14 Portland: Final Report, 21. Accessed July 3, 2015 at http://media.debconf.org/reports/)

In the report from DebConf14, Debian Project Leader Lucas Nussbaum described the significance of the conference:

> From the outside, DebConf could be seen as a hacking event. But it is actually primarily a social event. It enables Debian contributors to put faces to names (and nicknames), meet with each other, talk about future ideas and design plans, strengthen the ties within the Debian community, and smooth grudges that arise when communicating only over the Internet.
>
> (DebConf14 Portland: Final Report, 7. Accessed July 3, 2015 at http://media.debconf.org/reports/)

Opportunities to work, socialize, and spend concentrated time with each other thus allow Debian community members to work out difficulties that may have occurred in their online interactions. While the Internet is invaluable as a general mode of communication and collaboration, meeting in person is equally important for ongoing relationships and project development.

Alluding to conflicts that may arise in the process of collaboration, Nussbaum highlighted the importance of keeping such tensions in perspective in his statement following DebConf14:

> Debian is often pointed at for its flamewars and rather vocal development community. There's surely space for improvement, but what most people don't realize is that we are actually doing great when one looks at the context and the constraints. How many other organizations gather so many volunteer contributors, from various cultures, in a very flat structure, towards achieving common goals?
>
> (DebConf14 Portland: Final Report, 6. Accessed July 3, 2015 at http://media.debconf.org/reports/)

Debian conferences provide insight into the global nature of the Debian community. As a key gathering place for participants in the Debian Project, the conference provides a sense of the extent of international participation. Generally, the conference is attended by 300–400 people, primarily from Europe, the U.S., and Canada. Conference participants come from around the world, giving another indication of the global nature of the community. For example, at DebConf14 in Portland, participants came from 33 countries; this was similar to previous conferences (DebConf14 Portland: Final Report. Accessed July 3, 2015 at http://media.debconf.org/reports/). In 2016, Debian community participants organized the first DebConf in Africa, in an effort to expand and strengthen their work in the global South (accessed July 30, 2017; https://wiki.debconf.org/wiki/Debconf16/FinalReport).

Based upon its peer community structure, the Debian Project resonates with Benkler's (2006) characterization of peer production. Participants in the project engage in free labor (Terranova 2013), choosing voluntarily to work on projects without expecting to be paid for it. Of equal importance, they work within a community that does not have a traditional organizational hierarchy. They elect a Project Leader who oversees the broader operation and delegates key tasks to others; however, that leader does not have the authority of a traditional CEO to assign tasks that workers may not choose to do of their own accord. As a community of peer producers, the Debian Project has key qualities that would allow it to contribute to the development of a digital commons. Furthermore, Debian is organized internationally. The peer community thus has a global character that facilitates the development of a digital commons on a global scale, creating possibilities for the emergence of alternative forms of globalization from below. Nonetheless, it is important to explore the nature of the software itself. As discussed above, the potential for free software to create digital commons depends not only on the conditions of its production in a peer community. Indeed, the software itself provides the technological basis for the development of the commons. The catalytic property form, requiring all users to retain the freedom to modify, share, and redistribute the software, ensures that the software peer producers create retains its community-based character.

Debian Licensing and the Open-Source Property Form

On the Debian.org website, Debian is defined as a free operating system, including basic programs and utilities that make computers run. There is a link to a page discussing the meaning of the word "free," where the meaning is initially defined as follows:

> When we speak of *Free Software*, we mean freedom, not price…. While free software is not totally free of constraints (only putting something in the public domain does that) it gives the user the flexibility to do what they need in order to get work done. At the same time, it protects the rights of the author.
>
> (Accessed July 15, 2015. https://debian.org/intro/free)

The discussion of freedom is elaborated on that page, as well as on another linked page that explains the Debian Free Software Guidelines (accessed July 14, 2015. https://debian.org/social_contract#guidelines). Together, these pages emphasize the importance of users having the freedom to install the software on as many machines as they choose, to freely copy and share it with others, and to make changes to the software if they so desire. Similar to Stallman's initial development of the definition of free software, the Debian Free Software Guidelines stipulate that licenses for Debian components must allow for free redistribution, so that users are not prevented from selling or giving away the software. Programs must include the source code, as well as allowing users to change the software and distribute it under the same terms as the original software.

In itself, the Debian operating system is thus an example of the catalytic property form. In practice, however, the Debian Project makes it possible to introduce proprietary elements that are not completely separated from the main Debian distribution. On their website, the FSF explains that this potential for mixing free Debian software with proprietary elements occurs in several ways. First, this mixture may happen because the Debian Project hosts a repository of proprietary software on its main servers. It also offers a "contrib" repository that includes free software packages that are designed to load separately distributed proprietary programs. Users browsing Debian's online package database may thus discover and choose to use these proprietary programs. Up until the release of Debian 6.0 in February 2011, Debian releases included proprietary firmware files as part of the Linux kernel. After that time, those files were moved out of the main distribution and into the proprietary repository (accessed July 14, 2015. http://gnu.org/distros/common-distros.html).

In terms of the property form of the software, the Debian Project thus allows for a mixture of free and proprietary elements. The software itself is free; however, the project makes proprietary software available and leaves it to users to decide how they want to combine free and proprietary elements. Such a choice allows greater flexibility in the range of software available to users and has been characteristic of the open-source approach to software. For example, Bruce Parens (1999) reworked the Debian Free Software Guidelines in 1999. He removed references to Debian to recast the guidelines in more general terms and renamed it the Open Source Definition. He also analyzed the differences between major software licenses and the open-source approach. This analysis highlights the political differences between open source and the free software approach associated with Richard Stallman and the FSF. In reference to the GNU GPL, Parens (1999, 181) stated that it "is a political manifesto as well as a software license…This political dialogue has put some people off, and thus provided some of the reason that people have written other free software licenses." From its inception, the open-source approach was thus partly grounded in a desire to establish a different licensing system from the GPL, and particularly to differentiate it from Richard Stallman's politics.

Kelty (2008) shares this view that emphasizes the political and ideological differences between free and open-source software. He argues that "Free Software and Open Source shared everything 'material,' but differed vocally and at great length with respect to ideology" (Kelty 2008, 116). Kelty (2008, 116) depicts the FSF as emphasizing liberal values of individual freedom of expression, while the open-source approach emphasizes "organizations and processes," and particularly the pragmatic view that businesses need flexibility. For example, when the Debian Project makes proprietary software available on its website, this would be interpreted as offering a wider range of options for users, many of which might be businesses.

By contrast, while the ideological differences between free software and open source are certainly distinct, I view them as *secondary to the differences in the licenses*. I do not see free software and open source as sharing "everything 'material'" (Kelty 2008, 116), because their licenses are defined in critically divergent ways. Indeed, licenses legally constitute software's property form, which, in turn, is the critical factor shaping prospects for developing the digital commons. As discussed above, there are many important similarities between the definition of open-source software and the catalytic property form of free software. There is one key difference, however, that distinguishes the two with respect to their property form. Free software licensed under the GNU GPL prohibits the combination of free software with proprietary programs. It thus legally requires the software to remain free and separate from proprietary systems. For example, the GPL would not permit the combination of free software with proprietary software such as those made available in the Debian Project's repository discussed above. For this reason, Stallman (Gay 2002, 22) calls systems that mix open-source and proprietary software "freedom subtracted products." From his perspective, any software system that includes proprietary elements detracts from the collaborative project of building a software-sharing community. When software developers write programs that depend on the proprietary part of such a system, their work becomes tied into the proprietary system and cannot be integrated into completely free software (Gay 2002).

This is the crucial point that distinguishes the catalytic form of free software, since it is required to retain its community-based character. Such a requirement allows free software to create digital commons that, as Benkler (2013a, 1538) writes, "undergird and are interpolated throughout the proprietary system elements." Free software is the code for the digital commons, circulating whenever users modify, remix, or redistribute it and ensuring that future users will enjoy those same freedoms. Due to Debian's open-source licensing that allows combinations of free and proprietary elements, I thus consider Debian to be open source, rather than free software. Debian's open-source nature resonates with its historical relationship to the Open Source Definition and the Open Source Initiative, and has key implications for its relationship to the software market.

Debian's Relationship to the Market

Debian's open-source licensing facilitates corporate responses to what Bauwens (2009) calls "hyperproductivity," where peer production is so successful that it becomes a force to be reckoned with in the market. It creates new opportunities for profit, leading proprietary firms to adapt to it and integrate it into their operations. For example, by providing a high-quality operating system as an alternative to Microsoft and Apple, Debian creates the possibility for firms to contribute to the system and compete with those dominant firms in the market.

Over the years, corporations have played a key part in Debian's development. Robles, Dueñas, and González-Barahona (2007) studied the role of companies in free software projects, focusing on contributions to Debian source code over a seven-year period from 1998 to 2005. They chose Debian because it constituted the biggest collection of code available for Linux. The size of the distribution was important, since often, companies are interested in

> obtain[ing] a surrounding user community which serves both as a basic and fast feedback mechanism, but also as a marketing strategy, with the aim of getting software of better quality by letting external brainware access the project's source code, to lower the cost by letting volunteers enhance or fix the software, among others.
> (Robles, Dueñas and González-Barahona 2007, 122)

Corporations may thus benefit from the work of community participants, who provide a source of free labor (Terranova 2013). These peer producers willingly engage in work such as coding, tracking and fixing bugs, and writing documentation, without receiving any pay for their efforts. When large numbers of peer producers are contributing to a community, this expands opportunities for companies to reap the benefits of their work, as well as providing access to a broader base of potential users.

Over the course of the above study, the total amount of code in Debian doubled about every two years. During this period, the corporate contribution to that code remained steady at about 6–7 percent. Proprietary firms thus continued to contribute that proportion of the code, even as the total amount of code grew. For example, Sun Microsystems, a U.S. firm selling computers, computer components, software and information technology services, was the top corporate contributor to Debian version 2.0 and 2.1. Sun engaged extensively in software development;

it contributed almost a million lines of code to Debian 2.0 and 2.1, as well as developing the Java programming language, the Solaris operating system, and other programs. Sun's share of Debian development grew significantly when OpenOffice.org was included in Debian 3.1; it became the top corporate contributor at that point, with over 5 million lines of code. Netscape, a U.S. computer services firm known for its Netscape Navigator web browser, started out as another major Debian contributor; its total lines of code contributed rose from over a million in Debian 2.0 and 2.1 to over 2 million in Debian 2.2 and 3.0. Over time, however, Netscape's contribution fell to under 800,000 lines of code in Debian 3.1. As will be discussed further below, IBM's contribution rose considerably over time. It became one of the top 10 corporate contributors of about 220,000 lines of code in Debian 2.2; it then increased its contribution markedly to over 1,200,000 lines of code in Debian 3.0 and to almost 2 million lines of code in Debian 3.1. The third top corporate contributor to Debian 3.1 was Red Hat, a U.S. multinational software firm that produces the open-source Fedora software that competes with Debian; this was due to Red Hat's involvement in the GNOME project and the GCC compiler collection. Other smaller free software companies also made substantial contributions to Debian code, including Ximian and MySQL (Robles, Dueñas and González-Barahona 2007).

Companies have developed two major proprietary strategies toward the Debian Project, which we will explore in the following sections. First, a Debian developer who became frustrated with key constraints of peer production decided to start a for-profit company to distribute a version of the Debian software. In this case, the successful development of Debian, combined with organizational drawbacks of peer production, created the possibility and the incentive to found a business to develop and market it. Second, the extensive development and use of the Debian operating system is an example of hyperproductivity (Bauwens 2009), shaping market conditions and creating new opportunities for profits. IBM is an example of a proprietary firm that responded to these opportunities, contributing to the development of Debian in the process.

Proprietary Strategies Emerging from Peer Community: Ubuntu's Dual Process of Production

In 2004, Mark Shuttleworth, a South African software developer contributing to the Debian Project, made a bold business decision. He gathered a team of Debian developers and decided to found a firm called Canonical Limited. His corporate strategy was to create and commercialize a new version of the Debian operating system for the desktop, cloud, and server. Shuttleworth and his team called the operating system Ubuntu, which is an ancient African word meaning "humanity to others." It also means, "I am what I am because of who we all are."

According to the Ubuntu homepage, "the Ubuntu operating system brings the spirit of Ubuntu to the world of computers" (accessed July 30, 2017. https://ubuntu.com/about/about-ubuntu).

On a financial level, Shuttleworth's decision was made possible by his previous business endeavors. In 1995, while a student in Finance and Information Systems at the University of Cape Town, Shuttleworth founded Thawte, a highly successful company specializing in providing secure, authenticated, encrypted Internet transactions. According to Shuttleworth's website, Thawte "became the first company to produce a full-security encrypted e-commerce web server that was commercially available outside the United States" (accessed July 5, 2011. http://markshuttleworth.com/biography). Netscape and Microsoft recognized Thawte as a secure system for website certification, contributing to the firm's growing reputation as an international leader in Internet transaction security. In 1999, Shuttleworth made a fortune by selling Thawte to VeriSign, providing him the opportunity to found the HBD investment company, the Shuttleworth Foundation, and eventually to found Canonical and the Ubuntu project. He was CEO of Canonical from 2004 until 2010, when he shifted his focus at Canonical to leading design and product strategy (accessed July 5, 2011. http://markshuttleworth.com/biography).

Officially, Canonical is a market-based firm that is in the business of providing services to customers; toward this end, it charges substantial fees for those service contracts. A fuller consideration of Shuttleworth's motives and business practices, however, reveals that Canonical does not orient its activities primarily around making a profit. According to a 2010 interview with Alain Valk, a French software developer who works on Canonical's cloud project, the firm operated at a loss for the first five years. This was not a surprise; in fact, Shuttleworth did not expect to make a profit, at least in the beginning. He viewed the company as an experiment; he was happy to fund it to give it time to grow before putting the emphasis on profitability. In the short term, Shuttleworth would be satisfied if the company would break even by making enough money to pay for everyone working on Ubuntu. Thus, Shuttleworth's motivations in founding Canonical were social, rather than primarily economic. Canonical is philosophically committed to supporting Ubuntu as software that will always be free of charge for anyone to use.

Of equal importance, Valk (interview 2010) highlighted the convergence between these social and economic motivations. He noted that Shuttleworth started Canonical partly because he wanted to provide more direction for the software development occurring in the Debian community. What Benkler (2006) characterized as the heart of peer production, where each individual contributed to a project according to his or her own interests without centralized coordination, Shuttleworth viewed as a major problem. He wanted to create a commercial entity with a more defined authority structure to meet the needs of firms in the market. Companies that wanted to deploy the Debian operating system on a large scale would thus be able to get support from Canonical. Valk stated,

> We know that there's one thing that CIOs don't like, is to take chances. So one way of limiting the chances is to have a contract with someone else to get blamed. That's most of their job. That's why they went to Microsoft and that's why they can go a company named Red Hat or Novell or they can go to Canonical, for services, but they cannot go to the community called Debian or anything else.

Shuttleworth's business strategy in founding Canonical and creating Ubuntu was thus partly to remedy what he viewed as the drawbacks of peer production. As discussed above, the loose organization of peer communities allowed freedom for the participants to choose what projects they worked on without a boss telling them what to do. From a corporate perspective, however, this made it virtually impossible to integrate software like Debian into their business operations unless they could hire a firm to provide services to troubleshoot problems that might arise or otherwise customize the software to their business needs. Firms needed to know that such services would be available if they were going to consider using the software for their corporate operations. Otherwise, reliance on such software was unthinkable because it was viewed as unreliable. There was demand for a company like Canonical that could provide both a stable version of Debian packaged to fit corporate needs, as well as the services required to install and maintain the software.

Canonical's strategy of creating a stable, commercialized version of Debian spoke to problems of continuity in project development identified by researchers studying the process of volunteer participation in the Debian Project. For example, in a study conducted between 1998 and 2004, Robles, González-Barahona, and Michlmayr (2005) found that in most cases when developers left a project they had been working on in the Debian community, other developers would step in and continue the project. This practice of regeneration allowed for projects to be sustained over time, even when developers left. Regeneration did not occur in all cases, however, which meant that users of a particular software package were not supported once a developer left. This problem might be remedied by setting up clear ways to distinguish software packages that receive less support from those that would have longer-term support. Users could thus be aware of the potential problems they might encounter with certain packages. For example, if a project involved dozens of core developers working together in an active community, that package would have a much greater chance of being sustained over time than a project maintained by a single developer (Robles, González-Barahona and Michlmayr 2005).

Canonical's business model was designed to address such problems by ensuring more sustainable support for users. Under this model, Ubuntu is released every six months. Every two years, a release is issued that is designated to receive long-term support (LTS) from Canonical for the next two years. Users who do not want to adapt to changes in their operating system every six months can thus opt to use the LTS releases with guaranteed support for a longer period. Major changes to the operating system are generally reserved for the LTS releases. The first Ubuntu release, version 4.10 and code named Warty Warthog, was issued in October 2004. By 2010, Ubuntu 10.10 was listed in PC World's 100 top products in December 2010, based on its ability to "breathe new life into a PC or break free from commercial software," as well as the quality of Linux as "arguably the most secure PC platform you can find" (PC World 2010, 100). In 2011, Canonical began developing a mobile version of Ubuntu, highlighting the need for free software alternatives in the phone and tablet markets. In April 2017, however, Shuttleworth announced that he was terminating the project due to a lack of market interest (Sneddon 2017).

Canonical's business model is a prime example of the conditions under which market-based production can be designed to address what Shuttleworth and the above researchers viewed as problems with peer production. Shuttleworth and his team of developers created a hierarchical structure that built upon the work being done in the Debian community, where developers were engaged in a wide range of projects around the world. Establishing Canonical as a commercial entity transformed the way that the software was produced and delivered, as well as the ways that users were able to consume it. It offered users distinct options so that they could choose the type of release that best fit their needs. Creating Canonical and Ubuntu thus made the software developed by the peer producers in the Debian community available to the market in a more traditionally structured form. Toward this end, Canonical sought to enter the desktop software market by making Ubuntu accessible and easy to use for businesses and individuals alike. Ubuntu is one of the few free operating systems geared toward use on the desktop, as well as the cloud and server; it is designed to target individual users without programming or other technical knowledge, as well as businesses and software developers.

Canonical's dual cycle model of development involves collaboration between Debian developers engaged in peer production, the vast majority of whom are unpaid, and the paid workers at Canonical. In our 2010 interview, Alain Valk noted that Canonical's policy is not to fund or participate extensively in software development. By contrast, its mission is to take the software created by the Debian community and integrate it in a way that makes sense and is easy to use.

These social motivations, however, are combined with market-oriented goals of building a profitable business. This market orientation is reflected in Canonical's structure, comprised of an organizational hierarchy with considerable power for the CEO. Hence, Canonical can best be understood as a market-based firm that relies on peer production by the Debian community for the vast majority of its software development.

Peer Community Responses to Canonical's Business Strategy

Canonical's strategy is controversial, however; tensions arise between profit-oriented marketing activities and peer production based on unpaid, collaborative work in a community. Valk (interview 2010) describes this as Canonical's work of integration; nonetheless, such work is not highly valued by many participants in free software communities. As a result, community members criticize Canonical for taking from the community and not contributing back. They emphasize the importance of the shared contribution to the development of the software itself. Coding is generally valued above other kinds of work, especially among software developers. Indeed, the process of software development is often viewed as the foundation of free software communities, without which nothing else could exist.

In response to these critiques, Valk (interview 2010) emphasized that Canonical's work to integrate free software applications into Ubuntu allows those applications to become more widely available. He noted that at the time of the interview, Ubuntu had about 15 million users, all of whom would potentially learn about and use any particular application included in Ubuntu. Valk (interview 2010) discussed the example of the person who developed the "cheese" application so that people can take pictures of themselves; he questioned whether the developer of such an application should be unhappy that Canonical took his software, included it in Ubuntu, released it to 15 million people, but did not contribute back to further develop the application. Valk (interview 2010) thus highlighted the importance of the work of integrating and distributing the software. He noted that often, "developers think in developer terms, marketers think in marketers' terms, users think in users' terms" (Valk, interview 2010). He argued that most of the resentment in the community comes from the fact that people only think in some of those terms. Very often a developer will tell Canonical that the company is not contributing enough to the kernel. From Valk's point of view, however, the developer should be proud that Canonical takes the kernel, almost exactly as it is at a certain point in time, to make the next distribution of Ubuntu. The problem is that people doing particular kinds of work in the community often fail to appreciate the importance of contributions markedly different from their own.

Valk's interview (2010) thus illuminates intriguing unintended consequences of Canonical's profit-oriented marketing practices. By marketing the software and distributing it as widely as possible, Canonical enhances its own chances of eventually becoming profitable. Simultaneously, however, it contributes to the broader process of constructing the open-source software market by making that software available to a broader range of users. Paradoxically, over the long term, such marketing of open-source software may undermine the market position of proprietary software firms.

Prospects for Developing the Digital Commons: The Role of the Catalytic Property Form

Ubuntu is an intriguing case to explore the conditions under which the production of open-source software takes market-based rather than peer-based forms, as well as the implications of those forms for the prospects of developing the digital commons. Shuttleworth's critiques of the peer production model, combined with his financial wealth and commitment to building open-source software, led him to experiment with creating a market-based firm with strong ties to peer production. The result is a rich hybrid form, a mix of peer and market-based production, that both embodies and transforms capitalist practices.

Canonical is contributing to the digital commons in important ways by creating an operating system that anyone can download or contribute to, and that receives regular updates over time. With respect to the crucial question about the property form of software involved with Ubuntu, key changes occurred between 2013 and 2015. On the Ubuntu website, there is a page discussing licensing that notes that there are thousands of software packages available for Ubuntu; they are grouped into categories according to whether they meet Ubuntu's free software philosophy, as well as the level of support Ubuntu provides for the programs. In order to be categorized as a "main" component, licenses must include the source code, as well as permit modifications and distribution under the same license. Application software categorized as "main" or "restricted" is required to allow users to redistribute the software, either by selling it or giving it away. Users must not require royalty payments or other fees from others who want to change or share the software. They must also allow other users to have the same rights over the software as they have. All of these requirements fit with the definition of free software under the GNU GPL, as well as with the Open Source Definition.

Up until July 15, 2015, the Ubuntu licensing requirements, similar to other open-source requirements, diverged from the free software approach in their rejection of copyleft. For example, the Ubuntu licensing page stated that approved licenses

[m]ust not contaminate other software licenses. The license must not place restrictions on other software that is distributed along with it. For example, the license must not insist that all other programmes distributed on the same medium be free software.

(Accessed July 14, 2017. http://ubuntu.com/about/
about-ubuntu/licensing)

The key element of the catalytic property form, requiring all software to be free if it is included with free software, is thus depicted by the Ubuntu page as "contamination" of proprietary licenses.

As a result, some Ubuntu users found Canonical's licensing approach problematic. It did not fit with the overall free software approach to allow the freedom to share, modify, and redistribute software without limitations placed by proprietary programs. To express their concerns, they filed a report with the Software Freedom Conservancy, a nonprofit organization based in the U.S. whose mission is to promote, improve, develop, and defend free software projects. According to its website, Conservancy offers a "home and infrastructure" for these projects, allowing free software developers to focus on the work of software development (accessed July 16, 2015; https://sfconservancy.org/about/). Indeed, part of the work of maintaining free software projects is political and discursive, such as pursuing legal and technical questions involved with copyright license enforcement. In the case of Canonical, the Conservancy collaborated with the FSF to negotiate with Canonical about the users' concerns.

These negotiations bore fruit on July 15, 2015, when Canonical published a statement updating its intellectual property policy. The statement read as follows:

Ubuntu is an aggregate work of many works, each covered by their own license(s). For the purposes of determining what you can do with specific works in Ubuntu, this policy should be read together with the license(s) of the relevant packages. For the avoidance of doubt, where any other license grants rights, this policy does not modify or reduce those rights under those licenses.

(Accessed July 16, 2015; https://sfconservancy.org/
news/2015/jul/15/ubuntu-ip-policy)

Conservancy responded to this statement with a report on its website, detailing the history of the problem with the former policy and analyzing the implications of the policy change. Calling Canonical's statement a "trump clause," Conservancy noted that it was "sufficient for compliance with the GPL...[since it] mandates that when Canonical, Ltd.'s policy contradicts something that the GPL requires, or prohibits something that the GPL allows, the rights granted in the GPL shall prevail" (accessed July 16, 2015; https://sfconservancy.org/news/2015/jul/15/ubuntu-ip-policy/). This trump clause thus creates the legal foundation for Ubuntu to be free software and contribute to the development of the digital commons.

The case of Ubuntu and Canonical thus provides a clear example of the catalytic role of free software as a new form of property, and the crucial role of licensing in constituting this community-based property form. Indeed, the free software property form is so decisive in its effects that it can be created in the context of peer production in the Debian community or market-based production by Canonical.

As individual and organizational users enter the market and decide which kind of software to choose, the prospects for developing the digital commons are also shaped by a key characteristic shared by all software. As Weber (2004, 154) argues, all software has an "antirival" quality, where "the value of a piece of software to any user increases as more people use the software on their machines and in their particular settings." Major proprietary software firms like Microsoft and Apple are keenly aware of this, offering promotional deals to school systems, colleges and universities, and college students to broaden their user base among youth. In the process, it becomes easier to share files and communicate with other users whose systems run the same software. The knowledge and skills involved with using computers and the Internet may become identified with knowledge of particularly popular programs, like the Microsoft Office Suite. Proprietary software firms thus build upon the antirival nature of software to strengthen their user base and bolster their profits as increasing numbers of users rely upon their programs. At the same time, to protect their own profits, they must ensure that all users pay for the software. These firms thus oppose file-sharing, remixing, and other collaborative practices as illegal acts of "piracy."

Free software proponents also seek to broaden the user base, which has the potential to promote the development of the digital commons. Unlike proprietary firms, as long as a core group of developers continues to produce free software, expanding the numbers of users who neither pay for nor contribute to the software still facilitates market growth. The antirival nature of all software merges with the catalytic nature of free software as a new form of community created and owned property, giving rise to intriguing implications for constructing the software market and developing the digital commons. As Weber (2004, 154) puts it, *"the system as a whole positively benefits from free riders"* (emphasis in original). The task of free software proponents is to broaden the software's user base, often by giving it away for free. The more people who use free software, the larger the community becomes that can share files and communicate with each other without relying on proprietary systems.

One key way to develop the digital commons is thus to foster the market for free software, contributing to the development of the software itself as well as expanding the users of that software by building a customer base. The market provides a means to expand the digital commons as a global public good, as well as a venue for business opportunities.

Robert Young, the founder of Red Hat, the open-source software firm mentioned above, provided an example of this alternative approach to the market. In 1999, he identified the challenge for open-source firms as developing more users of free and open-source software, in the context of a market dominated by proprietary software. This challenge was considerable, considering that at that time, Microsoft's Windows operating system was used on over 90 percent of the world's personal computers (Pillar 2006). Young sought to address this situation by expanding the size of the market for free and open-source software as a whole, since more users of such software would potentially create more customers for Red Hat. He argued that you

> can't compete with a monopoly by playing the game by the monopolist's rules. The monopolist has the resources, the distribution channels, the R&D resources, in short, they just have too many strengths. You compete...by changing the rules of the game into a set that favors your strengths.
>
> (Young 1999, 118)

Young (1999) thus highlighted the need for his firm to approach the software market in a new way. He understood the expansion of the general market as in the interest of his company, rather than viewing all other software firms, and particularly free and open-source firms, as competitors with conflicting interests.

Based upon the nature of open-source software as providing source code so users can continually modify it to suit their needs, Young (1999, 116) and his colleagues sought to develop a unique software business model by looking at "industries where the participants benefit because of, not despite, the activities of the other participants." They explored models from the legal field, where winning arguments become public domain rather than being patented to restrict their use. They learned from the auto industry, based upon assembly and service using a collection of many different parts available to the industry as a whole. They adapted ideas from the commodity industry, where companies became successful by building brands that symbolized high quality and reliability to their customers. In the process, they fostered an ongoing process of innovations that "accrue to the community at large" (Young 1999, 125).

Weber's (2004) work, as well as examples like Red Hat, is thus useful in understanding more about why the catalytic nature of free software is decisive for the development of the market and the digital commons, regardless of whether that software is produced through peer or market-based processes. In a similar vein, Bollier (2008, 234) argues that commons-based peer production is spreading through the market:

> Especially when the commons has strong mechanisms to preserve its value-creating capacity, such as the [GNU General Public License] GPL, open networks are helping to convert more market activity into commons-based activity, or at least shifting the boundary between commodity markets and proprietary, high-value-added markets.

Indeed, by defining free software as a new form of property created and owned in community, the GNU GPL establishes legal conditions to challenge capitalism's dominant logic of private property. It is part of what Bollier (2008, 2) calls a "viral spiral," a "corkscrew paradigm of change." In the viral spiral, ideas posted on the Internet can be shared and remixed virtually instantaneously, potentially becoming "a platform used by later generations to build their own follow-on innovations" (Bollier 2008, 2).

From this perspective, Canonical is playing a key role in the development of both the market and the digital commons. As discussed above, the emergence of the commons is interspersed with proprietary systems and practices. As programs like Ubuntu become more widely used, proprietary firms view them as potential new sources of investment. The market is a terrain of strategic action, where proprietary firms develop a range of ways to respond to the opportunities offered by free software firms and programs. IBM is an example of a major proprietary hardware firm that has been engaged in such strategies since the late 1990s.

IBM's Strategies toward Open Source: An Additional Profit Center for Proprietary Firms

By 1998, IBM recognized the potential of open source to offer strategic advantages for its corporate operations. Seeking to extend its activities into profitable new markets, IBM was impressed with the quality of open-source software, as well as with the programmers engaged in its development. Members of IBM's Research Division and Software Group noted that

> the overlap between developers and users of a particular OSS [Open Source Software] project made possible excellent and open communication, rapid development cycles, and intensive real-environment testing, ultimately producing software that was often very good and sometimes excellent by our standards.
>
> (Capek et al. 2005, 250)

IBM developed a dual software strategy; it retained separate proprietary software activities and complemented them with open source as an alternative business model with distinct benefits.

To promote its work on open-source systems, IBM established the Linux Technology Center (LTC) in 1999. This Center's mission was to "increase collaboration with customers to innovate in ways IBM cannot do by itself" (IBM Corporation 2008, 2). Such collaboration involved contributing to Linux development, as well as allowing IBM products to operate smoothly with Linux systems and to be certified to work with them.

IBM's engagement with open source allowed it to take advantage of the hyperproductivity of peer production (Bauwens 2009), adapting some of its corporate activities to integrate open-source software into its operations. In 2001, IBM announced plans to invest $1 billion in Linux over a three-year period. For example, as noted above, IBM contributed substantially to the source code for Debian. It became the sixth largest corporate contributor for Debian 2.2, released in August 2000, contributing over 220,000 lines of code. Its involvement with Debian grew markedly by July 2002, when Debian 3.0 was released. It was the largest corporate contributor to that release, with over 1,200,000 lines of code. By the time Debian 3.1 was released in June 2005, IBM ranked as the second largest corporate contributor. It had boosted its contribution to nearly 2 million lines of code, however, indicating a strong level of involvement (Robles, Dueñas and González-Barahona 2007).

More recently, IBM's Power Systems hardware platform has become fully integrated with Linux. For example, the web page for IBM's Power-Linux Community notes that IBM's Power servers run Linux that meets the industry standard, using the Ubuntu software created by Canonical, as well as other software developed by Red Hat and SUSE (accessed July 7, 2015; https://ibm.com/developerworks/community/groups/service/html/communityoverview?communityUuid=fe313521-2e95-46f2-817d-44a4f27eba32).

In 2008, IBM released a brochure summarizing its commitment to Linux and open source, made available on its corporate website (IBM 2008). It described six main ways that IBM supports Linux development. First, IBM is one of the top commercial contributors to Linux code, with over 600 of its developers involved in more than 100 different open-source projects. Second, IBM offers services to design, deliver, and implement Linux solutions for businesses. For example, if a firm wants to migrate to a Linux system, IBM can assist with that process. Furthermore, by participating in Linux development, IBM can influence the process and seek to include features and functions that it sees as beneficial to its clients. Toward this end, engineers at the LTC work with open-source communities such as Debian to contribute code. Third, LTC engineers contribute by testing and deploying code developed by open-source communities, to troubleshoot and seek to improve the quality of the code. Fourth, these engineers develop documentation for open-source projects, as well as for an online repository for information on Linux and open source called the IBM Information Center. Fifth, IBM maintains the Linux Test Project, which includes test suites where open-source community participants can test for the reliability, stability, and robustness of Linux. IBM also contributes to efforts in the community such as autotest as part of testkernel.org; this work promotes the development and testing of high-quality Linux systems. Finally, IBM contributes to a range of organizations, such as the Linux Foundation and the Open Source Initiative.

IBM has thus responded to the hyperproductivity of peer production by supporting the development of open-source software since the late 1990s, and has contributed to the Debian Project since 2000. In the process, it has participated in Linux development and enabled its server and storage product line to operate with Linux. Through this combination of activities, IBM has increased the use of open-source systems, particularly by proprietary firms.

From Weber's (2004) perspective on the antirival nature of software, IBM's open-source strategies benefit all of the other open-source users by expanding the user base. Such strategies spread open source more widely throughout the market, making it more common and easier to access. Moreover, IBM has expanded the possibilities of firms to access services for their open-source systems, as well as supporting projects to troubleshoot bugs and thus improve software quality. It has thus strengthened the market for open source and bolstered its integration into the operations of a wide range of its corporate clients.

There are limits to the benefits of this antirival quality, however, in terms of contributing to the development of the digital commons. Indeed, IBM only funded the development of open-source systems that supported its proprietary activities, such as middleware software programs for corporate clients. IBM's financial support certainly encouraged the development of these projects. At the same time, however, a key reason that IBM became involved in these projects was to gain access to high-quality open-source infrastructure systems. It benefitted from the work of unpaid peer producers, as well as paid developers at open-source firms. Of most importance, IBM avoided using certain patents in its open-source work so that it could retain exclusive rights over those systems (Capek et al. 2005).

All of IBM's contributions to open-source development were thus forged within a broader strategy to maximize profits. Hence, the potential for IBM to contribute to the digital commons was consistently undermined by its efforts to use its involvement in open source as a strategy to position itself most effectively in the proprietary software market. In fact, IBM's open-source activities did not involve any of the qualities discussed above as central to developing the digital commons. It did not engage in peer production or disrupt the traditional organizational hierarchy. Neither did it contribute to the production of software with a catalytic property form. Overall, IBM took advantage of open-source software's hyperproductive nature to avail itself of high-quality programs developed by peer producers and contribute to the development and servicing of programs that offered an additional source of profit through marketing to its corporate clients. IBM did not want to miss out on the growing quality and popularity of open source, so it dedicated substantial resources to ensure that it could both shape and benefit from open-source software's development. For IBM, open source was thus a key part of its proprietary business strategy that served to complement its major focus on proprietary software and hardware.

The case of IBM highlights a key challenge involved in using an open-source strategy to develop the digital commons. Certainly, IBM's involvement in open-source development may expand the market and user base for the software, without strengthening the development of the digital commons itself. Google's strategy toward open source poses more insidious resistance to the development of the digital commons. In contrast to IBM's offering of open source as an additional option for its corporate clients, Google used open-source software as a gateway to attract customers who would use Google's proprietary applications on their mobile devices. It thus laid the groundwork to track user locations and activities, as they used their mobile devices for activities such as searching for restaurants, shopping, and posting photos of themselves on social media sites. This business strategy has problematic implications for the development of the digital commons that extend beyond software development into the realm of civil liberties and the right to privacy.

Google and Android: Open Source as a Vehicle for Corporate Control and Surveillance

In November 2007, a few months after the first iPhone was launched, Google announced the Android Open Source Project (AOSP). This project was part of a broader Open Handset Alliance (OHA), where Google collaborated with a consortium of firms that shared an interest in consolidating their positions in the emerging mobile market. Manufacturers of mobile devices such as HTC, Sony, and Samsung, as well as chipset makers like Qualcomm and Texas Instruments, viewed this as an opportunity to develop new products and extend their presence in the market. Similarly, wireless carriers, including Sprint Nextel and T-Mobile, sought to strengthen their positions, expanding their range of services as well as their user base (Amadeo 2013). Android's open-source nature allowed manufacturers and telecommunications companies to develop their own devices, as well as to gain access to applications and services developed by Google. It thus provided myriad ways that this alliance of firms could profit by building on the open-source platform.

Google had prepared the way for both the AOSP and the OHA by purchasing Android, Inc. in 2005 and building on the Linux kernel to develop a platform for mobile devices. At that time, industry observers discussed this purchase as an indication that Google was positioning itself in the mobile market and perhaps was developing its own mobile phone. Such views were supported in September 2007, when the global consulting and research firm Evalueserve released a report on Google's patent portfolio. Google had filed a number of patents related to mobile phones, several of which did not list Google as the owner but could be traced back to the company (Claburn 2007). The announcement of the AOSP and the OHA thus clarified Google's next major moves into the mobile market.

Google deployed Android as part of an ingenious open-source strategy. By giving Android away for free, Google used open source as a gateway to attract customers who would eventually become accustomed to using Google search and other services on their mobile devices. Google's business model involved making profits by harvesting the metadata of users to gain information on their interests, including tracking their movements and locations. These data allowed Google to create targeted advertising and services based on individual user interests and activities. This strategy was an insightful way to respond to the prospect of increasing use of mobile devices, and particularly to the specter of potential iPhone dominance in the mobile Internet sphere. Google's worst fear was that, over time, Apple might exercise its proprietary control over the iPhone to lock out Google search. If this happened, people might become so accustomed to using Apple's search on their phones that they would stop using Google search on their desktops. It was thus imperative for Google to offer an alternative to the iPhone in the emerging mobile market (Spreeuwenberg and Poell 2012; Amadeo 2013).

Somewhat paradoxically, and despite Google's open-source rhetoric, Google's open-source strategy is virtually the opposite of the catalytic form of free software. Instead of Android being a vehicle to ensure that users will retain the freedom to access, modify, and share the software, it is a vehicle through which Google seeks to profit from the myriad ways that users engage with their mobile devices and the Internet. With respect to peer production discussed above as central to the development of the digital commons, Android's development is controlled by Google. Individuals may contribute to Android as an open-source project; however, Android is not developed by an organized peer community that operates outside of a traditional organizational hierarchy.

The open-source model has been extremely successful in spreading Android in the mobile phone market. According to the research firm

Canalysis, Android's market share has grown remarkably, from 2.8 percent in 2009 to 33 percent in 2010 and about 52 percent in 2011 (accessed July 15, 2015. http://appleinsider.com/articles/09/08/21/canalys_ iphone_outsold_all_windows_mobile_phones_in_q2_2009.html; http://canalys.com/newsroom/google%E2%80%99s-android-becomes-world%E2%80%99s-leading-smart-phone-platform). According to the International Data Corporation (IDC) website, a majority of mobile phones have run on Android since 2012, with Android's share increasing from about 59 percent of mobile phones in 2012 to about 75 percent in 2013 and about 80 percent of the market in 2014 (accessed July 28, 2015. http://idc.com/prodserv/smartphone-os-market-share.isp). Data from the Statista website show Android with 76 percent of the market in 2015, rising to 79 percent in 2016, and holding steady at that position through March 2017. By comparison, iOS held 10 percent of the market in 2015, falling slightly to 9 percent during 2016, and remaining at that position through March 2017. The relative market positions of these operating systems have remained steady since 2012 (accessed August 22, 2017. https://statista.com/statistics/385022/ smartphone-worldwide-installed-base-operating-systems-share/).

The open-source nature of Android makes it possible for other firms to build upon it. In a twist on Bauwen's (2009) argument about hyper-productivity, the open-source code itself, rather than the peer production process, creates opportunities for firms to build on Android and compete with Google. In the context of Android's success in the market, this hyperproductivity creates tensions for Google and threatens its position in the market. This threat is rooted partly in the fact that Android is now installed on so many phones and also has an extensive amount of applications available. The strength of Android's market presence creates incentives for competitors to fork Android. As will be discussed in-depth in the next chapter, forking involves taking a shared code base and developing it into a separate, new software system. Through the process of forking, one of Google's competitors could build on the Android code base, improving and adapting it to add its own applications and shut out Google's applications and services. For example, Amazon employed precisely this strategy, using Android as the code base for its Kindle Fire. It shut Google out by banning most of its services. Amazon thus developed an alternative Android distribution that included its own app store, content stores, browser, cloud storage, and email. In a similar vein, the Chinese government banned most Google services, so Chinese customers use an alternative version of Android that does not include those services (Amadeo 2013).

Well aware of this possibility for competition from firms that build on Android's open-source code, Google has protected its control over the operating system in two major ways. First, as discussed at length above, licensing is the key to defining the nature of software and its potential to contribute to the development of the digital commons.

According to the Android web page on licensing, the AOSP employs several licenses recommended by the Open Source Initiative. The preferred license integrated into the majority of Android software is Apache 2.0, which allows for the combination of proprietary elements. Of most importance, the Apache licensing system allows for corporate control over all contributions to the software. This control is exercised through a process where anyone who contributes ideas, code, or documentation is required to sign a Contributor License Grant; contributors who work on Android as employees of a corporation are required to sign a Corporate Contributor License Grant. These Grants give Google the right to use the participants' contributions to Android in whatever way it chooses. Hence, while Android is officially an open-source operating system, the licensing allows Google and its partners full control over it.

Despite these grounds for corporate control built into the Apache 2.0 license, Google articulates a discourse of open source that emphasizes a particular form of user freedom. On the Android web page explaining licensing, the open-source philosophy is described as follows:

> Android is about freedom and choice. The purpose of Android is to promote openness in the mobile world, and we don't believe it's possible to predict or dictate all the uses to which people will want to put our software. So, while we encourage everyone to make devices that are open and modifiable, we don't believe it is our place to force them to do so. Using LGPL libraries would often force them to do just that.
>
> (Accessed July 28, 2015. http://source.android.com/
> source/licenses.html)

Android's version of open source, similar to other open-source approaches discussed above, thus views licenses like the GNU GPL, including the version Lesser General Public License (LGPL) mentioned in the statement, as restricting users' choices by requiring them to keep the code open for future users. Instead of viewing copyleft as ensuring users' freedoms, it sees it as a limitation on choice. Such an approach fits with corporate interests in having the maximum freedom to choose whether and how to combine proprietary software with open-source systems.

The Android web page on licensing identifies key reasons why Android does not recommend the LGPL. One is that the LGPL requires that users, who the website refers to as "customers," be able to modify the software once they have purchased it. Since Google's business model involves partnerships with a range of mobile phone and tablet manufacturers, the web page notes that most of these firms would view such restrictions as a "burden." The web page states, "It's critical to Android's success that it be as easy as possible for device makers to comply

with the licenses" (accessed July 28, 2015. http://source.android.com/
source/licenses.html). As noted above, a major way that manufacturers
and telecommunications services providers profit from Android as an
open-source system is by developing their own devices, which may come
bundled with certain applications and services. Such firms need the freedom to combine whatever applications or other elements they choose
in order to develop those products and services, and to engage in the
mobile market in a wide variety of ways.

Interestingly, the Android website extols the virtues of open source
and the value of other licenses. It states,

> We are passionate about this topic, even to the point where we've
> gone out of our way to make sure as much code as possible is
> ASL2.0 licensed. However, we love all free and open source licenses,
> and respect others' opinions and preferences. We've simply decided
> ASL2.0 is the right license for our goals.
>
> (Accessed July 28, 2015. http://source.android.com/
> source/licenses.html)

Despite this discourse emphasizing the benefits of open source, the limitations of the Apache 2.0 license provide some legal protections for
Google to exert more control over Android.

Furthermore, in addition to licensing, Google exerts control over
Android through its Google-branded applications. Android is based on
open-source code; however, a major source of Google's profits is derived
from proprietary applications. Google's use of the Apache license, and
its emphasis on the importance of choice in combining proprietary with
open-source code, allows it the freedom to pursue a particular business
model with respect to applications. In this model, proprietary versions
of applications take precedence over the ongoing development of open-
source versions. Once the proprietary version has been launched, development of the open version of the application is generally discontinued. In
the process, the open-source version becomes outdated, lacking the features that will attract users to the proprietary application. For example, in
2010, Google launched Voice Actions for the Google Search application.
It discontinued development on the open-source version of search (AOSP
Search), so all that service allows users to do is a basic web search. By
contrast, the proprietary version of Google search includes possibilities to
search by voice, audio, and text-to-speech. It also includes an answer service, as well as Google Now, a predictive assistant feature (Amadeo 2013).

As mentioned above, Google's proprietary applications are key to its
profits. When customers use the applications to engage in a range of
activities online, they provide a market for advertisers. Certainly, advertising is Google's main source of revenue. According to the 2015 Financial Tables on Google's Investor Relations web page, the company

made about $51 billion dollars in advertising revenues in 2013 and over $59 billion in 2014 (accessed July 28, 2015. http://investor.google.com/financial/tables.html). Data on the Statista website indicate a clear trend of Google increasing these advertising revenues, with over 67 billion in 2015 and over 79 billion in 2016 (accessed August 22, 2017. https://statista.com/statistics/266249/advertising-revenue-of-google/).

For example, through the AdWords program, advertisers target consumers as they are conducting Internet searches. Google's AdWords web page urges companies to "[b]e seen by customers at the very moment that they're searching on Google for the things you offer. And only pay when they click to visit your website or call" (accessed July 28, 2015. http://google.com/adwords/?subid=us-en-adon-aw-bing-sk&utm_source=bing&utm_medium=cpc&utm_campaign=us-en-adon-aw-bing-sk). The page promotes the service as a way to attract customers by targeting ads to people in particular cities, regions, or countries. Advertisers can also exclude certain users by identifying ranges of Internet Protocol (IP) addresses that will not receive their ads. Once advertisers pay to enroll in AdWords, they can pay an additional fee to use the AdSense program to help them decide how to best position the ads.

In order to develop user profiles for these advertising services, Google harvests metadata from users of its myriad services, from Google Search to YouTube, Google+, and more. This extensive collection of data shapes the broader ecology of the Internet and has implications for civil liberties, which will be discussed in detail in Chapter 6 on Internet Politics. In the process, Google's strategy toward open source undermines the development of the digital commons. This strategy fosters a range of corporate activities that depend on tracking users' locations and activities so that Google and its corporate customers can target those users through advertising. Google thus uses open source as a gateway for firms to engage in these advertising activities, as well as for device manufacturers and Internet service providers to offer an expanding array of goods and services to their mobile customers.

Google's activities have been a powerful influence over the development of the mobile phone market, as Android has risen to the top mobile phone operating system since 2011. This expansion of Android, accompanied by the growth in Google's proprietary applications, services and advertising revenues, promotes the development of proprietary firms and practices, rather than commons-based practices. Drawing upon the hyperproductive nature of open-source software (Bauwens 2009), Google uses open source as a strategy to attract business partners who want to build upon and profit from the opportunity to develop their own products and services. Open source, combined on a routine basis with proprietary elements, becomes an alternative vehicle for profit-making. Hence, Google is a prime example of open source as a proprietary strategy, rather than as a means for developing the digital commons.

Both Google and IBM provide cases where firms use open source to expand and promote their proprietary activities. They illustrate the challenges faced by peer producers who want to transform market dynamics. Indeed, Google and IBM reveal the power of proprietary interests and practices in making use of open source as a vehicle to facilitate profit-making. These proprietary constraints are formidable; however, there are myriad free software communities engaged in processes of peer production of programs that constitute the catalytic property form. These communities raise the possibility of transforming proprietary practices, contributing to the development of the digital commons and alternative forms of globalization from below.

One major such community is Drupal, a CMS used for web design that has been deployed extensively in high profile projects around the world, including the whitehouse.gov website for the U.S. White House during the Obama administration, the 2014 World Cup in Brazil (http://copa2014.gov.br/en), and the 2016 Summer Olympics in Brazil (http://rio2016.com/). The Drupal case provides a fuller picture of the challenges and possibilities involved with developing the digital commons.

Drupal: Free Software Built through Peer Community and Market-Based Production

Drupal was originally created by Dries Buytaert and Hans Snijder when they were students at the University of Antwerp. They began the project in Belgium in 2000, as part of an effort to develop a system to communicate with their friends. Toward this end, they built a news site with a built-in web board that allowed them to leave messages for each other. After graduation, they decided to put the internal website online and continued to develop it into a platform for new web technologies. According to the Drupal.org website, Buytaert released the software as an open-source project in 2001 (accessed August 5, 2015. https://drupal.org/about/history). He continues to be the Project Lead in the Drupal community.

Drupal is licensed under GPL version 2 or later. As discussed above, the GNU GPL is the basis for the catalytic software property form. In contrast to Debian, the Apache 2.0 license used for Android, and other open-source software licenses, the GPL does not allow proprietary elements to be combined with copylefted software.

In 2007, Buytaert collaborated with Jay Bateson to cofound Acquia, a for-profit, market-based company for which Buytaert is the Chief Technology Officer (CTO). Acquia uses the Drupal platform to offer software as a service, otherwise known as cloud services. These services include technical support and training for businesses, government agencies, and nonprofit organizations that want to use Drupal. Acquia also offers products such as the Acquia Cloud and Acquia Search. Private and public sector organizations have used these products to facilitate their operations in myriad ways. For example, New York's Metropolitan Transit Authority used Drupal and Acquia Cloud to offer commuters and other riders information about train schedules and services. Timex used Acquia Search, a web-based service integrated with Drupal, to expand the search options on its website so that potential customers could navigate it more easily to explore product features. Timex also used Drupal to add further security features to its website, allowing it to detect and reject suspicious transactions and reduce fraud. As of February 2015, Acquia had 600 employees and made over $100 million in revenue (https://acquia.com).

Drupal is developed through a collaboration between Acquia as a for-profit, market-based firm and the Drupal community of peer producers. There is a key difference, however, between this collaboration and Ubuntu's hybrid model of production discussed above. Certainly, Buytaert was one of the software's original developers, and he has consistently played a leading role in both the Drupal peer producer community and Acquia's for-profit operations. By contrast, while Shuttleworth started off as a Debian developer, he did not originally create the Debian Project. Of most importance, once he founded Canonical, he focused his work in that firm rather than in the peer community. Thus, there is not the same kind of synergy between Canonical and Debian as there is between Drupal and Acquia.

For example, the Drupal community is structured with an organizational hierarchy that allows Buytaert and the core committers to Drupal considerable authority over the project. They are the ones who have access to the code repository; they also conduct a peer review of all patches submitted to the issue queue, comprised of a database of bugs and feature requests. The community as a whole is actively involved in many other ways, such as monitoring the issue queue. If someone wants to contribute core code to the community, they do so by opening an issue for a patch on the issue queue or submitting a patch for an open issue (Moghaddam, Bongen and Twidale 2011).

The standard release of Drupal is known as the Drupal core. As described on the Drupal.org website, Drupal community members collaborate on the development of this code base, which can be extended through contributory modules. For example, as of April 2015, there were over 30,000 free community-contributed modules, or "addons," that allowed users to customize Drupal's behavior and appearance. The core contains features such as user account registration and maintenance, menu management, RSS feeds, taxonomy, page layout customization, and system administration, all of which are key features of most CMSs. If organizations install the Drupal core, they can use it to offer a basic website, a blog for one or more users, an Internet forum, or a community website that offers users the opportunity to create their own content. Drupal runs on any computing platform that supports both a web server capable of running PHP, as well as a database to store content and settings.

In addition to coding, community members engage in a diverse array of community projects and activities, such as participating in Drupal forums and discussion groups on various topics. Some of this work involves organizing Drupal community events and discussing options for planning future conferences, as will be discussed further below. Such work occurs primarily over electronic mailing lists and IRC channels on the Freenode network. Lists of these resources are kept updated on the main Drupal.org website, so that community participants can easily find out what kinds of projects are developing and think about how they want to become involved.

As discussed above with respect to Debian, it is difficult to give a precise estimate of the numbers of Drupal developers and community members. A study by Wang et al. (2014) noted that Drupal has over 17,000 developers around the world. A second way to estimate the number of members of the Drupal community is to visit Drupal.org, which lists 37,000 developer accounts as of March 2015. By contrast, there were over 1,167,000 million user accounts. A study by Gamalielsson et al. (2015) used this Drupal.org data to note that Drupal had over 1 million users in 228 countries, speaking 181 different languages. A third way to estimate the size of the Drupal community is by using the Drupal Project's LinkedIn page, which says that it is maintained and developed by a community of over 630,000 users and developers (accessed August 5, 2015. https://linkedin. com/company/2197069?trk=tyah&trkInfo=clickedVertical%3Acompany%2Cidx%3A2-3-6%2CtarId%3A1435695798091%2Ctas%3A Drupal). Based upon that range of data, it seems reasonable to estimate that there are at least 17,000 Drupal developers and between 600,000 and 1 million users. The Drupal community is thus exponentially larger than the Debian community, with its approximately 1,000 developers.

Developing Drupal: Dynamics of Participation within a Peer Community

Buytaert's vision for developing Drupal involved extensive interactions with large numbers of users, in an effort to appeal to those users by offering a high-quality experience. He emphasized the importance of usability after problems were reported with Drupal 6, particularly with respect to the administration interface. Some users critiqued this interface as confusing and intimidating, noting that this was particularly problematic for new web administrators. Researchers at the University of Minnesota and the University of Baltimore studied the problem and issued a usability report in 2008 (Scollan et al. 2008).

To address these problems, Acquia hired user interface designer Mark Boulton to work with the Drupal community to develop a new user interface. In developing Drupal 7, the community implemented most of the usability design work done by Boulton's team. When researchers at the University of Minnesota Office of Information Technology conducted further usability tests on Drupal in 2011, they found that the main usability problems identified in Drupal 6 had been eradicated or at least markedly improved. They also identified new usability problems, signaling the need for further work in that critical area (Rosencrans 2011).

In March 2009, in a key example of Buytaert's role as leader of the Drupal community, he announced that there would be a code freeze on Drupal 7 in about six months, on September 1. For software developers, announcing a code freeze is the most definitive way to signal that a project has entered its final phase of development. In a keynote address at a Drupal conference, as well as on his blog, Buytaert explained the reasons for this decision and the upcoming process of Drupal 7 development. He stated, "Announcing a code freeze date is always a little bit dangerous in light of a possible slip, but doing so helps prioritize development efforts and helps end-users in their planning" (accessed August 6, 2015. http://buytaert.net/drupal-7-code-freeze-september-1st). Buytaert thus acknowledged the potential risks involved with a code freeze, since the developers would make no further changes to the code after that time. If unexpected problems arose, that could jeopardize the planned timeline. Nonetheless, the code freeze conveyed to Drupal users that a new release was close to being ready. This information could facilitate their planning if they wanted to migrate to the new version.

Such advance planning was particularly important for large institutional users, such as the U.S. government. For example, in November 2009, the Obama administration decided to migrate to Drupal for the official Whitehouse.gov website. President Obama had used Drupal extensively during his presidential campaign, and chose it over the custom-built proprietary CMS that had been used by the outgoing Bush administration. The migration of Whitehouse.gov to Drupal created conditions for other federal Chief Information Officers to consider using Drupal as well. Since 2009, a growing number of other government websites have used Drupal. These include the We The People petition tool; a platform for the House of Representatives that provides support for a wide range of committees, conferences, as well as individual Representatives; the Departments of Energy, Education, Commerce, Defense, Health and Human Services, Homeland Security; and the Federal Emergency Management Agency (FEMA) (accessed August 8, 2015. https://drupal.org/whitehouse-gov-launches-on-drupal-engages-community). The Trump administration continued to use Drupal after taking office in 2017. A complete list of U.S. government websites running Drupal is available at drupal.org (accessed June 16, 2017. https://groups.drupal.org/government-sites#USA).

Buytaert's decision to announce the Drupal 7 code freeze six months ahead of time thus allowed large institutional users to consider the possibility of migrating to the new version of Drupal in their long range planning. In this announcement, Buytaert noted that after September 1, 2009, work on Drupal would focus on issues of performance, stability, and usability of the code that had been built by that time. Such work involved preparing for the release of Drupal 7, fixing bugs, and integrating usability improvements recommended by the usability design team discussed above. Buytaert outlined the process by which he made the decision about when to implement the code freeze. He highlighted the influence of input and collaboration from the Drupal community of peer producers:

> I decided...after talking with people in the community (including my Drupal 7 co-maintainer webchick), reading forums topics, listening to users and examining the download and usage statistics. Now that most of the major modules work with Drupal 6, it's clear that Drupal 6 has really taken off. As an example, Drupal.org is humming along on Drupal 6.
>
> (Accessed August 6, 2015. http://buytaert.net/
> drupal-7-code-freeze-september-1st)

Drupal 7 was released on January 5, 2011. Over 250 release parties were planned in more than 90 countries to celebrate the extensive work that the community had invested in the project. These efforts included strong coordination between teams focusing on the areas of usability, accessibility, and design (accessed July 1, 2015. https://drupal.org/drupal-7-released).

Wang et al. (2014) illuminated the dynamics of participation and interaction during the process of developing Drupal 7. They studied tweeting behavior within the Drupal community, and particularly among the 12 developers who committed the most to the code base of Drupal 7 between 2008 and 2012. They also studied the two Drupal 7 project coordinators, who one of Wang et al.'s (2014, 3) study participants described as "cat herder[s]"; these were two committed core developers who sought to promote participation from the community.

Within the Drupal community's participatory governance structure, project coordinators did not assign tasks directly. By contrast, they used Twitter to reach out and let the community know what work needed to be completed. One coordinator quoted by Wang et al. (2014, 8) tweeted the community to come to a "[c]ore hack sprint tomorrow on IRC! Help D7 be more kick-ass, learn new tricks, and have fun, too!" Through this kind of social media communication, coordinators thus called on the broader Drupal community, as well as the general public, to participate in the hack sprint through IRC. As Wang et al. (2014, 8) noted, these "crowdsourcing tweets often come from the two coordinators...[and] are often combined with short motivational phrases to encourage participation." Such tweets were one way that community leaders attempted to elicit participation in particular tasks or events. Despite these efforts, Wang et al. (2014) did not find any examples where these crowdsourcing tweets were effective in communicating with prospective volunteers or spurring them to action.

Wang et al.'s (2014) analysis of Twitter usage and content also focused on distinct communication patterns between tweets by individual developers compared to group tweets. They showed that developers' individual tweets were more "versatile, interactive, and revealing of the affective states" than tweets from group accounts, which were "impersonal and informative" (Wang et al. 2014, 7). For example, 53 percent of individual developers' tweets contained web links to information related to the project, compared to 87 percent of group tweets. When sending updates about their work, individual developers also included personal emotions about the projects, such as describing the new Drupal 7 release as "friendly," "powerful," and "awesome" (Wang et al. 2014, 7). By contrast, only two of the tweets in the sample communicated negative sentiments. The tweets expressing positive emotions were retweeted, while the negative tweets were not.

This study showed key ways that the Drupal community used Twitter, which shed light on how the community functions. First, developers employed Twitter as what Wang et al. (2014, 8) called an "information radiator," to share information about their work with each other. This was extremely useful, since they might be working in different parts of the world and might not see each other face to face. They might be working in different time zones, and thus use the updates over Twitter to keep them abreast of tasks that may have been completed while they were sleeping or otherwise occupied. Such tasks included "submitted requests and changes, crucial decisions, important milestones, or even team retrospectives" (Wang et al. 2014, 8). Second, developers used Twitter for "knowledge preservation...[to] externaliz[e] tacit knowledge during informal communication, sav[e] it persistently, and mak[e] it publicly available" (Wang et al. 2014, 9). In this sense, developers made information available to potential contributors in the wider community, who might be among the many followers of the Twitter accounts. By publicizing key tasks that needed to be done at a particular time, developers provided access to this knowledge and left the door open for more people to become involved in the community. Third, as mentioned above, the Drupal community worked through a process where participants chose what tasks they wanted to work on, cooperating with each other without a formal coordinating structure. Wang et al. (2014, 9) argued that even though some community members "play coordinating roles," they did not have formal authority to give permission for specific tasks or to approve releases. Finally, community members used Twitter to express positive emotions, thank each other for contributions to a project, and generally maintain their connections with each other. They maintained a sense of community bonding through these interactions.

Beyond these insights gleaned from Twitter usage, participation in the Drupal community can be understood through attendance at the semi-annual Drupal conference, DrupalCon. According to Drupal.org, attendance at the conference grew from 500 in 2008 to over 3,700 in 2014. Apart from giving a sense of the community's growth in sheer numbers, a closer consideration of the process of planning the conference provides insight into Drupal's emergence as a global community. Indeed, the community's global character is one of its key distinguishing features that provide the potential for it to contribute to the development of the digital commons and alternative forms of globalization from below.

Building the Global Drupal Community

To provide a foundation to understand the Drupal community's international character, it is useful to consider the work it has done in language localization. For example, according to the web page on language-specific communities on Drupal.org, there are 36 such communities with third-party websites offering a range of resources to community participants. These resources include language-specific support forums, handbooks, and directories of companies and freelancers offering Drupal services. Language-specific communities may offer their own workshops and seminars for Drupal users, as well as hosting projects for translating Drupal content and documentation into native languages. These communities include Drupal Belarus, Belgium, Brazil, Catalan, China, Croatia, Czech, Denmark, Esperanto, France, Finland, Germany, Greece, Hispano, Hungary, India, Indonesia, Israel, Italy, Japan, Korea, Lithuania, Mauritius, Norway, Iran, Poland, Russia, Serbia, Slovakia, South Africa, Sweden, Taiwan, Thailand, and Ukraine. In addition, there is a wide range of other Drupal groups that are not formally language-specific but that reveal the extent of the Drupal community's global development, including Drupal Vietnam and Drupal Sweden (accessed July 8, 2015. https://drupal.org/language-specific-communities).

Similar to the above discussion of the Debian conferences, the development of DrupalCon sheds light on the growth of Drupal as a global community. Furthermore, the processes of planning DrupalCon illuminate the participatory nature of this community. As noted above, these conferences are key sites where community participants interact face to face, complementing their collaboration via online forums throughout the rest of the year. DrupalCon is held more frequently than DebCon, however, providing further opportunities for such communication and interaction. Similar to DebCon, between 2005 and 2013, the Drupal conference alternated between Europe, the U.S., and Canada; it was located in Australia in 2013. The Drupal community, however, developed a strong sense of the importance of expanding its work beyond North America and Europe into the global South.

I learned about this aspect of the Drupal community's work while engaging in participant observation at the International Free Software Forum (FISL) in Brazil in 2014. At the conference, I met Jorge da Costa, an active member of the Brazilian Drupal community. In several informal conversations as well as a 2014 interview, da Costa emphasized that Drupal community participants were becoming increasingly committed to fostering community development in Latin America and other parts of the global South. They viewed such expanded community development as a key way to combat the digital divide. In fact, grassroots organizers had spurred the growth of a Drupal Latino community with its own annual meeting and Drupal camps in several countries in the global South (da Costa, interview 2014).

These local community development efforts in the global South bore fruit in 2013. The DA, the organizers of DrupalCon, decided to add a third annual conference that would complement the two conferences that had traditionally been held in Europe and North America. In March 2014, a member of the DA with the handle stephaniet66 posted a blog stating that the conference would take place in a "region where Drupal is gaining traction, and having a Con could help further Drupal adoption" (accessed July 16, 2015. https://assoc.drupal.org/content/drupalcon-goes-latin-america-2015). This post followed up on an earlier post in September 2013, where stephaniet66 stated that the third DrupalCon would be held "in a region where there is opportunity for significant Drupal growth and adoption" (accessed July 16, 2015. https://assoc.drupal.org/node/18453). She explained the process of selecting sites for DrupalCon, which involved long range planning three years in advance. Such planning facilitated negotiations with hotels and event venues, with the goal of keeping costs to a minimum and maximizing participation. In selecting a site, the DA first considered input from the community. It conducted a survey asking for suggestions for locations of future conferences. Second, the DA developed selection criteria, including a "popular city" with hotels and event venues that would accommodate large numbers of people; the existence of a local Drupal community, which might involve prior hosting of Drupal camps or other community activities; and relatively inexpensive travel. Finally, the DA consulted with a destination travel company to gain further input on whether particular locations could accommodate the conference (accessed July 16, 2015. https://assoc.drupal.org/node/18453).

In March 2014, stephaniet66's posted a blog entry entitled "DrupalCon Goes to Latin America in 2015." She announced, "[h]ere is the much awaited blog post to consider our options for the location of our

2015 Latin American DrupalCon" (accessed June 30, 2015. https://assoc. drupal.org/content/drupalcon-goes-latin-america-2015). She asked for feedback from the community about the decision. She gave some background on the work that had already been done, explaining that the Executive Director of the DA met with members of the Latin American Drupal communities at a regional conference in January 2014. Based on discussion with Drupal community members from several Latin American countries who attended that meeting, Bogotá, Colombia and São Paulo, Brazil were selected as the two top choices of location for the conference. Two active Drupal community participants from Brazil and Colombia volunteered to organize teams within their communities to research costs and travel considerations involved with holding the conference in each city. Stephaniet66 expressed her appreciation for the enthusiastic participation of the communities in gathering the information and advocating for their respective cities. She noted, "As far as community support goes, I am confident that in either place we would have a groundswell of passionate volunteers who would help produce the event" (accessed June 30, 2015. https://assoc.drupal.org/content/ drupalcon-goes-latin-america-2015).

With that background, stephaniet66 summarized the DA's assessment of the differences in the two locations and the reasons why they thought it best to hold the conference in Colombia. She noted that prices for airfare, hotel, event venues, Internet, and catering were all considerably higher in Brazil. Visa considerations were also important, since Brazil required visas for travelers from the U.S. DrupalCon planners were concerned that this visa requirement would affect attendance and perhaps make it more difficult to book key speakers they hoped would participate in the event. One key factor in Brazil's favor was that it had a larger business community than Colombia, raising the potential to get more sponsors and earn more revenue. After weighing the information, however, the DA recommended holding the conference in Bogotá.

This recommendation prompted extensive debate on the blog, revealing some of the dynamics of decision-making within the Drupal community, as well as the process of its global development. Drupal community members engaged in a lively discussion about the advantages and disadvantages of the two sites. For example, math3usmartins, a Drupal community participant who did not identify his or her nationality, posted a spreadsheet with data on the numbers of Drupal developers from different Latin American countries who were on LinkedIn. It included a pie chart with percentages of Drupal developers on LinkedIn who were from each country. About 29 percent of those developers were from Brazil, compared to about 21 percent from Argentina, almost 15 percent from Mexico, and almost 11 percent from Colombia; in terms of total numbers of developers, there were 1878 from Brazil, 1383 from Argentina, 951 from Mexico, and 701 from Colombia. There were also 404 developers from Peru, 399 from Chile, 218 from Venezuela, and smaller numbers from 7 other countries (accessed July 10, 2015. https://docs. google.com/spreadsheets/d/1czb4__OlrDzOliwD9zp2C4NlctxyBZ0I BFB6j0vKR58/pub?single=true&gid=0&output=html). Based on these data, math3usmartins commented that São Paulo seemed to be the best choice, "considering the benefits for the local community (developers, companies, and market); the ease to bring them; and the overall impact of the Drupalcon" (accessed July 10, 2015. https://assoc.drupal.org/ comment/7033#comment-7033).

A number of Brazilian community members argued in favor of holding the conference in São Paulo. They questioned the cost estimates for hotel, food, and Internet, which led the DA to conclude that it would be more costly to hold the event in Brazil. They suggested that there were ways to lower the cost, such as considering a wider range of hotels. Others discussed the question of visas for U.S. citizens to go to Brazil, which could involve a 4–8-week process and cost $160–$180, depending upon whether one applied in person. Stephaniet66 remarked that the visa question was a major concern for the DA planners. Math3usmartins replied that more input into the discussion was needed by U.S. citizens, to get a sense of how many were planning to come to the DrupalCon in either São Paulo or Bogotá. Math3usmartins commented that the DA was concerned about people coming to the DrupalCon from the U.S., while perhaps that "shouldn't *really* affect the choice" (emphasis in original) (accessed July 10, 2015. https://assoc.drupal.org/content/drupalcon-goes-latin-america-2015). For example, if a keynote speaker from the U.S. ended up having visa issues and not being able to attend, local speakers could be found instead. The main point of having a DrupalCon in Latin America was to promote attendance and exchange between Drupal users and developers in the region, while also bringing in participants from the U.S. and Europe.

A community member with the handle rafaelcichini urged consideration of Brazil due to the strength and size of the Drupal community there. He identified himself as Rafael Cichini, Chief Operating Officer at Just Digital and Vice-President of Drupal Association Brazil. He noted that 250 Drupal developers attended the last Drupal Camp in São Paulo. He continued, "[s]o… think about it… because São Paulo is just one city and if you think in entire Brazil…. If in a Drupal Camp it is possible to have 250 people. Imagine with a DrupalCon" (accessed July 11, 2015. https://assoc.drupal.org/content/drupalcon-goes-latin-america-2015). He estimated that perhaps 500 people would attend the conference in Brazil. In a later post, Cichini emphasized the importance of Brazil's organized community, including an official DA, as well as the importance of São Paulo as a center for global business.

A Colombian member of the Drupal community, with the handle cesabal, responded that he owned a Drupal company and knew many others who did as well. He noted that Bogotá was also a major city, where many global companies sought to do business. He stated,

> when we think of what is best for Drupal, we also need to think what is best for Drupal in the Latin American Region. Don't we need every country represented in as large number as possible? Don't we need to think [about] Dupalers in countries that are not so greatly developed as Brazil?
>
> (Accessed July 12, 2015. https://assoc.drupal.org/content/ drupalcon-goes-latin-america-2015)

Other members of the Colombian Drupal community also highlighted the importance of Bogotá as strategically located in the middle of the Americas. They noted that it had excellent international transportation connections. Furthermore, they emphasized the city's booming business community, high-quality hotel infrastructure, and multicultural urban space that could draw conference participants interested in exploring its parks, cycling paths, and other amenities.

As the discussion evolved, members of the Brazilian community posted the research they had done about the venue, general location, and costs in an open letter to the Drupal community. They asked that the Colombian community post similar information to supplement that provided by stephaniet66 in her original recommendation for where to hold the conference. The Colombians never posted such information, and neither did stephaniet66. At that point, one of the advocates for locating the conference in Brazil called the argument for Bogotá being more centrally located "bullshit," and reiterated the call for Colombia to post their proposal. Stephaniet66 then interceded, stating,

> This isn't a "who is better" discussion. It is simply a discussion about where we can best produce a successful event for the whole of the Latin American community.
>
> When we look at all the factors, we feel that Bogota offers us the most chance for a successful event. It is the easiest and cheapest location to travel to for most of Latin America, it is a less expensive option all the way around...(and we have looked at the budget much more closely than these general statements suggest), and it will allow us to bring in outside speakers, including Dries [Buytaert] with less complications.
>
> We feel both communities are equal in community support and enthusiasm, but stand behind our recommendation for Bogota.
>
> (Accessed July 12, 2015. https://assoc.drupal.org/content/ drupalcon-goes-latin-america-2015)

At that point, Rafael Cichini questioned whether the process for choosing a venue was truly participatory, or whether the decision had already been made by the DA. He asked stephaniet66 to "explain the real reason to start this discussion…this sounds to me like a TOP DOWN decision, not [a] DEMOCRATIC decision" (emphasis in original) (accessed July 12, 2015. https://assoc.drupal.org/comment/7033#comment-7033). Stephaniet66 replied by describing the process that had occurred to date. She reiterated what had been included in her original post, that the Executive Director of the DA met with members from a range of Drupal communities in Latin America, who initially chose the two best options for cities to hold the conference. She stated, "[t]he participants in that discussion who were from Brazil wanted the event in Brazil, while most of the participants from other Latin American countries, wanted it in Bogotá" (accessed July 13, 2015. https://assoc.drupal.org/comment/7033#comment-7033). With respect to the question of whether the decision to hold the conference in Colombia was "top down," stephaniet66 defended the collaborative nature of the process. She emphasized that they had "gathered data from both locations, and the responses associated with this blog post have also provide additional data. All of this input has come directly from the two communities (São Paolo and Bogotá)" (accessed July 13, 2015. https://assoc.drupal.org/comment/7033#comment-7033). In response, stephaniet66 noted that the DA was considering the "data" from the blog, including the range of responses from the two communities most involved in the decision. She stated:

> We, the Drupal Association are making the final decision on location based on the sum of this community feedback, combined with all of the research on both locations we have been gathering. We feel this has been a VERY collaborative process, and will be making a final decision later this week that will be communicated in another blog post.
>
> Both communities are passionate, committed and have done a great job in stating their cases to come to their cities. I sincerely hope, that, whichever city we select, everyone will support us in creating a fabulous DrupalCon Latin America.
>
> (Accessed July 14, 2015. https://assoc.drupal.org/
> comment/7033#comment-7033)

Stephaniet66 thus reiterated the DA's commitment to community participation in the decision-making process about where to hold the conference. Moreover, she appreciated the enthusiastic commitment of all the Latin American Drupal participants that had engaged in the discussion, as well as in the work to research possibilities for holding the event in their cities. Once the decision about location was made, these qualities of community commitment to the larger Drupal Project would be essential for people who had disagreed on the blog thread to put aside their differences and work together to make the conference a success.

As the discussion on the blog continued, one other contributor also raised the question of whether the DA genuinely wanted feedback or whether the decision had already been made. Another user responded with a call for calm and patience, emphasizing the importance of everyone working together to make the conference happen. Rafael Cichini then replied that he was calm, but simply wanted to pursue the discussion. He stated,

> If the event will happen in Bogotá, no problem, but while there is a chance to bring the event to Brazil I want to try. When the final decision is announced I will start to plan how I can involve me and my company to help the event, in Brazil or in Bogotá.
> (Accessed July 15, 2015. https://assoc.drupal.org/content/ drupalcon-goes-latin-america-2015)

Passionate, extended exchanges on the blog thread illuminated how much the Drupal community participants valued the chance to discuss the question of where the conference should be located, and particularly to air their differences. A participant with the handle develCuy posted apologies to the Drupal Association Board, as well as to the international community, noting that "in this thread there are comments that cross the line of friendliness and fraternity." Moreover, develCuy stated that he or she did not want people to think "that the Drupalcon Latino community is a kind of 'madhouse,' please excuse the strong language, redundance and agressions seen in this thread" (accessed July 16, 2015. https://assoc.drupal.org/content/drupalcon-goes-latin-america-2015). Nick Vidal, the Brazilian Drupal community member who organized and presented the research on costs for the São Paulo venue and identified himself by name, responded to develCuy. Vidal said, "We are not fighting. We are just discussing this important matter in an open manner. I do agree that a minority has crossed the line on this thread, but I think most have been respectful" (accessed July 16, 2015. https://assoc. drupal.org/content/drupalcon-goes-latin-america-2015). He explained that he and the other Brazilian organizer had

> explicitly told the community NOT to bring Colombia down, but to respect them and argue why São Paulo should host a DrupalCon. It might seem a bit confusing, for sure, but this open discussion is healthy and promotes transparency. Now we know each others' proposals and we can analyse the pros and cons.
> (Accessed July 16, 2015. https://assoc.drupal.org/content/ drupalcon-goes-latin-america-2015)

Nick Vidal's support of an open process, including disagreements and debates, was supported by the participant mentioned above, whose handle was math3usmartins. Math3usmartins noted that there were about 230 comments on the post so far, and that only 5 might be considered "aggressive." This community member stated, "I think that contributing with ideas and comments should be considered part of the work to make a successful DrupalCon no matter where it goes. And dealing with inadequate comments or different views/culture is part of that work" (accessed July 16, 2015. https://assoc.drupal.org/content/drupalcon-goes-latin-america-2015).

Indeed, the participants in the blog discussion provided vital input into the DA's decision about where to hold the first DrupalCon in Latin America. Their thoughtful involvement, as they made the case to hold the conference in their respective countries, reflected the commitment and enthusiasm of the Colombian and Brazilian participants. Eventually, the DA stayed with its initial recommendation to hold the conference in Bogotá. Once the conference was held, it had 263 participants; this attendance seemed to support the Brazilians' argument that they could have gotten more people to attend a conference in São Paulo. Brazilians certainly attended the conference, however, as did others from different Latin American countries. They were pleased to have held the first conference in Latin America and to have participated in the process of its organization.

In 2015, the DA decided to hold a 2016 DrupalCon in India. They engaged in a similar process to that described above, eliciting input from the Indian community about which city would be the best choice. A member of the DA with the handle megansanicki provided a more detailed explanation of the Association's approach to planning. She posted a blog inviting community members to help in the planning of the 2016 DrupalCon in India. She described DrupalCon as "an important community event that brings a diverse group of Drupalers together under one roof to share knowledge, grow skills, and strengthen community bonds" (accessed June 30, 2015. https://assoc.drupal.org/blog/megansanicki/help-us-plan-drupalcon-india). She noted that over the years, the DA had tracked attendance at the conferences and found that they were primarily attended by people from the region, as well as neighboring countries. Conference participants were drawn by the opportunity to hear speakers from around the world, as well as to meet with trainers and community leaders. She stated, "[k]nowing this, the Drupal Association is committed to hosting DrupalCon in regions other than just North America and Europe" (accessed June 30, 2015. https://assoc.drupal.org/blog/megansanicki/help-us-plan-drupalcon-india). She highlighted that India was viewed as a good choice for a conference because of the extensive development of the community, including business, Drupal leaders and contributors, and end users. In fact, India was the country that originated the second highest amount of traffic to the Drupal.org website, with 450,000 sessions compared to 1 million from the U.S. Moreover,

India had many communities with strong leadership across the country, several of which had organized Drupal camps over several years.

Megansanicki informed the Indian Drupal community that they had asked community participants to research possibilities for hosting a conference of 1,000 people in their cities. After discussions with the communities, the DA chose Bangalore, Mumbai, and Delhi as the three most viable options. They provided information about potential venues, including cost estimates for food, hotel, and travel.

Interestingly, the discussion about where to locate the Indian Drupal-Con was very different from the one concerning the Latin American conference. Participants in the Indian blog thread made encouraging comments noting the convenience of reaching their city and the success of their annual organization of Drupal camps. Posts such as this were made to advocate Delhi, Mumbai, and Bangalore. Participants from Bangalore advocated it as a hub for information technology development. Participants from Mumbai noted the ease of transportation around the city, as well as the impressive size of its business community and the pleasant climate in that region. In contrast to the Latin American case, the blog thread did not involve much back and forth discussion between the participants or points about why one city would be preferable to another. Instead, the Indian participants made positive comments about the benefits of their particular city. No one questioned the DA's intentions to gather community input, or suggested that perhaps the decision was being made in a top-down manner rather than through genuine community engagement. After consideration of the discussion, the DA chose Mumbai as the location for DrupalCon Asia in 2016.

The Drupal community is thus engaged in an ongoing process of expanding, through the interactions between the DA leadership and the grassroots organizers in local communities around the world. This expansion is promising for the development of the digital commons and alternative forms of globalization from below, particularly since Drupal is an example of the catalytic property form, spreading through the market and transforming capitalist practices in the process. It offers the possibility for peer production to become transcendent in Bauwens (2009) sense, since the Drupal community operates on an alternative logic of peer production and global community development that challenges the private property form. By building these community-based practices into the nature of the software and the organization of its community, Drupal contributes to the growth of alternative knowledge, property, and power structures in the context of informational capitalism.

Drupal: Capitalist Transformation through Peer Community and the Catalytic Software Form

Indeed, Drupal's "post-capitalist aspects" (Bauwens 2009, 122) include its development in a peer community that is organized on a global scale.

As noted above, this community collaborates with Acquia as a market-based firm, so the development of Drupal is simultaneously organized through peer production and more traditional capitalist practices. Nonetheless, as the previous discussion of the process of organizing DrupalCon Latin America suggests, the peer communities are actively engaged in much more than the technological development of Drupal. These communities are involved in the spread of Drupal events that provide opportunities for participants to gather, share knowledge, and deepen their collaborative work on projects. This alternative logic of peer community development is thus a vital and growing part of the Drupal Project.

Drupal's presence within the global political economy is rooted in this community participation, as well as in its extensive deployment in both the private and public sectors.

The Drupal.org website lists 158 countries in Asia, Latin America, Africa, and the Middle East, as well as the U.S. and Europe, whose governments are using Drupal at the state or federal level. Organizations such as embassies, parliaments, governmental portals, police, research centers, ministries and departments, and monarchies in these countries may deploy Drupal in their operations (accessed August 4, 2015. https://groups.drupal.org/government-sites). To give a sense of how Drupal is employed within these countries, the Drupal.org website includes an extensive list of municipal, district, department, county, and other local government agencies and departments that currently use Drupal (accessed August 4, 2015. https://groups.drupal.org/node/24119). In a similar vein, Drupal.org also lists all the examples of known implementations of Drupal in intergovernmental organizations, such as the United Nations, the European Union, and others (accessed August 4, 2015. https://groups.drupal.org/node/79093).

Drupal is thus employed extensively around the world, by a wide range of organizations. This deployment gives a sense of the expansion of the digital commons, as these organizations take advantage of the quality of Drupal technology, as well as the ability to cut costs associated with proprietary systems. For example, in an interview with Nikhil Deshpande, Director of an office within the Georgia Technology Authority (GTA), he discussed reasons for shifting to Drupal when the state decided to replace its outdated CMS. He noted that the state wanted to keep costs down, since the proprietary system had become very expensive. Beyond cost, however, he emphasized the importance of having a high-quality system with a major share of the market. He stated, "'What really sold us on Drupal was its enormous market share in government and the public sector in general. The success of all the federal government sites convinced us'" (Meyer Maria 2012).

Since Drupal is licensed under the GNU GPL, it allows users to freely share and modify the software. These freedoms are appealing to public sector organizations that want to engage in a process of influencing the software's development. Such agencies adhere to high level standards for security as well, so government participation in software development ensures that systems offer the security provisions that they need. Certainly, the U.S. government has contributed substantially to Drupal development, including modules released by the White House; the Departments of Commerce, Education, and Energy; the Federal Communications Commission; and the General Services Administration. A list of Drupal modules contributed by U.S. government agencies is available on Drupal.org (accessed August 31, 2015. https://drupal.org/node/1497356).

Due to its extensive implementation by government, nonprofit, and market-based firms and organizations, many Drupal developers are able to make a living as independent contractors. For example, in an interview, a Belgian Drupal developer noted that she had developed her own web design business by tailoring her skills to fit the needs of a range of different customers. She enjoyed the freedom of working for herself, and found that there was substantial demand for her skills since so many organizations needed high-quality web pages as part of their business models (Marie Daalman, interview 2014).

Implicit Communities of Resistance, the Digital Commons, and Globalization from Below

The Debian and Drupal cases provide intriguing comparisons that illuminate the prospects and challenges involved with developing the digital commons and alternative forms of globalization from below. The examples of IBM and Google offer further insights into these interconnected processes.

Both Debian and Drupal are produced in peer communities by participants who perform free labor, where they voluntarily engage in production without pay (Terranova 2013). As Benkler (2006) argues, these peer communities operate outside of a traditional organizational hierarchy. Community participants collaborate in a wide range of activities essential to the software's development, from writing software code to creating documentation, translating into a range of languages, and organizing workshops and conferences for others to learn about and become involved in the community. They perform most of this work online through email lists and IRC. Face-to-face interaction is vital as well, as community members gather on a regular basis at conferences to engage in intensive periods of collective work, discussion, and decision-making.

In these communities, processes of software development are thus integrally related with processes of community building. These processes are intertwined, ongoing, and deeply collaborative, resonating with Hess and Ostrom's (2006) conception of the commons as a complex ecosystem. Certainly, both the Debian and Drupal communities provide shared resources of knowledge and skill central to the software's development. These communities involve structured relationships where peers collaborate with each other. As discussed above, the Drupal community is structured with more direction from the Project Leader. Both of these communities are part of a commons ecosystem, offering vibrant examples of the commons as a shared resource that is continually growing and changing as it is created by community participants.

Simultaneously, however, these commons coexist within the proprietary structures of capitalism, and particularly within the structures of capitalist markets. Benkler (2013a) offers an apt analysis of the complex, fluid relationship between markets and commons. He argues that the commons provide a foundation that is interspersed in intricate ways throughout proprietary markets.

The Drupal and Debian Projects provide insights into this relationship between markets and commons. As emphasized above, peer production is a key foundation for both communities. Furthermore, both projects involve strong collaboration between peer communities and market-based firms. In Debian's case, the Canonical corporation takes the operating system built by the peer community to produce and market Ubuntu as a new version of that system. There is thus a clear separation between the peer producers in the Debian community and Canonical's activities as the creator and distributor of Ubuntu. By contrast, Acquia's profits arise from offering cloud services based upon the Drupal platform. At the same time, there is strong coordination and collaboration between Acquia and the Drupal community. Part of this coordination involves the leadership structure, since Dries Buytaert plays a leadership role in both Acquia and the Drupal community, while Mark Shuttleworth confines his work to Canonical and does not become involved in the Debian community. The collaboration between Drupal and Acquia extends beyond this leadership structure, however, since changes in the development process are coordinated as well. For example, when Buytaert decided that Drupal needed to strengthen its user interface, Acquia hired consultants who worked with a team of its employees as well as with volunteers in the Drupal community. Changes in the user interface were thus designed and implemented through a collaborative process between Acquia as a market-based firm and the peer producers in the Drupal community. Hence in the case of Drupal, the commons are integrated with proprietary elements as part of the ongoing operation of both the market-based firm and the peer community. Even with Debian, Canonical's market-based operations continue to rely on software production in the Debian community. In both the Debian and Drupal cases, software production thus involves a mix of commons-based and proprietary processes.

Work in market-based firms and peer communities thus contributes to the ongoing development of the digital commons, which are interspersed with capitalist markets. Commons and markets develop together in a complex mosaic of hybrid forms of work and production. Certainly, commons and markets can be conceptualized by distinguishing processes of peer production from paid labor in market-based firms. In practice, however, work processes in peer communities and market-based firms often contribute to each other, as well as to a broader process of interconnected development of both markets and commons.

Thus in the Debian and Drupal cases, the major challenges for developing the digital commons do not arise from this interaction between peer communities and market-based firms. By contrast, these challenges are rooted in the nature of the software that is produced. Free software's nature as a community-based, catalytic form of property is the vital quality distinguishing it from proprietary software and allowing it to contribute to the development of the digital commons. The GNU GPL legally ensures that current and future users of the software will be free to use, modify, and share the software as they see fit. This catalytic form of free software is the code for the digital commons, since it makes it possible to use, share, and further develop the software as a collective resource. Free software transforms capitalism with an alternative logic of community sharing, undermining the proprietary logic of profit-making.

The Drupal and Debian cases provide insights into the ways that free software can be produced either through peer production or in a market-based firm. Drupal is licensed under the GNU GPL, thus constituting an example of the free software, catalytic property form. This software is created by both peer producers in the Drupal community and paid software developers at Acquia. By contrast, Debian can best be characterized as open-source software, since it permits the inclusion of proprietary elements. In response to Ubuntu users' concerns that this open-source approach limited user freedoms, Canonical changed its intellectual property policy to comply with the GNU GPL. As of July 2015, the Ubuntu software thus constitutes free software, while Debian remains open source. Thus the market-based Canonical is producing free software that contributes to the digital commons, while the peer producers in the Debian community are making open-source software that fits with the proprietary logic of profit.

Indeed, a wide range of firms have developed strategies to increase their profits by engaging with open-source software. Such strategies do not contribute to the development of the digital commons, since they produce software that limits users' freedoms by including proprietary elements. Furthermore, these strategies focus on strengthening the firms' positions within the proprietary structures of capitalism, rather than on building communities or software that offers a collective resource.

IBM and Google offer two examples illuminating the ways that open-source strategies create challenges for developing the digital commons. First, since 1998, IBM has contributed to the development of Debian and other open-source software that it views as offering attractive additional options for its corporate customers. Such efforts bolster IBM's market position, while simultaneously expanding the market for open-source systems. By consistently including proprietary elements, however, these strategies limit opportunities for users to modify and share software. Such constraints on user freedoms undermine the development of the commons as a collective resource. Second, in one of the most striking corporate successes in recent decades, Google used the open-source Android software to attract mobile device manufacturers and telecommunications service providers as corporate partners. By giving Android away for free, it also lured customers who became accustomed to using Google search on their mobile devices. This expanding user base became Google's major source of profits, as it harvested metadata about their interests, activities, and movements to create targeted advertising and services. Google's open-source strategy was like the proverbial Trojan horse, where a free (of charge) search service gave Google access to valuable consumer data and billions of dollars in profits from advertising. As will be discussed further in Chapter 6 on Internet Politics, Google's strategy provides the basis for consumer surveillance, creating threats to privacy and other civil liberties. Furthermore, Google's activities underscore the importance of the choice of license for prospects for developing the commons. Android is licensed under Apache 2.0, which allows for the combination of proprietary elements. Similar to other open-source software discussed above, Android thus does not contribute to the development of the digital commons since it limits users' abilities to modify and share the software. By contrast, the Apache license allows Google to develop proprietary applications for Android, providing another key source of profits.

Both IBM and Google use open source primarily as a strategy to increase their profits and strengthen their position in the proprietary and open-source software markets. They contribute to the development of open-source software, which has provided a growing customer base as well as access to the development work of peer producers. They consistently integrate proprietary elements and use open-source software as part of their overall proprietary strategy. This approach creates challenges for the development of the digital commons, since the software's proprietary elements undermine users' freedoms to access, modify, and share the software as a collective resource. Neither does the proprietary approach contribute to the development of free software communities that are such an integral part of growing the digital commons as well as free software itself.

Like the digital commons, alternative forms of globalization from below are rooted in the related processes of community building and free software development, as well as in free software as a catalytic form of property. These interconnected processes of community and property counteract the proprietary interests of capital. They contrapose the dynamic of neoliberal globalization that promotes the expansion of capital in markets around the world. In contrast to this dynamic, free software community participants from a wide range of countries contribute to the ongoing development of the digital commons.

Both Drupal and Debian are organized as global communities. Debian is smaller, with 1,000 or more developers in its peer community compared with Drupal's 17,000 or more developers. In addition to this difference in overall size, the Debian community is more concentrated in the U.S. and Europe. It meets less frequently, gathering once a year compared to Drupal's recent shift from two to three conferences a year. Of most importance, Drupal has recently employed a conscious strategy to promote the community's expansion outside the U.S., Canada, and Europe. Toward this end, one of its annual gatherings is intentionally located in the global South, organized through a process of grassroots community involvement in choosing conference venues and mobilizing participants to attend.

Drupal is a key example of a free software community that is contributing to the development of the digital commons. Through its extensive deployment in the private and public sectors, Drupal is spreading the catalytic form of software into a wide range of organizations in the market. Organizations like the U.S. government are participating in the ongoing development of Drupal; they have a stake in this development process, since Drupal is integrated into their major operations. These commons activities and practices take place side by side with proprietary activities, since most of the organizations that use Drupal also use other computer systems that run proprietary software. Drupal itself, however, is a catalytic form of software that will remain free and open to sharing and modification. It thus contributes to the development of a digital commons that coexists with a range of other proprietary practices.

On an international level, the Drupal community is an example of an alternative form of globalization from below, rooted in the production of free software as a catalytic, community-based form of property. The Drupal community is similar to other communities promoting alternative forms of globalization from below, since its participants organize themselves on a global scale. Diverse local participants collaborate across borders to develop a global project. In this respect, Drupalers from 228 countries, speaking 181 languages, collaborate on software development, engage in translation, write documentation, and more (Gamalielsson et al. 2015). They comprise a global community that does most of this daily work via the Internet, while gathering for conferences a few times a year.

In other ways, however, the Drupal community is distinct from other efforts to promote globalization from below. As discussed in Chapter 1, such alternatives often focus on resisting economic and political efforts to prioritize the interests of transnational corporations and states from the global North over the interests of diverse local communities. In the process, they struggle to promote environmental justice, or the rights of women, workers, immigrants, or other groups. They often organize consciously and explicitly as communities of resistance against neoliberalism (Portes 2000; Sassen 2005; Della Porto, Andretta and Mosca 2006; Langman 2012). In the case of Drupal, it is integrated into the operations of a wide range of corporations and governments. By producing and disseminating the catalytic property form of free software, the Drupal community thus transforms capitalist practices from the inside. It develops alternatives to neoliberalism and informational capitalism that are integrated within corporate and government operations, as well as in alternative communities that exist in the commons alongside those operations. Drupal community participants do not generally organize, however, to explicitly resist neoliberalism or the proprietary interests of global capital. I thus view Drupal as a global community that implicitly resists neoliberalism by building an alternative form of globalization from below. It contrasts with the explicit communities of resistance discussed in Chapters 5 and 6, where free software and net neutrality activists organize to oppose proprietary interests.

Larry Garfield, the Drupal 8 Web Services Lead and Drupal Database system maintainer, portrayed a vivid image of this global Drupal community. He delivered the keynote speech to the Drupal conference in Bogotá in February 2015, which was posted as a YouTube video (Garfield 2015). He addressed an enthusiastic group of developers to highlight the features of the new eighth version of Drupal. He emphasized that Drupal was being built by large numbers of people in communities around the world, who shared a vision of the importance of being able to access the web independently, without it being centralized and controlled by large corporations. To cheers from the audience, Garfield kept asking the questions, "Who are we? Who built Drupal?" As photos of Drupal developer communities around the world flashed across the screen, he called out their names: top core contributors from Latin America; DrupalCon Bogotá; DrupalPicchu (in Peru); Drupal Camp Costa Rica; Drupal Camp Mumbai; Drupal South Wellington, New Zealand; DrupalCon Amsterdam; DrupalCon Austin, Texas; and a group of random people from a PHP conference, who Garfield noted could be considered Drupal developers even though they had never directly worked on Drupal before or talked to a Drupal developer. Garfield argued that since Drupal runs on the scripting language PHP, the 80 percent of the web that runs on PHP is now part of the Drupal development team.

Indeed, PHP is a prime example of free software as a catalyst transforming capitalism to create alternative forms of globalization from below. PHP has become ubiquitous on the web, and Drupal has become ubiquitous in organizations that use it to manage web content. In the process, free software has spread throughout the Internet. Garfield (2015) noted that the Drupal community is constituted by people working together as colleagues, as a development team, even though most of them have never met each other. This is a clear image of the digital commons, open to everyone to create and employ, from diverse parts of the world. The peer nature of their collaboration, and the flexible organization of their community, facilitates their collective work outside of a traditional organizational hierarchy. To illustrate this point in his Bogotá address, Garfield (2015) asked for people to stand who had done a wide range of different kinds of work, from writing a core patch for Drupal, to working on documentation, helping people out on IRC, answering someone's question in person, or building something with Drupal for themselves or for anyone else. He then called for applause for all of those people as part of the Drupal community. He noted that at the time of the address, over 2,600 people had contributed code to Drupal 8. This international community, combining volunteer peer producers with paid developers at Acquia, other market-based firms, and government organizations, is a key example of an alternative form of globalization from below. This alternative form of globalization is rooted in the structure and process of creating the global community itself, as well as in the catalytic form of software that it contributes to the digital commons.

4 Forking toward the Commons

Struggles to Sustain Freedom through Organizational Change

The Drupal community offers a vibrant example of globalization from below. It resonates with Benkler's (2013b, 246) conception of peer production as building "a degree of freedom in the world of interlocking systems that we inhabit." It reveals the integral connection between processes of free software development and community building as constituent elements of the commons. These collaborative processes simultaneously create and require shared resources and skills in technological development, documentation, translation, and more. They involve the organization of events, from entire conferences to participation at panels or exhibits within conferences sponsored by others. Benkler's (2013b, 246) analysis of peer production allows us to grasp the importance of free software communities as

> a pathway we can use to bob and weave between the continuous flow of efforts of others, in particular others who occupy positions that allow them to project power onto us through market or state institutions that the peer solution has allowed us to dodge.

A range of scholars has conceptualized the commons as a kind of "third way" between the market and the state, an alternative to either state or private property that allows participants to navigate the oppressive limitations of those established institutions (Bollier 2008; Benkler 2013a,b). As Boyle (2008, 200) argued, "there are other methods of generating innovation, expression, and creativity than the proprietary, exclusionary model of sole control."

Free software communities provide such alternative methods and structures to circumvent some constraints of the market and the state by organizing the production of software as a collective resource. Those communities are an indispensable resource in themselves, providing an ecosystem of relationships, skills, and work processes that allow peer producers to collaborate with each other, as well as with market-based firms that may contribute to the software's development.

As noted in Chapter 2, Benkler (2013a, 1533) builds upon Hess and Ostrom's (2006) conception of the commons as a shared resource, arguing that this resource "can occur at a wide range of scales and, critically, raises challenges of use, governance and sustainability that can be viewed as social dilemmas." In this chapter, I highlight some of those social dilemmas by exploring the importance of free software communities in governing and sustaining the shared resource of the digital commons, as well as the technical development of free software itself. Sustaining such a community is challenging in the context of neoliberal pressures to integrate proprietary practices to compete in capitalist markets. I thus consider such communities to be implicit global communities of resistance. Struggles emerge around vital processes of developing organizational structures to support community activities, including software development and dissemination.

I focus on the case of LibreOffice and The Document Foundation (TDF). This project was formed in 2010 when participants in the OpenOffice.org free software community decided to take that project in a new direction. To understand the broader context that shaped this decision, I analyze the historical development of OpenOffice.org as a free software office suite deployed extensively around the world. I highlight the importance of language for the process of developing free software as a global community, by examining the development of OpenOffice. org's Native Language Confederation. In this project, community participants volunteered to translate, document, and support OpenOffice in their native languages.

Despite the impressive development of OpenOffice.org, a core group of participants decided to leave the project and establish a new community, through a process known as forking. To explore the reasons for their decision, I examine tensions between proprietary interests and efforts to build free software communities, emphasizing the power relationships between the Sun and Oracle corporations and the OpenOffice.org community. I analyze the struggles that emerged when Oracle bought Sun, exploring how they gave rise to the creation of LibreOffice and TDF in September 2010. I identify the conditions that led to the decision to fork OpenOffice.org, as free software community participants decided that they needed to defend against corporate actions that could undermine the free nature of the project.

The fork of OpenOffice.org provides a key case study of the broader strategy of forking. Historically, this strategy has sparked controversy in free software communities. I explore the implications of forking for the development of free software communities and the digital commons. The conditions of the fork of OpenOffice.org exemplify what Robles and González-Barahona (2012) characterize as a community-driven development strategy; those conditions also resonate with what Gençer and Özel (2012) call an independent fork.

The case of LibreOffice and TDF offers insights into the dynamics of this community-driven development strategy (Robles and González-

Barahona 2012). I explore how a core group of committed community members applied their political will and skill to fork the project. They organized effectively to garner support from a diverse range of free software advocates, from community volunteers to corporations, governments, and associations. This broad base of support made it possible to accomplish the fork on both the technical and political levels.

TDF advocates organized support by clearly articulating the project's underlying values. They issued a *Next Decade Manifesto* that proclaimed their commitment to digital inclusion, highlighting the importance of making free software office suites available to people around the world who spoke many languages and had been historically disenfranchised from engaging with the benefits of software. TDF participants thus effectively communicated their commitment to democratizing access to the LibreOffice free office suite. As part of this process, they sought to eradicate the digital divide between those who had historically had access to software, computers, and the Internet and those who did not (The Document Foundation 2015b).

The TDF case provides insights into the possibilities for the strategy of forking to contribute to the broader project of developing the digital commons and alternative forms of globalization from below. It highlights the importance of developing organizational structures to strengthen the community, as well as the ways that participants in local communities collaborate to develop those structures as a key part of their common global project. As mentioned above, the historical background for this case begins with the development of OpenOffice.org.

Developing OpenOffice.org as a Free Software Office Suite

On July 19, 2000, Sun Microsystems announced the release of the source code for its StarOffice Suite under the GNU General Public License (GNU GPL). This was the "single largest open-source software contribution in GPL history," according to Marco Boerries, Sun vice president and general manager of webtop and application software. In a press release, he noted that "[s]ince innovation happens in many places, making the source code...available will enable the enormous community of developers to bring their expertise and energy to improve and expand the reach" of this office suite (accessed June 19, 2017. http://www.openoffice.org/press/sun_release.html). At the same time, Sun announced that OpenOffice.org would serve as the hub for coordinating the source code, as well as the definition of XML-based file formats and language-independent office application programming interfaces (APIs). Many free software proponents viewed this as a momentous move, primarily because it challenged the dominance of Microsoft's proprietary Office file formats. Since the StarOffice source code enabled users to read and write Microsoft Office formats, it made it possible for other open-source projects to provide compatible functionality as well. In the process, this release expanded opportunities to use the GNU-Linux operating system on the desktop (accessed June 19, 2017. http://www. openoffice.org/press/sun_release.html).

From the inception of the OpenOffice.org project, there were plans to create an OpenOffice.org Foundation. In an announcement on its website on November 4, 2001, OpenOffice.org stated that the OpenOffice. org Foundation would be a nonprofit organization that would "oversee the operations, technology strategy, incorporation of technology contributions, and establishment of standards in conjunction with other standards bodies and open source projects as appropriate." The vision was to model the foundation after the Apache Software Foundation; it would be run by a Steering Committee or Board with membership from the open-source community, with Sun Microsystems holding a minority representation in the governance structure.

This original vision of shared governance of a foundation to promote the development of OpenOffice.org never came to fruition. By contrast, corporate interests were a consistently strong presence in the project, since Sun became the dominant supporter of OpenOffice.org. There were ongoing tensions between Sun's commitment to free software projects and its efforts to control those projects through patent and copyright mechanisms. Many developers viewed Sun as a trusted supporter of free software projects, however, so this arrangement was largely accepted (Hillesley 2010).

OpenOffice.org and Digital Inclusion: A Language-Based Strategy for Community Development

Despite this strong corporate presence in the project, OpenOffice.org contributed to the development of the digital commons in a fundamental way: it made a high-quality, free office productivity suite accessible to millions of people around the world. Since it did not require licensing fees like proprietary software, this free office suite offered historically disenfranchised groups a better chance of access to office productivity tools. It thus contributed to a process of digital inclusion. From 2000 until 2010, users in many parts of the world adopted OpenOffice.org. As discussed in the last chapter with respect to Drupal and Debian, it is impossible to measure the exact number of users, community members, or developers participating in free software projects. It is clear, however, that users downloaded OpenOffice.org hundreds of millions of times. Furthermore, the OpenOffice.org website documented public information about major deployments by governments, schools, and universities, and the private sector in Africa, Asia, Europe, North America, Oceania, and

South America through April 2011 (accessed June 19, 2017. http://wiki.services.openoffice.org/wiki/Major_OpenOffice.org_Deployments).

This extensive, global use of OpenOffice.org signals its contribution to the digital commons, as individual, government, and other institutional users engaged with the project. In many of these countries around the world, language was key to OpenOffice.org's contribution to the process of developing the digital commons, as well as to its emergence as a global community. One of the most striking achievements of the OpenOffice.org project was the development of the Native Language Confederation. The Confederation was comprised of a wide range of locally based projects that provided information and resources, such as documentation and support, in over 100 native languages. It began with localization projects for French, German, Italian, and Dutch, and then expanded to other languages.

In a 2010 interview with the Project Leader of the Native Language Confederation, he highlighted three strategic reasons for choosing a language-based approach for the global expansion of OpenOffice.org. First, on the technical level, the nature of the tool as an office suite increased the need for language localization. Such suites are targeted toward individual users of applications like word processing and slideshow presentations. To make it possible for non-English-speaking people to use the OpenOffice.org suite, many words needed translating. Volunteers participating in language localizations thus developed a glossary of terms in the local language to make it available to those who spoke it. Thousands of strings needed to be translated, including terms like file, open, new, document, and more. Language thus played a central role in making the OpenOffice.org office suite globally accessible to people speaking myriad languages. The role of language in this process was quite different in the office suite than it was for other tools, such as an Internet browser.

The role of language was especially clear in the Brazilian case, where a dedicated group of seven volunteers initially created the local Brazilian OpenOffice.org community; they called themselves OpenOffice.org.br. In 2002 and 2003, their first big project was to translate OpenOffice.org into Brazilian Portuguese. Olivier Hallot assembled the team for the translation project and completed much of the work himself. In a 2010 interview with Hallot about this work, he emphasized the importance of providing access to OpenOffice.org for millions of Brazilians who do not speak English. In fact, language was a central aspect of the Brazilian OpenOffice.org community's early work. Translating OpenOffice into Brazilian Portuguese was a necessary step to facilitate digital inclusion of Portuguese speakers in the global free software community. In addition to the translation project, Brazilian volunteers wrote documentation in Portuguese and created key tools like a spelling dictionary and a grammar checker. They sponsored several regional and national events attended by a mix of developers, service providers, and corporate users. They remained active over many years.

Certainly, Brazil offers a case of one of the most extensive national deployments of OpenOffice.org. The Brazilian government supported this deployment as part of its broader policy of promoting digital inclusion, so that historically disenfranchised groups in Brazil would have access to skills, knowledge, and resources to use computers and the Internet. Starting in October 2003, the Lula administration gave preference to free software solutions that offered equal functionality and performance with proprietary solutions. President Lula directed government offices to employ free software operating systems, servers, web servers, and email solutions. Free software systems made it possible to save on licensing fees, as well as complying with open and international standards for software. They strengthened national control over sensitive data files, since those files were not vulnerable to changes in the file format executed by a private firm that might make older files inaccessible (Schoonmaker 2007; Olivier Hallot, interview 2010).

As part of this process of promoting digital inclusion, a wide range of organizations adopted BrOffice.org. These included the state-owned *Banco do Brasil*, which installed 71,000 copies of BrOffice.org on almost every computer in the business. The state government of Paraná deployed BrOffice.org throughout its state offices; this included over 40,000 installations in the education sector alone. Furthermore, the state governments of Sergipe and Bahia migrated to BrOffice. The government deployed it in a range of sectors, from airlines to the public information technology company, Dataprev (accessed June 20, 2017. http://wiki.services.openoffice. org/wiki/Major_OpenOffice.org_Deployments). Years later, in response to the fork of OpenOffice.org and the launch of LibreOffice in the fall of 2010, organizations using BrOffice.org began a process of migrating to LibreOffice. This migration allowed them to maintain the open nature of the project (Ghedin 2011; filhocf 2011).

Brazil is one example of how OpenOffice.org community participants in individual countries faced the challenge of developing and spreading the free software office suite within their own national contexts. Around the world, community participants strategized about the most effective ways to build the OpenOffice.org brand.

In many cases, these communities collaborated with participants in other countries to organize language localization projects. Since Brazil has such a large potential population of OpenOffice.org users, it made sense for community participants to focus on providing access to the office suite in their language. Smaller countries who spoke similar languages to each other, however, found it useful to pursue a collaborative approach. In a 2010 interview with the Project Leader of the Native Language Confederation, he emphasized the benefits of the language-based approach to the localization of OpenOffice.org. This strategy allowed participants to organize on a broader, cross-national scale, while also avoiding political tensions. It helped to create conditions for people from different countries to work together in deploying the office suite. For example, Israelis, Palestinians, and Iranians collaborated on the Arabic language localization. This strategy was similar to the Creative Commons project to translate licenses into Arabic and other languages, discussed in Chapter 2.

Equally important, the language-based approach encouraged more involvement by a broader range of the software's users than a country-based approach. It involved what the Project Leader of the Native Language Confederation called a "guerrilla strategy" (interview with Native Language Confederation project lead 2010). This strategy developed from the bottom up, rooted in the work of volunteers in local communities who wanted to make the office suite available in a particular language. Developing a localization required resources and connectivity generated primarily by particular local communities. Certainly, OpenOffice.org had some resources and tools to help guide localization projects. The key to the success of such projects, however, depended on local people as well as the resources available in particular parts of the world. For example, the project lead noted that there were only a few successful localization efforts in Africa, due to the lack of resources and connectivity. Localizations had better success in South Africa due to its greater resources, with projects done in Afrikaans, Zulu, and other languages spoken in that country.

Language localization has thus been central to the development of OpenOffice.org as a global community. As participants speaking similar languages collaborated with each other, they strengthened and expanded the project. They simultaneously contributed to the process of digital inclusion, making it possible for users who spoke a wide range of languages to access the project. One source of evidence for the development of the global community is the OpenOffice.org wiki. It lists all language localizations and their current status; members of the community can edit the status of their projects as they develop (Interview with Native Language Confederation project lead 2010). Language localizations include a wide number of lesser known languages, such as Bulgarian, Bosnian, Catalan, Czech, Gujarati, Hindi, Icelandic, Khmer, Kannada, Marathi, Pashto, Sindhi, Tamil, Tswana, and Ukrainian. There is a complete list in the OpenOffice.org wiki (accessed October 20, 2015. http://wiki.services.openoffice.org/wiki/Languages).

Proprietary Interests Conflict with Community Development

Despite these achievements in promoting the development of free software as a global community, the OpenOffice.org project was fraught with contradictions. These tensions were rooted in Sun's proprietary interest in the marketing and development of the suite. Developers encountered high barriers to entry under the OpenOffice.org licensing system, since they were obligated to sign a contribution licensing agreement (CLA) that gave Sun joint legal ownership over the code that they wrote (Gamalielsson and Lundell 2014). Under this agreement, OpenOffice.org required that developers share the copyright to their contributions with Sun as a commercial entity. Sun benefitted from this copyright assignment process. Each individual developer had joint ownership over their contribution with Sun; however, the company's joint ownership of all of the software created by contributors to OpenOffice.org gave it control over the software project as a whole.

Many developers did not like this arrangement, since Sun's control over the code made the OpenOffice.org project vulnerable to the company's actions and interests (Phipps 2011a,b; Interviews with The Document Foundation Board member 2011, 2012). For example, in September 2007, when OpenOffice.org was seven years old, IBM decided to start participating in the project. A press release on the OpenOffice.org website noted that IBM would be collaborating on software development, contributing technology and engineering resources, including code it had been developing for its Lotus Notes project. A key part of this process involved IBM's plans to "package and distribute new works that leverage OpenOffice.org technology" in its products (accessed September 26, 2015. https://www.openoffice.org/press/ibm_press_release.html). IBM thus supported the Open Document Format (ODF) standard integrated into OpenOffice.org. Many free software proponents viewed this support as a major step forward in spreading the use of open formats through the market.

One week after IBM announced its collaboration with OpenOffice.org, it released a beta version of IBM Lotus Symphony, a suite of document, spreadsheet, and presentation applications designed for a wide range of users in universities, businesses, and governments, as well as the general public. Symphony was based on OpenOffice.org version 1.2. It ran on both Windows and Linux platforms and supported multiple file formats, including ODF. By releasing Symphony at no cost, IBM sought to compete with Microsoft Office and attract users who were interested in the possibility of free access to an alternative office suite (Fontana 2007).

Since IBM was able to release Symphony only one week after announcing its formal collaboration with OpenOffice.org, it was clear that IBM had been developing this arrangement for some time. Certainly, IBM and Sun had negotiated the collaboration, which fit with IBM's strategy for increasing its presence in the open-source market. One crucial aspect of this arrangement was that when Sun released the OpenOffice.org code to IBM for use in developing Lotus Symphony, Sun did so under a proprietary contract rather than an open-source license. Sun thus used its legal control over OpenOffice.org code to make proprietary arrangements with IBM, furthering corporate profits and undermining the power of the community over software development. Simon Phipps, President of the global nonprofit The Open Source Initiative (OSI), critiqued arrangements such as Sun's CLA as "introduc[ing] private business-model reasoning into the community where it doesn't belong" (Phipps 2011a). Phipps (2011a) argued that successful open-source communities are grounded in the "equality of every participant," where each participant brings distinct abilities to contribute to the project and particularly to the software code itself. These participants choose to become involved in the community either at their own or their employer's expense. Such communities are not based on monetary obligations or business strategies, and participants who do have a business interest in the software pursue those interests in other contexts. CLAs such as Sun's contradict these principles of community, since they are designed to benefit the business in ways that are not available to individual members of the community. In other words, the CLA gives Sun rights of ownership that allow it to profit from the software, while the other members of the community may contribute to the code without enjoying similar benefits. Directing his comments to corporations, Phipps (2011a) argues that in such cases, corporations should realize that "[y]our attempt at control will either result in the failure of the community to grow as you hope, or ultimately in the community you create forking and working around you."

In this article, Phipps (2011a) focused on central principles of participating in open-source communities, rather than the specifics of the relationship between Sun and OpenOffice.org. Nonetheless, he highlighted the kinds of contradictions between community values and corporate interests that led to the fork of OpenOffice.org. These contradictions were rooted in the nature of the property defined by Sun's CLA, giving Sun legal ownership of the software. Hence, this software did not take the catalytic property form that protected users' freedoms and created the foundation for the digital commons. By contrast, the CLA served to retain corporate control over the software. Sun's involvement with OpenOffice.org was thus similar to the examples of IBM and Google, where for-profit firms developed proprietary strategies toward community-based software projects. As explored in the last chapter, such strategies undermine the software's community-based character as well as prospects for developing the digital commons. A range of research highlights the importance of licensing in creating conditions for community growth, confidence, and security. When licensing is perceived as fair, it encourages developers to contribute code and thus strengthens the community (Bacon 2009; Engelfriet 2010; Gamalielsson and Lundell 2014).

These tensions between community and corporate interests came to a head when Oracle, the world's largest enterprise software company, purchased Sun for $7.4 billion in 2009. In a press release on Oracle's website on April 20, 2009, Oracle President Safra Catz stated that she expected Sun to contribute over $1.5 billion to Oracle's profits in the first year and over $2 billion in the second year. Sun Chairman Scott McNealy commented in the release, "'Oracle and Sun have been industry pioneers and close partners for more than 20 years...This combination is a natural evolution of our relationship and will be an industry-defining event.'"

When he stated that Oracle's acquisition of Sun would be a defining event in the industry, McNealy probably imagined the growth of new business opportunities for the companies. It is unlikely that his vision of shaping the industry involved laying the groundwork for a fork. Nonetheless, the conditions for forking began to emerge as questions arose about the future of the OpenOffice.org project under Oracle's ownership. Oracle's decision to assert its ownership over Java by suing Google for copyright and patent infringement heightened these concerns, as did its cutoff of support for OpenSolaris (Hillesley 2010). Hence, Oracle's acquisition of Sun threw a spotlight on key problems posed by the OpenOffice.org structure. Reliance on one company to maintain the project made it virtually impossible to protect the broad community involvement essential for the development of the digital commons. As highlighted in the last chapter, the process of developing the digital commons requires participation from free software communities, as well as the ongoing development of those communities themselves. Control by one corporation is antithetical to such a process and sparked action by the OpenOffice.org community to redirect the project.

In August 2010, a core group of 20–25 people who had played major roles in the OpenOffice.org community gathered at a conference in Budapest. They came from countries all over the world, including France, Germany, Sri Lanka, and Brazil. They discussed their interest in creating a foundation that would ensure a more stable, community-based structure for the project and support its development as a free software office suite. They agreed upon the need to avoid OpenOffice.org's problems of reliance on Sun as a single commercial entity. Toward this end, they planned to encourage a wide range of corporate participation.

On September 28, 2010, this committed group of volunteers from the OpenOffice.org community announced that they were breaking away to form a new organization. This group included members of the Community Council and several project leads. They formed a Steering Committee of developers and national language project managers to create TDF. TDF's mission was to build the OpenOffice.org suite into a free software office suite that was more widely accessible to users and developers. They gave this new office suite the provisional name of LibreOffice. Unlike OpenOffice.org, LibreOffice would not rely upon one firm's commercial interests. By contrast, it would be structured through an independent foundation, as envisioned in OpenOffice.org's original charter. TDF would thus provide a new ecosystem for individuals, corporations, governments, and other interested users to contribute to the software's development. By expanding the range of contributors, TDF advocates hoped to encourage greater innovation and involvement. Since the foundation would be independent from a single corporate vendor, this would provide incentives for a range of companies to become involved, stimulating competition and eventually increasing consumer choice (Corbet 2010).

Contradictory Dynamics of Forking within Free Software Communities

These community leaders thus launched LibreOffice as a free office suite that would both protect and promote community, as well as corporate, participation in the software's development. They engaged in the process of forking, which Nyman et al. (2011, 1) define as "a situation in which several versions of a piece of software originating from a single, shared code base are developed separately." In a similar vein, Robles and González-Barahona (2012, 2) view forks as "two independent software projects, deriving both from the same software source code base." They note that the forking process has not been studied extensively, partly because hacker ethics see forks as potentially wasting the effort of community members who become involved in solving problems more than once. For example, if coders compete with each other on incompatible versions of what was originally a common software project, this undermines the broader process of innovation. Equally problematically, forks may "split the community,…reduce communication and…produce incompatibilities" (Robles and González-Barahona 2012, 2). Furthermore, forking has been understood in a more general sense that occurs routinely during open-source software development, whenever developers draw upon an existing code base to develop a distinct project (Nyman and Lindman 2013). In studying this broader concept of forking, Nyman et al. (2011, 1) argue that forking constitutes "the invisible hand of sustainability" of open-source software. Hence, forking is key to sustainability because it provides a way for the community to ensure that the code remains open, and that the code most useful for fulfilling community needs is maintained. In the process, the community secures its own survival and contributes to the development of the digital commons. As Nyman (2015, 56) states, "[t]he right to fork is the guardian of freedom and the watchdog of meritocracy."

Forking is thus a complex process with a contradictory, dual dynamic. In fact, forking can simultaneously threaten and ensure a project's survival. From this perspective, the possibility of a fork is inherent in free software and open-source projects, by virtue of their open code (Nyman et al. 2011). This theoretical possibility in itself provides incentives to resolve conflicts in communities, as well as raising the prospect of investing participants' time and energy to move the software in a new direction. Forking can be a free software community's "ultimate sustainer: insurance that, as long as users find a program useful, the program will continue to exist" (Nyman et al. 2011, 3).

Creating new forms of governance structures can be an important part of the forking process. As discussed above, more than the code was at stake with the fork of OpenOffice.org and the launch of LibreOffice. The structure of the community, and particularly the relationship between the peer producers and the corporations involved with the project, was a key issue. de Laat (2007, 172) offers insights into the importance of organizational structures by identifying phases of development of open-source projects, where they move from looser, self-directed action by community participants to what he calls "governance toward outside parties." Peer communities develop these more formalized types of governance as firms, national and international organizations, and nongovernmental organizations are increasingly drawn toward the possibilities of participating in open-source software projects. Such emerging relationships may threaten what de Laat (2007, 172) calls the "regulated source code commons." He highlights increased efforts to patent software in the U.S. as the major threat to the commons, noting that "[i]n order to deal with these challenges and threats, projects were forced to consciously manage their relations with parties outside of OSS [Open Source Software]" (de Laat 2007, 172).

De Laat's perspective is useful in understanding the LibreOffice project's attempt to manage its relationship with Oracle during the time of the fork of OpenOffice.org. As discussed above, many participants involved with the fork viewed it as a way to promote greater community control over the project, both in the aftermath of Oracle's purchase of Sun and over the course of its future development.

Despite these potential advantages of forking for preserving the community-based aspect of the software project, the forking strategy simultaneously posed considerable risks. Most important, since OpenOffice.org was so widely employed around the world, forking the project to launch LibreOffice raised the possibility of losing vast numbers of users. Ten years of development work on OpenOffice.org was potentially threatened, since current users might not decide to migrate to LibreOffice.

The TDF Steering Committee sought to address this problem by inviting Oracle to become a member of TDF. Of equal importance, they asked Oracle to donate the OpenOffice.org brand to the community. Such a donation would resonate with the culture of free software communities that emphasized the importance for all software users to be able to use, share, modify, and redistribute software code as they saw fit. By October 5, 2010, Oracle gave its answer. It announced that it would continue to develop OpenOffice.org and encouraged community members to remain active. Oracle stated that it would not be working with TDF and LibreOffice, but wished them the best in their project (*The H Open* 2010; Interview with The Document Foundation Board member 2010). In June 2011, Oracle solidified the separation between OpenOffice.org and LibreOffice by donating the OpenOffice.org project to the Apache Software Foundation, which named the project Apache OpenOffice (Gamalielsson and Lundell 2014). TDF's effort to govern its relationship with Oracle as what de Laat (2007) calls a powerful "outside party" was thus unsuccessful. Consequently, TDF ran the risk of losing years of development work in the process of the fork.

As the emerging LibreOffice community strategized ways to navigate the risks involved with the fork, they found that organizational structures were an important resource. Indeed, foundations such as TDF are examples of the organizational forms advocated by de Laat (2007). Such forms are rooted in practices and principles of representation, decentralized decision-making, and independence from pressures from interests outside the community. In the case of the LibreOffice community, they created TDF as a structure to protect representation from the community and ensure its independence from one dominant corporate influence such as Sun or Oracle. Such organizational forms fit with Markus's (2007, 152, emphasis in original) definition of Open Source Software (OSS) governance as *the means of achieving the direction, control, and coordination of wholly or partially autonomous individuals and organizations on behalf of an OSS development project to which they jointly contribute.* Markus (2007) highlights the importance of identifying particular kinds of governance configurations in open-source projects, as well as understanding why such configurations develop.

The fork of OpenOffice.org and the launch of LibreOffice and TDF provide insight into the processes of developing a foundation as a governance structure for a free software project. As discussed above, community participants in OpenOffice.org decided to fork the project largely because they wanted to create an organizational structure to ensure community participation and protect the project from domination by one corporate actor. These participants were working to sustain not only the code, but the structure of the community itself. They sought to craft an organized way for members to continue to participate in the project. In this respect, the fork of Openoffice.org and the launch of Libreoffice are an example of what Gençer and Özel (2012) call an independent fork. Such forks generally arise as a result of internal power conflicts and licensing issues. In fact, this case resonates with a scenario posed by Nyman et al. (2011, 3) where a company "shepherding the code make[s] decisions which run counter to the interests of the larger community and developers." Certainly, the tensions between community and corporate interests discussed above fit with this characterization. Forking provided community participants with a way to strengthen their control over the project.

Since the OpenOffice.org fork and the launch of LibreOffice were rooted in an effort to protect a central role for the community in the ongoing development of the office suite, this fork fits with Robles and González-Barahona's (2012) characterization of some forks as driven by a commitment to more community-driven development. Interviews with key participants in the project highlight the importance of community-driven development in their decision to fork the project.

For example, Charles-H. Schulz was a member of the TDF Steering Committee, a group of OpenOffice.org participants who engaged in intensive organizing and planning to launch TDF. When I interviewed Schulz soon after the launch, he emphasized that OpenOffice.org involved a "flawed model" that relied too heavily on one company. He called the fork a "sad story"; however, he also viewed it as liberating (Charles-H. Schulz, interview 2010). On his blog the day TDF was launched, Schulz posted an article aptly entitled, "Give up spoon-feeding: Use a fork instead." In the post, he highlighted the problems associated with Sun's dominance of the OpenOffice.org project. He noted, "10 million lines of code that are not easily hackable, a certain heaviness in our process and governance structure made us feel like we had to change something" (Schulz 2010). The key change was a shift back to emphasizing resources coming from the ground up, from the community, to take the project to a new level. For example, in the first four days after TDF and LibreOffice were launched, volunteer developers integrated software updates and bug fixes that had been stalled for three years under Sun's control of the project (Charles-H. Schulz, interview 2010).

Schulz's critiques of the OpenOffice.org model fit with research on open-source software communities that emphasizes the importance of leadership in pursuit of shared goals. As Gamalielsson and Lundell (2014, 129) note, "clear leadership, congruence in terms of project goals, and good team spirit are of fundamental importance." In a similar vein, Currie, Kelty, and Murillo (2013) propose a continuum of forms of participation in free software projects, understood along three key dimensions. They argue that strong forms of participation allow participants to make decisions about the broad goals of a project, rather than simply performing tasks that are decided upon by others. Such involvement might mean that participants could engage in policy or goal-setting discussions, or at minimum have access to decision-making through some form of representation or voting rights. Moreover, strong participation entails what Currie, Kelty, and Murillo (2013) call availability, where individual participants can access the resources they produce, as well as participate in processes of collective control over those resources. If participants lack any of these opportunities, they have only pseudo or weak forms of participation in the project (Currie, Kelty and Murillo 2013).

Indeed, project goals and access to resources became central points of community discussion, coherence, and identity in the process of forking

OpenOffice.org. Such discussions were particularly significant in the context of the tensions with Sun. Many of these tensions arose from Sun's use of CLAs in ways that contradicted values of sharing and openness central to free software communities.

Forking to Promote Digital Inclusion and the Digital Commons

As mentioned above, when the emerging LibreOffice community decided to fork OpenOffice.org, they articulated fundamental project goals and values in the *Next Decade Manifesto*. These goals and values were expressed as commitments, emphasizing the importance of strategies for action to put them into practice. Each of the commitments was paired with actions that they rejected. This contrast between commitments and rejections clearly delineated TDF's position on key struggles to promote free software programs and communities in the face of the dominant proprietary form advocated by a range of corporations and governments. These positions reflected the centrality of software in economic, political, social, and cultural life; equally important, they resonated with software's role as a productive force within informational capitalism.

The Manifesto highlighted the question of digital inclusion, stating that TDF committed itself to "eliminate the digital divide in society by giving everyone access to office productivity tools free of charge to enable them to participate as full citizens in the 21st century" (The Document Foundation 2015b). Such action to transform the digital divide involved rejecting "the ownership of office productivity tools by monopoly suppliers which imposes a de-facto tax on global electronic free speech and penalises the economically disadvantaged" (The Document Foundation 2015b). The community authors of the Manifesto thus viewed free software office suites as a vehicle to democratize access to free speech on a global scale. By subverting proprietary control over office productivity software, TDF sought to make such software widely available around the world, including to those unable to pay for it.

Through the Manifesto, the LibreOffice community expressed a second commitment that was integrally related to eliminating the digital divide. This second commitment was to "support the preservation of mother tongues by encouraging people to translate, document, support, and promote our office productivity tools in their mother tongue" (The Document Foundation 2015b). It extended the work discussed above, carried out by the Native Language Confederation of the OpenOffice.org project. It was a way to further democratize the use of computers and office productivity tools by making them accessible to those who do not speak English. As noted above, such an endeavor required people from local communities to do a range of work; it thus served to deepen the participation and contribution to the project by people from different language groups around the world. In the process, TDF community members rejected "[t]he creeping domination of computer desktops by a single language, forcing all people to learn a foreign language before they can express themselves electronically" (The Document Foundation 2015b).

Beyond addressing the digital divide, community authors of the Manifesto articulated two other key project goals and values. They stated that the LibreOffice community was committed to "allow users of office productivity software to retain the intellectual property in the documents they create by use of open document formats and open standards" (The Document Foundation 2015b). TDF community members thus rejected proprietary ownership of file formats by software companies, which could create problems for users if the software is updated to employ formats that make earlier ones obsolete. For example, documents that were written in Word Perfect in the 1980s and 1990s were incompatible with Microsoft Windows NT released in 1995. Since Microsoft succeeded in getting its office suite bundled into a wide range of computer sales at corporations and universities, it thus became difficult to use other file formats such as Word Perfect. This created pressure for many Word Perfect users to switch to Microsoft Windows. By contrast, ODFs are not tied to a particular corporation, so they are not vulnerable to market decisions by any one firm. LibreOffice programmers designed it to allow users to save their files in 19 possible file formats, including 5 versions of Microsoft Word such as doc, docx, pptx, and xml; ODF (odt); rich text (rtf); text (txt); and more. In other words, as the Manifesto states, TDF rejects "the ownership of file formats by proprietary software companies – documents belong to their creators, not software vendors" (The Document Foundation 2015b).

In an interview with a TDF Board member, he noted that offering LibreOffice users a wide range of choices for their file formats is one way to smooth the transition from proprietary to ODFs. Users of the Microsoft office suite thus might find that LibreOffice allows them to work in their customary proprietary formats such as docx or pptx, or to exchange files easily with others who do. At the same time, they might become comfortable with using LibreOffice and find that transitioning to the ODF within that office suite can be quite easy (Interview with The Document Foundation Board member 2012). Increasing users' familiarity with and ease of access to ODFs could thus be part of a longer-term process where more users migrate away from proprietary formats and gain greater control over the documents they create.

Finally, the Manifesto committed TDF to "an open and transparent peer-reviewed software development process where technical excellence is valued" (The Document Foundation 2015b). Toward this end, programmers designed LibreOffice to differ from OpenOffice.org in fundamental ways. As in many free software projects, LibreOffice has no copyright assignment; individual developers thus retain ownership of the code that they write (Hillesley 2010). Hence developers who write for LibreOffice can do whatever they want with that code. They thus enjoy the kind of access to the resources that they create that Currie, Kelty, and Murillo (2013) view as a basis for strong forms of participation in free software projects. This access is grounded in the licensing for Libre-Office. All the code for LibreOffice is licensed under the GNU Lesser General Public License (LGPL v3+) and the Mozilla Public License (MPLv2.0). Like the GNU GPL, the LGPL is published by the Free Software Foundation (FSF), which posted an explanation of the differences between the licenses on its website (accessed June 20, 2017; http://www. fsf.org/news/openoffice-apache-libreoffice). The LGPL is more permissive than the GPL, since it does not include the strong copyleft provision that legally requires developers and companies to release the source code of all software components included with a program. For example, under the GPL, a company would not be allowed to mix software components licensed under the GPL with proprietary software components, unless the company was willing to release the source code for those proprietary components. In other words, the GPL does not allow companies to mix proprietary and free software components. By contrast, the LGPL is a weak copyleft license that allows programs that merely link to the software to be released under proprietary terms. For example, a company would be permitted to use and integrate LGPL software with its own proprietary components without having to release the source code for those proprietary components. Nonetheless, the copyleft provisions in LibreOffice's LGPL require all software covered under that license to be released along with its source code. It thus provides collective control over the software as a digital commons, where all contributors and other users can access, modify, and share the software. This form of community control fits with Currie, Kelty, and Murillo's (2013) framework for strong participation in free software projects.

Thus, LibreOffice is an example of the free software catalytic property form, covered by a partial copyleft license. Its weak copyleft provisions give companies the option of combining LibreOffice with their own proprietary components. These provisions do not, however, undermine the catalytic nature of the LibreOffice software itself. Any users of LibreOffice may make changes to the code, while simultaneously being required to allow future users the same freedom to modify the code. As discussed in previous chapters, Richard Stallman and the FSF designed copyleft licenses to promote quality software, since bugs and other problems in the software could be worked out by members of the community on an ongoing basis. As a result of its commitment to free software, TDF's *Next Decade Manifesto* rejected a "closed software development process where errors can lie hidden and poor quality is accepted" (The Document Foundation 2015b).

Largely due to its free software copyleft license and emphasis on community involvement, there was significant community support for TDF from the time of its initial launch in September 2010. TDF promoted its commitments to digital inclusion by designing its organizational structure to ensure independence from specific corporations, while also encouraging broad involvement by corporations as well as the community. This created opportunities for a range of corporations to support the project from the beginning, including Google, SUSE, Canonical, and Red Hat. When TDF participants launched the project, they posted statements of support from a wide range of organizations on their website. For example, Mark Shuttleworth, the founder of Canonical discussed in the last chapter, stated his intention to ship LibreOffice with future Ubuntu releases. He noted that "The Document Foundation's stewardship of LibreOffice provides Ubuntu developers an effective forum for collaboration around the code that makes Ubuntu an effective solution for the desktop in office environments" (accessed November 20, 2015. http://www.documentfoundation.org/supporters/). In a similar vein, Chris DiBona, Open Source Programs Manager at Google, viewed TDF as "'a great step forward in encouraging further development of open source office suites'" (quoted in Corbet 2010). He noted that Google was proud to be involved, since "[h]aving a level playing field for all contributors is fundamental in creating a broad and active community around an open source software project" (quoted in Corbet 2010). Ralf Flaxa, the Vice President of Engineering at SUSE, called LibreOffice a "crucial component of SUSE's Linux Desktop" (accessed November 20, 2015. http://www.documentfoundation.org/supporters/).

In addition to these major corporate players in the open-source field, a range of free software community organizations expressed support for the LibreOffice project. Notably, FSF President Richard Stallman commended TDF for its policy not to recommend proprietary add-ons that had been part of OpenOffice.org. Community and activist groups from France, Ecuador, the Czech Republic, Germany, Turkey, and Norway also expressed support. Simon Phipps, Director of the OSI discussed above, stated that OSI looked "forward to the innovation [TDF] is able to drive with a truly open community gathered around a free software commons" (accessed November 20, 2015. http://www.documentfoundation.org/supporters/).

This diverse range of support created enthusiasm for the project of forking OpenOffice.org and developing LibreOffice as a free software office suite. The project also involved a range of challenges, however, due to the sheer size of OpenOffice.org. In facing these challenges, the knowledge and commitment of the community constituted a solid base upon which to build an alternative to the problems that had plagued OpenOffice.org. The most pressing issues were to promote community participation in the project, as well as to create a foundation as an alternative organizational form. Indeed, community participants viewed this alternative organizational structure as key to providing a legal basis for widespread community participation. Moreover, they strove to design the foundation to avoid the problems of dependence on a single commercial entity such as Sun.

Dynamics of Community-Driven Development

Forking OpenOffice.org was a massive undertaking. With such immense amounts of code, OpenOffice.org was what TDF Steering Committee member Charles-H. Schulz called the "aeroflot of free software" (Interview with Charles-H. Schulz 2010). I interviewed Schulz nine days after the Steering Committee announced the launch of TDF and Libre-Office. Events were unfolding rapidly, and the Steering Committee was making a series of strategic decisions. Schulz emphasized that during this process, the founders of TDF allied with the technical team. The founders had to trust that the technical team could accomplish the fork. They were conscious of taking risks in this process, however, since they were not completely sure how it would work (Interview with Charles-H. Schulz 2010).

During the process of forking, hundreds of free software community participants decided how they would relate to both OpenOffice.org and LibreOffice. While some sought to participate in both projects, most participants chose one project or the other. In the first two months after the fork, many of the leading members in the OpenOffice.org community left the project to join TDF. One of the most publicized examples occurred in October 2010, when 33 leading members of the German-language section of the OpenOffice.org project announced their resignation in an open letter to the OpenOffice.org community. They stated,

> Although it has been stressed several times that there will be collaboration on a technical level, and changes are possible – there is no indication from Oracle to change its mind on the question of the project organization and management. For those who want to achieve such a change, but see no realistic opportunity within the current project and are therefore involved in the TDF, unfortunately this results in an "either/or" question.
>
> The answer for us who sign this letter is clear: We want a change to give the community as well as the software it develops the opportunity to evolve.
>
> (Rahemipour 2010)

This announcement reflects the views of many free software community participants who saw the fork as a time to choose between the two projects. They viewed work on LibreOffice as consistent with earlier goals of building a global community that made a free office productivity suite available to users all over the world. On the LibreOffice website, the description of the project credits 1,241 people who either contributed to the development of OpenOffice.org and had those contributions imported into LibreOffice, or contributed to LibreOffice between September 2010 and January 2017 (accessed June 20, 2017. http://www.libreoffice.org/about-us/credits/).

A study by Gamalielsson and Lundell (2014) explored the involvement of committers, developers in free software projects who are able to modify the source code; committers have "commit bits" on their user accounts that give them permission to commit changes to the code. Through these changes, or "commits," developers contribute to the ongoing evolution of the code. Gamalielsson and Lundell (2014) studied contributions to LibreOffice from when it was launched in September 2010 until about two and a half years later, in May 2013. They found that of the 645 committers to LibreOffice during this period, 553 or 85.7 percent had been recruited to the project. The researchers base this conclusion on data revealing that these committers had not participated actively in the continuation of OpenOffice.org after the formation of LibreOffice, or in the subsequent development of Apache OpenOffice. Furthermore, 75 of the 645 committers to LibreOffice had previously contributed to OpenOffice.org; 66 of these 75 committers stopped contributing to OpenOffice.org once they became involved in LibreOffice.

These data indicate that these 66 committers were recruited from OpenOffice.org to LibreOffice. Gamalielsson and Lundell (2014) view those committers as a particularly important group, since they provided 58.7 percent of the commits to LibreOffice between September 2010 and May 2013. This group illustrates Nyman and Mikkonen's (2011) point that forking may have a range of effects on a free software community. Certainly, if forks precipitate the loss of users and developers, drawing away participants who contribute to the project's development as well as those who make use of the software in their daily activities, they can damage such a community. On the other hand, however, forking may also create conditions where developers are drawn to participate in the community. In situations where developers become frustrated with a project, forking can provide incentive for them to continue their work by focusing on the new version. As Weber (2004) argues, forking may promote innovation, as well as the overall health of a free software project, since the highest quality code will survive over the course of the forking process.

Concerns about quality free software code may have motivated developers to work on LibreOffice instead of OpenOffice.org. In fact, such concerns were accentuated about six months after the fork. As mentioned above, in the summer of 2011, Oracle, IBM, and the Apache Software Foundation announced that OpenOffice.org was becoming an official Apache project and would be licensed under the Apache License.

This shift introduced significant changes in the licensing of OpenOffice. org. In a statement about this change on its blog on June 10, 2011, the FSF noted the implications of the change in licensing. It warned that "users and contributors should be aware that…it will become easier for proprietary software developers to distribute OpenOffice.org as nonfree software." Since the Apache License did not include copyleft provisions, individual and corporate users, and developers were legally allowed to distribute the software under proprietary terms. This license thus undermined the catalytic property form, as well as prospects for developing the digital commons. Previous participants in the OpenOffice.org community may have decided to leave due to these potential problems with the quality and freedom of the software itself.

Due to a combination of the above factors, substantial numbers of developers were attracted to the TDF project. By early 2012, there were about 400 developers contributing, with about 55 percent of them working as volunteers and the rest divided among the participating corporations. In interviews in 2011 and 2012, a TDF Board member noted that this situation was very different from the case of OpenOffice.org, where it was more difficult to get new developers involved. As discussed above, developers encountered high barriers to entry under the OpenOffice.org licensing system, since they were required to sign a copyright licensing agreement that gave Sun legal ownership of all of the code they wrote. Many developers did not like this arrangement, since they were required to share their copyright but Sun was not. The project thus lacked transparency and reciprocity, two key values in free software communities. Certainly, this arrangement conflicted with the free software culture of freedom to share, modify, and redistribute work both between individuals and within a larger community (Interviews with The Document Foundation Board member 2011, 2012). By contrast, LibreOffice's copyleft licensing gave developers collective ownership over the software they produced. Of equal importance, it provided developers with individual access to the code they created. As Currie, Kelty, and Murillo (2013) argue, the availability of this kind of high level of control over resources produced in a free software project, as well as individual access to those resources, reflects a strong degree of participation in the project.

As noted above, organizational structures can be central to the successful forking of a software project. In this vein, during the initial process of forming TDF, community participants sought to establish an independent, self-governing democratic foundation that would function on a nonprofit basis. They articulated these goals in the *Next Decade Manifesto*, stating that the foundation would "own assets and conduct financial and legal transactions on behalf of the Community" (The Document Foundation 2015b). Membership in the foundation was open to anyone who supported TDF's core values and contributed to the project in some way, from development to translation, documentation, volunteering at trade shows, and more. An extensive process unfolded, where community members from around the world discussed possibilities for how to structure the foundation.

Indeed, due to TDF's global nature, there were comprehensive discussions about which country would be the best place to legally establish the foundation. Eventually, community participants chose Germany because of the stability of foundations under German law, dating back over 500 years. A critical German legal provision required foundations to have objectives that cannot be changed. Due to this provision, once a foundation has been legally established, the German government has an interest in the foundation prospering as it accomplishes its stated objectives. The government thus oversees and supports a foundation's work. This was one key reason why TDF chose to set up its organizational structure in Germany, rather than in France or the United Kingdom; there is not such strong government support in those other countries (Interview with The Document Foundation Board member 2012).

Establishing TDF in Germany thus had organizational advantages; however, it posed financial challenges. German law required that foundations have approximately 50,000 Euro of capital stock to provide financial stability. To raise these funds, TDF launched a public fundraising campaign four months after launching the LibreOffice project. In the first two days of the campaign in February 2011, they raised 15,000 Euro from people in a range of countries including Germany, France, Spain, Brazil, and elsewhere. Most contributions were small, between 10 and 100 Euro, and came from private individuals. In eight days, 2,000 donors from around the world made contributions that allowed them to raise the 50,000 Euro that they needed. By the end of this fund-raising campaign, TDF raised over 90,000 Euro (Interview with The Document Foundation Board member 2011).

Once TDF community had mobilized to secure financial stability, they crafted the details of the organizational structure. The design included a Board of Directors to conduct the main administration of projects and teams, as well as to serve as TDF's legal representatives. There was diverse global representation on the Board of Directors, which included two Germans, one Brazilian, one person from the United Kingdom, one from Ireland, and one from Italy. They were a mix of people with experience working in development, marketing, and infrastructure, as well as a mix of volunteer community members and people who made a living working for corporations (Interview with The Document Foundation Board member 2011).

Currie, Kelty, and Murillo (2013) provide a framework to understand this structure's potential to promote community participation in the project. They view project governance as a key way for community members to participate in free software projects.

From their perspective, such participation is necessary to engage in the development of project goals. Moreover, engaging in the governance process offers free software project participants a way to gain access and control over the resources that they produce. To enjoy strong participation in project governance, individuals need the autonomy to speak their mind about how a project is unfolding. Of equal importance, they need the freedom to leave the project without risking some kind of loss or reprisal. Participants must know that they can protest or raise questions through an established form of community procedure.

TDF's structure resonates with Currie, Kelty, and Murillo's (2013) model of strong participation in free software project governance. In fact, TDF contributors designed the foundation to promote community participants. They ensured this participation primarily by providing a formal legal role for community members. For example, each Board member appoints one community member as a deputy who serves on the Membership Committee (MC); the MC oversees membership applications and renewals, as well as the election of the Board of Directors. Community members thus have a formal organizational basis to challenge, and potentially change, Board decisions. If the Board of Directors does something with which community members disagree, those members have a formal governance structure through which to respond. They can go to the Board, propose an alternative, and legally enforce it. This governance structure thus ensures a strong element of power to each community member. Certainly, the participatory power of TDF community members goes considerably beyond raising questions about how the project is running or leaving the project without risk of reprisal, as emphasized by Currie, Kelty, and Murillo (2013).

Of most importance, the MC serves as a formal check on the power of the Board. It is an example of an organizational structure designed to achieve community control, as discussed above with reference to work by de Laat (2007) and Markus (2007). In 2011, I did a series of three interviews with a TDF Board member who was intensively engaged in the process of formulating this organizational structure. He noted that providing such strong governance rights to community members is very innovative. As a result, it took extensive consultation with a lawyer to develop a way for the German authorities to accept this arrangement. Through these consultations, TDF community leaders worked with their lawyer to comply with the requirements of creating a foundation under German law. They worked for months to formally establish the foundation, completing the process in the fall of 2011 (Interviews with The Document Foundation Board member 2011).

During these early months of establishing TDF through the fall of 2011, community members faced the key challenge of figuring out how to make money and to work with corporations. As O'Mahony (2005) emphasizes, foundations generally provide organizational structures to facilitate the relationship between community-based projects and corporations. In a similar vein, Currie, Kelty, and Murillo (2013) argue that free software projects often tend to shift from volunteer peer communities to more formal legal structures with at least one paid employee. Such formal organizational structures provide a basis to coordinate software development, as Shuttleworth did by founding Canonical to market the Ubuntu software based on development by the Debian peer community. Moreover, formal structures facilitate processes of fund-raising, developing partnerships, and overseeing potential problems with patents and copyrights (Currie, Kelty and Murillo 2013).

Since TDF's foundation structure was unusual, many corporations had been waiting for it to be finalized before deciding how they wanted to participate. In a 2012 interview, a TDF Board member noted that corporations had been impressed with the extensive legal process that TDF participants pursued to establish the organizational structure. He emphasized the importance of this process to reassure corporations that TDF was not just "a group of hackers who aren't happy with Oracle – we're serious people" (Interview with The Document Foundation Board member 2012).

TDF's efforts to develop relationships with corporations bore fruit in the constitution of the Advisory Board, staffed by organizations that contributed substantially to TDF in a range of ways. As noted on TDF's website, the Advisory Board includes organizations that offer a basic level of financial or other support, as well as advice to the Board of Directors. It has no institutional status and thus no rights to veto any decisions (The Document Foundation 2013). In an interview with a member of TDF's Board of Directors in 2011, he emphasized that it is not possible to simply buy a seat on the Advisory Board. For example, at that time, Novell/SUSE supported TDF's work by paying about 15 developers to contribute to LibreOffice. These developers from Novell/SUSE worked full time on LibreOffice. Other corporations donated money to finance the foundation. In the future, an Internet Service Provider might offer servers or bandwidth for free; an organization might also donate use of a venue for a TDF event. Such organizations may appoint one representative to the Advisory Board and are required to pay an annual fee. The Advisory Board offers proposals, guidance, and advice to the Board of Directors; however, the Board of Directors is not required to follow it. As a safety measure to avoid problems with dependence on a single corporation encountered with OpenOffice.org, there cannot be more than three people from the same corporation on the Advisory Board.

Once the foundation structure was established, the lead organizers of TDF faced challenging questions about how to proceed in building the community. They continued to reach out to corporations, governments, and key organizations in the free software field, to encourage diverse kinds of involvement.

Growing TDF as a Global Community

Similar to the cases of Drupal and Debian discussed in the last chapter, LibreOffice participants developed a global community by working at both the grassroots and broader organizational levels. They combined processes of community building with the development of free software as a catalytic form of property. They created an organizational structure that integrated key actors from around the world, including corporations, governments, activist or advocacy organizations in the free software field, and local community participants. LibreOffice's licensing and software development practices appealed to this diverse range of actors, encouraging their participation. Over time, projects such as language localization and document liberation facilitated the growth of LibreOffice as an international community, largely due to their global span and participation from a diverse range of local advocates. Finally, an emerging certification program created possibilities for professional development and employment for LibreOffice developers, further strengthening the community's global expansion.

Building International Relationships

From the inception of the LibreOffice project in 2010, key international organizations supported its work and participated on the Advisory Board. On the community level, the FSF commended the project as vital to the larger free software community. On the corporate front, Google, SUSE, Canonical, and Red Hat consistently served as Advisory Board members. As TDF continued building relationships with corporations, a major shift occurred in February 2012 when Intel joined the Advisory Board. This was significant, since Intel is a leading manufacturer of processors, graphic cards, and chips. In 2013, the chip manufacturer AMD joined the Advisory Board. Both Intel and AMD contributed to the work on LibreOffice, and particularly on the arithmetic operations for the spreadsheet program, Calc (The Document Foundation 2013).

As part of its development as a global community, TDF developed relationships with key governmental organizations in France, Germany, and Saudi Arabia.

In 2013, the Inter-Ministry Mutualization for an Open Productivity Suite (MIMO) joined the Advisory Board. MIMO is a working group of the French government that represents 500,000 workplaces. MIMO contributes to the development of LibreOffice as part of its work to promote a free desktop environment and to migrate French ministries to LibreOffice (The Document Foundation 2013).

In 2012, TDF developed a relationship with the city government of Munich, Germany, where they were undergoing a migration from proprietary to free software systems in city government as part of Project

LiMux. City officials invited TDF community members to come to Munich to help them to troubleshoot problems and to discuss the migration process so that they could continue to implement it effectively. TDF was interested in supporting the city's effort to promote the use of free software and open standards.

In 2015, Munich extended its commitment to the use of free software by joining the TDF Advisory Board. In a January 12, 2015 announcement about this decision on TDF's blog, TDF staff member Italo Vignoli noted Munich's valuable experience with Project LiMux. This project involved the migration of 16,000 public employees' personal computers and laptops from proprietary to free software between 2003 and 2013. As a result of this project, the city government of Munich is the largest public sector free software stakeholder in Germany. The city has reduced its dependence on proprietary software, fostering the use of open standards in employee workstations and a standardized IT platform with consolidated applications and databases. Project LiMux began by deploying OpenOffice.org and then shifted to LibreOffice (Hillenius 2011; Interview with The Document Foundation Board member 2012; The Document Foundation 2015a).

Christian Ude, mayor of Munich, took a visible stand on the importance of such migrations by writing a public letter to the European Commission and the European Digital Agenda Commission. Ude, who was also head of the German association of municipalities, argued that use of ODFs should be compulsory for all public institutions in the European Union. Such a requirement would ensure that data remain accessible to public officials, regardless of which software was used to create the documents; it would also save money. Toward this end, he urged European officials to install either LibreOffice or OpenOffice.org on their computers and to use the ODF. Ude wanted public administrations to use free software "'so that public knowledge remains accessible in the future'" (quoted in Hillenius 2011).

Finally, King Abdulaziz City for Science and Technology of Saudi Arabia (KACST) joined the TDF Advisory Board in 2013. KACST is a key supporter of the National Program for Free and Open Source Software Technologies (Motah), designed to promote free software.

Motah has made critical contributions to LibreOffice development, particularly with respect to Arabic language localization. This localization program was launched in 2012, with the goals of enhancing Arabic language support in LibreOffice. A September 13, 2012 announcement about the program on TDF's blog highlighted the importance of supporting languages written from right to left. Motah sought to solve bugs related to all functions and operations involved with the Arabic language, including improving the graphical user interface. Motah participants also worked to strengthen documentation and help services for Arabic-speaking users (The Document Foundation 2013).

By initiating and advancing these relationships with governmental organizations, TDF solidified itself as a global community. Rooted in the history of OpenOffice.org as a free software office suite employed around the world, TDF continued to expand and strengthen its international ties to diverse local communities. Volunteers in communities on five continents work to promote and market LibreOffice in their countries, seeking to attract new participants.

TDF's international relationships go beyond the peer producers engaging in software and community development. On the organizational level, TDF depends upon the financial contributions of its supporters. In 2014, 67,500 contributors made donations in 47 currencies. With an average donation of 8.81 Euro, these contributions amounted to a total of almost 595,000 Euro. Furthermore, TDF's technical infrastructure is global; it includes 167 mailing lists in 38 languages, with about 20,000 subscribers from a range of countries around the world. Both the TDF and LibreOffice websites provide content in 50 languages to more than 40 million visitors per year (The Document Foundation 2014).

Projects with Global Span and Local Participation

As TDF advocates continue to grow the global community, they engage in a wide range of projects. As will be discussed below, these projects are diverse; however, they share key common characteristics. They are all rooted in the work of local community participants that is organized and coordinated at a global level. Indeed, as Boyle (2008) and Benkler (2006) argue, these projects are examples of how free software communities create innovative ways to solve problems and engage in their work outside the proprietary model of sole control. Some of these projects involve processes of peer production of the software itself, while others focus on extending the availability of LibreOffice to a broader range of users for a broader range of purposes.

Native Language

For example, TDF's commitment to making the free office suite available to people in their native language sparked volunteers to participate in Native Language Projects. As discussed above, language localization was an important way that communities fostered the growth of OpenOffice.org. LibreOffice community participants continue to build on this history of language localization work, through Native Language Projects in Brazil, China, the Czech Republic, France, Germany, Italy, Japan, Uruguay, and the U.S. A team is working to translate a new version of TDF's website, as well as other blogs and social media sites, into Spanish. A volunteer is also translating LibreOffice into Guarani, a native South and Central American language. Once completed, this will be the first time that an office suite has been available in Guarani (The Document Foundation 2014). In September 2012, TDF Chairman of the Board Florian Effenberger announced the LibreOffice language localization program in Saudi Arabia on TDF's blog. He stated, "[o]nly the balanced mix between organization and volunteer activities within TDF can guarantee the global reach of LibreOffice, and offer users a free office suite in their native language independently from their geography or language" (accessed June 21, 2017. https://blog.documentfoundation. org/blog/2012/09/13/libreoffice-localization-program-in-saudi-arabia-announced-to-enhance-arabic-language-related-features/).

Document Liberation

In 2014, TDF initiated a new Document Liberation Project (DLP). Like language localization, DLP is organized on a global level, while simultaneously depending upon grassroots work in a diverse range of local communities. DLP participants share a common goal of giving users complete control over the files that they create. With the motto, "own your content," these participants created the project to "empower individuals, organizations and governments to recover their data from proprietary formats and provide a mechanism to transition that data into open file formats, returning effective control over the content from computer companies to the actual authors" (TDF 2014, 29). The project is based on the premises that people who create content should own that content, and that access to that content should not depend on whether a corporation decides to maintain a particular operating system. As discussed above, users may encounter problems when corporations make changes to proprietary formats that make it impossible to access files on the new systems. For example, after an upgrade of operating system and office software, users may be locked out of their own documents, since the new systems are configured in ways that will not read the old files. Such problems are magnified when large organizations such as governments experience this process of being locked out of their documents. Citizens, government employees, and businesses may risk losing valuable data and other records if they cannot access their earlier files.

In the DLP, community participants developed import filters that would allow users to free their documents from proprietary formats that locked in content. As stated on the DLP's website, "a significant amount of our legacy digital content is encoded in proprietary, undocumented formats" (accessed November 20, 2015. http://www.documentliberation. org/). To respond to this problem, DLP participants seek to understand the structure of proprietary, undocumented file formats and to extract as much information as possible from those formats. They develop ways to export users' files and encode the data into a variety of open file formats, including ODF; the open standard e-book format EPUB; and the free software word processor AbiWord (TDF 2014). Over the long term, ensuring that users have control over their documents will involve using free and open standards to encode digital content. As stated on the DLP website, "implementation of Free and Open Source Software that can read proprietary file-formats is the best solution to escape vendor lock during the transition period to truly open and free standards" (accessed November 20, 2015. http://www.documentliberation.org/).

Hackfests and Quality Assurance

In order to make it easier for developers to get involved in projects like document liberation or language localization, and especially to contribute to ongoing software development, TDF sponsored hackfests. They provided a list of "easy hacks," things that people with some development experience could readily do. By choosing to work on one of these relatively simple projects, developers had a clear idea of where to start; they could get some pointers about how to fix bugs and what needed to be done in the project. Such a list fit with the overall TDF effort to promote a transparent work process where everyone who chose to contribute to the project knew what was going on and had the same rights. The goal was to foster a trusting atmosphere for firms as service providers or large adopters, as well as for individual developers (Interview with The Document Foundation Board member, 2012).

Of equal importance, hackfests are a key way that TDF has organized focused work on particular aspects of the LibreOffice project. As discussed in the last chapter, most developers in free software communities are part of global communities where they are geographically dispersed around the world. They work primarily over Internet Relay Chat (IRC) or other modes of Internet communication. Hackfests provide a chance for developers to gather in the same room for a period of time, working intensively side by side to solve problems. In 2014, TDF created hackfests after the Free and Open Source Software Developers' European Meeting (FOSDEM) in Brussels, one of the main European free software events. Organized by volunteers and attended by about 4,000 people, it has been held annually since 2001. As noted above, major conferences like this provide opportunities for free software developers to come together in person to learn about the latest changes in the software, organize themselves as a community, and sometimes engage in concentrated periods of collective work.

TDF organized hackfests for a range of other purposes as well, all of which contributed to its construction as a global community. At a range of events in different parts of the world, LibreOffice developers effectively used hackfests to make key updates to the user interface, as well as completing work in the areas of accessibility, memory issues, and unit tests. For example, in April 2014, they held a hackfest as part of a strategy to strengthen relationships with organizational users of LibreOffice. This hackfest was held in conjunction with the University of Las Palmas on the Canary Islands. The city of Las Palmas had implemented a migration of over 1,000 desktops to LibreOffice in 2012, so the TDF community decided that it would be useful to hold a hackfest to foster the development of local knowledge about the software. This hackfest included talks about the history of the LibreOffice project, the importance of open standards, and the ODF, and how to engage in work on quality assurance (QA). These talks provided a background to the programmers' coding work. In Paris, TDF held a hackfest at Simplon.co. This "digital school" offers intensive courses in coding, website, and mobile applications development primarily geared toward youth under 25 with little or no formal education. As described on its website, Simplon. co seeks to provide training for groups that have been underrepresented in technical fields, as well as retraining for women and seniors (accessed June 21, 2017. Simplon.co). In Toulouse, France, TDF developers gathered for a hackfest at the *Capitole du Libre*, or Capitol of the Free, a community event for several free software projects. In Boston, TDF organized a hackfest at the mobile development company Xamarin, with participants from the U.S. and Canada (TDF 2014).

As emphasized in the cases of Drupal and Debian in the last chapter, ongoing work to develop free software as a catalytic form of property is a vital foundation for global free software communities. In the case of LibreOffice, these processes of software development are organized periodically through hackfests, and in a continuous way through the work of the QA team. For example, the QA team engages in ongoing efforts to respond to users' reports of errors, flaws, or failures in the software, known as "bugs," and to strategize about how to build momentum for continued improvement. Like many free software community participants that collaborate on projects, QA team members are dispersed in different parts of the world. They rely on an IRC channel to maintain close contact through biweekly meetings. Responding to users' bug reports often requires discussions of complicated cases, so the IRC channel facilitates this direct communication and fosters a sense of community. It also provides an easy way for QA members to reconnect with the team's work if they have become disengaged for a period of time.

The QA team is a key example of how TDF operates as a global community, integrating volunteers from a range of countries around the world into common projects to improve the ongoing development of the software. In 2014, the number of volunteers on the QA team grew from 19 to 32, making it possible to respond to a record number of bug reports. From a high of over 2,500 bugs in 2012, the QA team reduced the number of unconfirmed bugs from 1,100 to 387 during 2014. They accomplished this partly by holding five bug hunting sessions during 2014, as part of the process for preparing for different LibreOffice releases.

In these sessions, ongoing members of the QA team collaborated with developers and other occasional volunteers to test and identify problems. For example, over 100 bugs were filed at the bug hunting session before the release of LibreOffice 4.4, and almost a third of those bugs were fixed over the following week (The Document Foundation 2014).

LibreOffice for Android

In 2014, the QA team became energized about a new beta version of LibreOffice for Android. The prospect of LibreOffice running on new platforms and configurations, such as Ubuntu Touch and LibreOffice Online, led to more involvement by users interested in testing on mobile platforms.

The development of a mobile version of LibreOffice had been a priority since 2012. Community members recognized mobile phones and tablets as key to the software's future development, since growing numbers of users were relying on these devices rather than laptops or desktops. In 2014, the Board of Directors decided to invest some of the donations TDF received to develop a mobile version of the suite, since it appeared to be too extensive to accomplish with independent volunteers. On September 4, 2014, TDF posted an online tender calling for companies to submit proposals to "develop the base framework for an Android version of LibreOffice with basic editing capabilities." Over time, community volunteers would work with this base framework to develop concrete features of a mobile version ready for end users. In the tender, TDF asked firms to submit proposals by the end of February 2015, detailing the nature of the work they proposed to do, as well as timing and cost estimates for the additional work required to produce a fully fledged Android version of LibreOffice.

In January 2015, TDF announced the results of the Android tender on its website (accessed June 21, 2017. https://blog.documentfoundation.org/blog/2015/01/27/the-document-foundation-announces-the-results-of-the-android-tender/). After reviewing proposals from a range of companies, the Board chose two companies to conduct this work: Collabora, which had a good track record after developing the LibreOffice Viewer; and Ignalia, an open-source software development consulting firm (The Document Foundation 2014).

Developers released the LibreOffice app for Android in May 2015; however, it got critical reviews. For example, a review in the British technology news and opinion website *The Register* noted difficulties in viewing documents. These problems made the LibreOffice viewer "feel like an experiment" that would likely make many people want to uninstall the app. The review stated that those who continued to use the app would find "a competent document viewer and an editor that seemed stable enough but was tricky to use on a smartmobe's small screen" (Sharwood

2015). A comment on that review noted that there were several alternative apps on Google Play that handled the LibreOffice file formats more smoothly than the official app (accessed November 10, 2015. http://forums.theregister.co.uk/forum/1/2015/05/29/libre_office_comes_to_android/). Developing a high-quality mobile version of LibreOffice for Android thus poses an ongoing challenge for the community, from the QA team to other developers interested in the project. Addressing such challenges would allow TDF to build on the above interconnected processes of creating a global community, as well as improving the quality of free software as a catalytic form of property.

As discussed in the last chapter with respect to Debian and Drupal, dual processes of community and software development contribute to the emergence of the digital commons. As global communities grow, they give rise to alternative forms of globalization from below through free software projects that are coordinated globally, yet developed through the local actions of community participants. The diverse projects discussed above are key examples of how peer producers organize themselves to promote the development of the software and the community itself.

Certification

Certification programs have unique potential to contribute to the development of free software communities, as well as to the broader construction of the digital commons. Such programs give developers a formal opportunity for training, to improve their skills and enhance the pace and quality of their professional development. They are one way of addressing what Moreno et al. (2012, 1607) call the "sizeable challenge" of "[a]ligning SE [software engineering] education with industry." Certification provides developers with official recognition for their skills. It makes developers' expertise visible and credible when they apply for jobs, and potentially makes them more highly valued by their employers as well as their peers. Furthermore, nonprofit and for-profit firms, as well as government organizations, can have a clearer sense of prospective employees' skills in areas like software development and system administration. Certification thus facilitates efforts to hire employees with particular areas of expertise.

Broad-based certification programs are designed to assess software engineers' professional knowledge of the whole field. By contrast, product-specific certifications test the knowledge of a particular operating system. Certification shares similarities with other historical efforts by professional communities to govern the process of entering the profession and establishing standards of behavior. For example, professional bodies developed recommendations for licensure, program accreditation, and curricula for software engineering programs (Seidman 2008). The major professional association of technical professionals, Institute of Electrical and Electronics Engineers (IEEE), offers a Certified Software Development Professional (CSDP) certification that is recognized internationally. Lethbridge, Díaz-Herrera, LeBlanc, and Thompson (2007) view such certifications as playing a vital role in strengthening the educational levels of software engineers. They see certification programs as a key way to improve software education, so that it can be a vehicle for software professionals to maintain their professional competence. In turn, such programs may contribute to the broader process of creating higher-quality software by strengthening processes of software development and professionalism. Moreover, Adams and Demaiter (2008, 345) emphasize the symbolic benefits of educational credentials as a form of cultural capital, which "signal that an employee is competent and trainable." In an economy where knowledge and skills are highly valued, employers view credentials as evidence not just of particular skills, but of a flexible ability to learn and adapt to changes on the job. As Adams and Demaiter (2008, 358) argue, information technology workers "have to be adaptable, flexible, and to upgrade their skills constantly through their network contacts and self-learning activity."

Over the long term, certification contributes to broader processes of professionalization in the free software field. It helps to create clearer career paths and to institutionalize the presence of free software professionals in the market. Both the professionals seeking work and the organizations seeking their skills benefit from this institutionalization process. Increased training, recognition, and hiring of free software professionals contributes to the construction of the professional labor market as well as to the broader market for free software office suites, web content management systems, and more.

A number of nonprofits and professional societies have developed certification programs over the years. One of the best known is the Linux Professional Institute (LPI), a nonprofit organization founded in 1999 that offers certification courses for professionals working in open-source and free software fields. LPI is "vendor neutral," so its courses do not focus on a particular software program. As noted on its website, LPI has delivered over 500,000 exams in nine languages; it has over 400 training partners working to help certify professional in over 180 countries. LPI offers certification courses and exams in thousands of locations around the world, with the support of employers, vendors, and trainers (accessed June 21, 2017. http://www.lpi.org/about-lpi/our-purpose).

By contrast, a number of firms offer product-specific certifications. For example, the website for the Red Hat certification program states that professionals with this certification are "qualified to work with your Red Hat products" (accessed June 21, 2017. https://www.redhat.com/en/services/certification/rhcp/success-stories). In a similar vein, Acquia, the for-profit firm offering software as a service on the Drupal platform discussed in the last chapter, initiated a certification program in March 2014. Acquia's certification program is designed to help Drupal developers to strengthen and market their skills. Equally important, a growing number of businesses and other organizations are interested in hiring professionals to integrate Drupal into their organizations' operations. The Acquia Certification Program (ACP) provides a formal way for these organizations to recognize candidates with particular areas of expertise, such as site building, configuration, and management; module development; theme development; and front-end and back-end development. To facilitate involvement from Drupal developers around the world, the ACP makes the Acquia Certified Developer (ACD) exam available either online or in person. If it is easiest for Drupal professionals to take it online to save on travel time, the exam is proctored through Webassessor to ensure its integrity. If developers want to take an in-person exam, they can do so at events like DrupalCon; alternatively, they can go to one of over 700 Kryterion test centers located in more than 100 countries around the world (Manijak 2014).

In 2012, TDF joined this array of certification programs by launching one of its own. TDF participants designed a certification program to assess developers' competence in critical areas, including development of LibreOffice, migration from other systems to LibreOffice, and training in LibreOffice. The goals of this program are different, however, from commercial certification programs. While commercial certification emphasizes processes of improving technical skills and thus enhancing professional development as discussed above, TDF views certified professionals as "ambassadors" for the community. According to the TDF web page describing the program, "certified professionals have the objective of extending the reach of the community to the corporate world, by offering CIOs and IT managers a recognition in line with proprietary offerings" (accessed November 10, 2015. https://www.documentfoundation.org/certification/). Such a vision promotes the development of TDF as a global community, since these certified professionals "are supposed to become a valuable channel for a deeper engagement with the corporate world" (accessed November 10, 2015. https://www.documentfoundation.org/certification/). TDF certification thus promotes relationships between the TDF community and the market, while simultaneously seeking to increase customer satisfaction.

The TDF Board of Directors initiated the certification process by appointing 44 certified developers and 13 certified specialists in migration and training. They chose these professionals based upon their contributions to the LibreOffice code, as well as their experience working in the field. The migration and training specialists played a particularly important role, since they worked with governments, nonprofits, and corporations that wanted to migrate to LibreOffice. In the process, these professionals worked with employees to teach them how to use the LibreOffice software. By February 2015, the certification team had trained and certified eight new people to be LibreOffice development professionals (The Document Foundation 2015a).

Until April 2015, the TDF Board pursued the certification project by making it open only to TDF members or active project contributors. They organized it this way so that TDF could improve the process of certification training. By developing the training with TDF members, the trainers could pinpoint problems and improve the process before opening it to the broader market. TDF offers certification at a range of levels. For example, support professionals address problems raised by customers, solving technical issues by gathering information, and exploring solutions. Migration professionals coordinate migration to LibreOffice from proprietary systems. Certified developers engage in a range of high-level work, offering support services to enterprise users, developing solutions to address problems, and sometimes adding new features to the code (accessed November 10, 2015. https://www.documentfoundation.org/certification/).

Certified LibreOffice developers work in a range of firms. Their presence in the free software market is indicated by the TDF website that lists certified developers. As of July 2017, nine firms or organizations each had one certified LibreOffice developer working for them; these were Canonical, Ericsson, Igalia, ITOMIG, Landeshauptstadt München, Linagora, SIL, SUSE, and TDF. Moreover, there were 7 certified LibreOffice developers working at CIB, 15 working at Collabora, and 5 working at Red Hat. In addition, there were 20 certified LibreOffice developers who were unaffiliated with any firm. The website includes a disclaimer that the list is not necessarily complete, and that it includes only a small fraction of the participants who have committed code to the project (accessed July 5, 2017. https://www.documentfoundation.org/certification/developers/).

As discussed above, certified professionals such as these expand the presence of free software communities in the market, facilitating the use of LibreOffice by a range of organizations. Increasing the number of certified professionals makes it possible for a wider range of organizations to migrate to LibreOffice, potentially shifting away from proprietary systems. As stated on the website, "by communicating with the LibreOffice community through certified professionals, organizations should be able to improve the way they leverage the advantages of free software and the features of LibreOffice, and get a better value added support" (accessed November 11, 2015. https://www.documentfoundation.org/certification/). In a similar vein, these professionals offer a way for organizations to communicate their ideas to improve the development of the office suite, potentially becoming involved in the development process.

TDF participants in communities around the world thus collaborate on myriad projects. They organize their work around their common interests, contributing their skills and expertise. They shape the global community in diverse ways, from translating for Native Language Projects to empowering users to recover their data from proprietary formats through document liberation. They hunt for bugs and troubleshoot problems with code through hackfests and other work by the QA team. Some coders create and refine a mobile version of LibreOffice for Android, while others specialize in migration to LibreOffice from proprietary systems or work on the certification program. Through this rich mosaic of talent, knowledge, and skill, TDF advocates from across the globe collaborate to create a multifaceted international community.

Conclusion: Forking, Globalization from Below, and the Digital Commons

Through this spectrum of globally organized projects, TDF advocates built a global community that constitutes an alternative form of globalization from below. In the process of sustaining the LibreOffice office suite and TDF as an organizational structure, they constructed alternatives to neoliberal globalization with its dynamic of prioritizing the proprietary interests of global capital. Similar to the free software communities discussed in the last chapter, they created an implicit form of resistance to neoliberalism. By nurturing the growth of free software as a community-owned form of property, as well as the communities that are so critical for developing that software, these free software advocates engaged in alternative practices that challenged the dominance of private property. The case of LibreOffice and TDF thus highlights the vital importance of community structures as an organizational foundation for free software itself, as well as for the digital commons.

By creating the foundation structure for TDF, free software advocates contributed to developing the commons as a shared resource. In the process, as Benkler (2013a) argued, they faced challenges fraught with social dilemmas. When the Oracle Corporation bought Sun, free software advocates organized to assess the conflicts involved with greater corporate control over the OpenOffice.org project. This increasing corporate presence was the catalyst for free software proponents to fork the project. They realized the importance of community organizational structures as a basis to protect software freedom. They devised an organizational form to legally protect the community-based nature of the project, integrating contributions from a diverse range of participants from around the world.

As they built this alternative foundation structure, however, TDF advocates encountered further dilemmas inherent in the strategy of forking. By figuring out how to resolve these dilemmas, TDF participants forged an alternative organizational structure with potential to solidify the project's contribution to the digital commons.

The launch of Libreoffice is thus a significant recent example of the forking process. As Gamalielsson and Lundell (2014, 129) state, Libre-Office "is one of the few OSS [Open Source Software] projects which have had an active community for more than 10 years...with significant commercial interest." They base this definition of the longevity and commercial interest in the LibreOffice project upon the fact that it built upon OpenOffice.org. Moreover, they highlight the extensive deployment of LibreOffice in a range of organizations in countries around the world. In the years since the launch of LibreOffice, it has become widely used by individuals, corporations, governments, and nonprofits. Such deployment indicates the quality of the software and the high regard in which it is held by both private and public sector organizations (Gamalielsson and Lundell 2014).

As detailed in this chapter, four interrelated sets of conditions contributed to the success of the fork of OpenOffice.org.

First, a core group of community members employed their considerable political will and skill to develop a strategy to fork the project. They won support from a range of corporate, government, and peer contributors committed to the development of free software. This community and corporate support for the project made it possible to accomplish the fork, both technically and politically. Both volunteer and paid developers contributed hours to the project, while other participants engaged in translation, worked on documentation, and crafted the organizational structure.

Second, LibreOffice advocates built upon a 10 year history of extensive community investment by hundreds of OpenOffice.org volunteers. In the process, they pursued what developers studied by Nyman (2015, 59) considered to be a best practice, "to attempt to develop the versions in such a way that code can still be shared between the fork and the original." In his research, Nyman (2015, 59) found that developers do not have clear general rules for how to best accomplish a fork; however, "[t]he most commonly held opinion relates to the significance of crediting previous contributors who have created the original program from which the fork is made." TDF and LibreOffice participants followed such an approach, by acknowledging the work of previous OpenOffice.org contributors. They configured the project to allow code to be shared between the projects, and encouraged OpenOffice.org contributors to continue to participate in LibreOffice.

Third, Oracle and Sun's actions to pursue their private economic interests sparked concern in the OpenOffice.org community about the future of the project. These actions threatened to undermine the project's commitment to developing software that was freely available to develop, share, modify, and redistribute, as well as community members' hard work.

Last but certainly not least, TDF advocates clearly articulated the underlying goals and values of the project, through early statements by

TDF founders and the *Next Decade Manifesto*. They publicized these goals and values widely over the Internet, drawing interest from participants around the world who supported them.

In addition to these conditions that fostered success, LibreOffice and TDF face challenges that are instructive in understanding the process of developing the digital commons. Since the foundation structure is still relatively new, participants need experience to learn how to run it. Gamalielsson and Lundell (2014, 142) call this organizational form a "tailor made foundation," noting that "contributors shaped TDF with a view to support their preferred way of working." In a 2011 interview, one TDF Board member emphasized that difficulties may arise in the effort to involve the community so closely in the foundation's formal work. Other free software projects that are run by peer communities are often more loosely organized. TDF thus constitutes an organizational experiment that requires participants to learn through experience.

For the LibreOffice brand to continue to solidify its user base and garner support, TDF will need to continue building relationships with free software communities around the world, as well as with governments, nonprofits, and corporations. It is breaking new ground in certain ways, largely due to the nature of a free software office suite as integral to the work of every computer user. Such a program is used by individuals for a range of purposes, both in their personal activities and in their work with diverse kinds of organizations, such as governments, school systems, nonprofits, and corporations. Since LibreOffice is available on Windows, Mac, and Linux platforms, it crosses boundaries between proprietary and free software systems. Challenges may arise in the attempt to be relevant to the myriad interests of such a diverse user base.

Improving the code and further developing the software is an ongoing challenge for coders working on bug hunting, QA, and developing the mobile version of LibreOffice. Furthermore, developing LibreOffice in a global community, crossing barriers of language, technical resources, and more, involves a continual process of communication and effort.

Despite these challenges, TDF and LibreOffice participants were able to use forking as an effective strategy to solidify the organizational basis for their free software community. In the process, they sustained the community-based nature of the software as well as the project itself. As Nyman (2015, 58) concluded after studying developers' perceptions of forking,

> forking is considered unproblematic and favourable when it is done for the good of the code...the right to fork serves as a means of protecting the software and its community's interests through taking the work done so far and continuing it in the direction of their choosing.

Indeed, TDF and LibreOffice advocates chose to move their community in a direction of stronger community control. After employing the forking strategy, they created an innovative organizational structure to formally solidify community participation and control over the project. They constituted an implicit global community of resistance to the proprietary dynamic of neoliberalism. This implicit global community of resistance, as well as the communities studied in the last chapter, was instrumental in developing free software as a foundation for the digital commons. Building on this foundation, free software activists forged explicit global communities of resistance. They organized to defend free software and free software communities against challenges from corporations and governments.

5 Software Politics
Building Communities to Defend Software Freedom

As software is increasingly integrated into economic, political, social, and cultural practices, it becomes a terrain of struggle. Since software powers computers, industries, and communications networks, it provides an underlying commonality to these myriad practices. Free software advocates, corporations, and governments engage in software politics, where they apply diverse strategies to shape the terms for software use. Through software politics, they target the conditions for development and access to key productive forces of informational capitalism.

Over the past decades, free software proponents played a key role in these struggles over software politics. They waged these battles within the broader context of neoliberal globalization, with its underlying dynamic to privatize multiple forms of property, from state-owned public utilities to intellectual property. As discussed in Chapter 2, U.S. free software advocates employed the freedom discourse to create an alternative form of property that challenged closed proprietary software. In this chapter, I examine a range of activist strategies, from defending free software in legislative battles to educating consumers about potential problems of surveillance involved with cell phones and other products powered by software. These distinct struggles over software politics contribute to the effort to develop a digital commons. They transform political conditions that frame, and largely define, information and software. They contest the corporate and government interests promoting neoliberal globalization, building global communities of resistance that explicitly engage in political activism.

Activists engaged in software politics make a different contribution to the digital commons than the free software proponents discussed in the last two chapters. Those proponents created *implicit* communities of resistance focused on the development of particular free software projects and communities, such as Drupal and LibreOffice. Exploring software politics contrasts with such efforts, as well as with previous research such as Coleman's (2004, 2012) studies of Debian software and community development, Kelty's (2008) work on Creative Commons and Connexions, or Takhteyev's (2012) study of free software communities of practice. My approach to software politics resonates with the Peruvian free software community activism studied by Chan (2013); however, the focus of this chapter is on struggles over conditions for developing and employing the software, as well as building international alliances to resist corporate and government efforts to impose a proprietary software regime.

Specifically, I explore how French free software activists developed a global free software community of resistance with an explicitly political focus. I highlight the work of the *Association pour la Promotion et la Recherche en Informatique Libre* (April) or the Association for Promotion and Research on Free Computing. This organization was founded in 1996 by a group of five French student activists. As these activists continued their work over the years, April became the major free software association in France. April's motto, displayed prominently on its website, is "to promote and defend free software" (accessed June 29, 2017. http://www.april.org/, my translation). Furthermore, April's website highlights its campaign to prioritize free software, "to retake control of our digital life" (accessed June 29, 2017. http://www.april.org/, my translation). Such activism is a vital part of the development of the global free software community of resistance, as free software becomes a site for political struggle over policies involving copyright, patents, and Internet access. Equally important, April's activism is a vehicle for citizen empowerment. These activists seek to educate and mobilize citizens to protect their rights to access, share, and create free software.

April activists developed their work over three phases. For the first five years after they created April in 1996, the activists engaged in education work to raise awareness among the general public. In the process, they began building relationships with free software companies that offered key support for their organizing work. Software politics thus extended to the broader process of constructing the market for free software. In the second phase of their work between 2001 and 2010, April activists developed a multipronged strategy. They continued their public education work, focusing on threats to free software from corporate efforts to protect their interests by reforming copyright law. Moreover, April strengthened the global free software community of resistance by joining forces with free software activists across Europe; united, these activists opposed legislation extending beyond France to the European Union. They pressured the French government and the European Union to shape conditions for applying copyright law to the software field. In the third phase of work after 2010, April activists placed greater emphasis on consumer education. They highlighted the importance of consumers' choices about buying and using technologies that allowed corporations and governments to target them with surveillance. The significance of consumer and citizen engagement in promoting and defending free software came to a head during April's work on the Digital Republic bill in 2015 and 2016.

French Activists Build the Global Community of Resistance

As discussed in Chapter 1, Sassen (2005, 54) argued that alternative forms of globalization from below involve the development of "transboundary public spheres" rooted in the connections between a range of local struggles and global networks. Since 1996, French free software activists have engaged in such a process of local struggle to build upon the work that the Free Software Foundation (FSF) began in the U.S. April activists applied the freedom discourse to the French context, while also seeking to build relationships with free software communities in other European countries. Through this combination of national activism and international alliance building, French activists made vital contributions to the creation of free software as a global community of resistance.

The FSF is an international organization; however, most of its work has focused on developing the free software community in the U.S. This occurred in part because, despite international conventions, each national government can impose different licensing requirements that may conflict with the freedom discourse. Activists in particular countries have thus worked to organize local communities to address the particular challenges within their national contexts. These local struggles all contribute to the broader process of developing a global free software community. The FSF does not provide an organizational structure to connect these local communities. As discussed in Chapter 2, however, it does articulate a freedom discourse about the value of free software to society. Furthermore, it established free software as a new form of property through copyleft. To promote the freedoms of software users and the ongoing implementation of software licensed under the General Public License (GPL), the FSF offers ongoing position statements and analyses of conflicts involved with promoting and legally defending free software around the world.

Inspired by the FSF, April activists worked to translate its approach to their national context. They sought to advance the FSF's work by building an activist group focused on promoting and defending free software in France. As a result, April is an associate organization of the FSF France, which is a sister organization of the FSF. The leader of these activists, Frédéric Couchet, recounted the process of founding April and developing the French free software community in an interview in 2010. These events capture key biographical events of what Couture and Proulx (2008) call "militants of code."

Couchet and the other cofounders of April were computer science students at the prestigious Paris 8 University. According to Couchet (interview 2010), "at Paris 8 the philosophy was that you were there to learn, so you could work on the machines and do roughly what you wanted." Students were encouraged to work together, and when the software involved was free software, they were able to install programs and run tests on the systems to look for potential problems. Thus, they learned through practical experience how to develop the software and understand how it worked.

The students' early relationship with the FSF strengthened when Richard Stallman came to do a conference at the university and discuss the application of the FSF's approach to free software to the French context. This exchange of ideas fostered the relationship, creating a space for further interaction and the emergence of a global community spanning France and the U.S. Anton Chastain, a member of April's board who has been involved with the association since the early years at Paris 8, described April's relationship with Stallman and the FSF in an interview. He noted that when Stallman came to France to meet with April activists, he began his presentation by saying "I can summarize free software in three words: *liberté, égalité, fraternité*. It fits very well in French, evidently" (Chastain, interview 2010). By drawing upon the French values of freedom, equality, and brotherhood, as well as by speaking fluent French, Stallman used the freedom discourse to highlight how the ethic of free software resonated within the French cultural context. In turn, Chastain drew upon this discourse to extend the parallel between the philosophy of free software and French culture. He stated that free software involves

> the freedom to share. And equality is that there is nobody who will say to you, 'you must do this, but not that.' And brotherhood is that there is no barrier between the developers and the users. For me, this is truly the ethic of free software.
>
> (Chastain, interview 2010)

The April activists thus identified strongly with the freedom discourse and its resonance within the French context. Once Couchet finished his studies, his primary goal was to build upon the FSF's work. He stated,

> And I thought [...] we could create an association with the goal of making people understand about free software, like the FSF did in the US. And in 1996 we created April with five students, without knowing concretely our objectives or how we would go about them; we just wanted to bring the understanding of free software to the people of France.
>
> (Couchet, interview 2010)

From the beginning of their organizing efforts, April activists thus pursued political goals of raising public awareness about free software. Indeed, Couchet (interview 2010) emphasized that the April activists were not lobbyists, but advocates. He explained this vital distinction, noting that to "lobby is to defend a private interest, and [to] advocate is to defend the public interest" (Couchet, interview 2010). Because April activists viewed free software as quintessentially a public good that contributes to society, "[w]e don't defend the interests of our members, of our companies, we defend free software" (Couchet, interview 2010). This defense of free software as a public good goes to the heart of free software as a community of resistance to neoliberalism. The political goal is to protect the public good, rather than any one group or actor's particular interests. Furthermore, the fundamental distinction between lobbying and advocacy characterizes the community's resistant nature. Couchet stressed that corporations like Microsoft hired professional lobbyists, whose job was to defend corporate interests. By contrast, April's advocacy work was rooted in a process of political education. A key part of this work involved educating politicians about the importance of free software to broader societal freedoms and processes of sharing and cooperation.

Free software activists thus identified themselves as doing a completely different kind of work than professional lobbyists. Couchet (interview 2010) did not use the language of defending the commons; however, April's efforts to promote societal freedom and sharing through free software resonate with the processes of constructing the commons discussed throughout this book. From the perspective of coding the digital commons, free software activists are engaged in vital struggles to create the political conditions for the commons to emerge.

In April's early years, the activists focused on promoting greater understanding of free software among the general public. One of their strategies was to translate works about the Internet and free software into French. In the late 1990s, many of these writings were only available in English, including the information about the FSF and its approach to free software. Translation work was thus germane to constructing a global community including advocates from France and the U.S. The April activists synchronized their work with the FSF and collaborated directly with Stallman, who Couchet (interview 2010) described as "very, very happy" to support April's efforts.

Hence, during the initial development of the French free software community, April activists engaged in a process of applying and interpreting the freedom discourse within the French cultural context. They sought to make that discourse relevant to the concerns of French citizens. Couchet (interview 2010) described the period from 1996 to 1998 as the first stage of developing the French free software community. The activists focused their attention on local conditions in France, as they were "constantly adapting to the situation, slowly getting stronger" (Couchet, interview 2010). April grew to about 15 or 20 members, most of them students from the Paris 8 university. This was a period of learning about issues that were central to developing a free software community, including how to work with the media. Many journalists had little knowledge about free software; however, as the activists increased their public education work, they were able to interest more journalists in their project.

After 1998, the activists reached more people with their message about the value of free software. They organized some larger actions, including a weeklong event at the Science and Industry museum in Paris. There, they demonstrated how to use free software and educated people about its benefits. These kinds of educational events drew more involvement and interest in April's work.

Of equal importance, the activists began working with companies to promote the use of free software in the private sector. They sought to garner support from those companies for April's organizing efforts. To create a global free software community, activists thus collaborated with free software firms. Through this collaboration, they contributed to broader processes of constructing the free software market.

Software Politics, Activism, and the Market

Some free software companies recognized the importance of building understanding and awareness about political issues that affected the conditions for the use of free software. They believed that it was important to have an organization like April to raise and defend alternative positions.

The first company to support April as a corporate member was AdaCore. AdaCore is a free software company with offices in both the U.S. and France. As described in the 2014–2015, edition of AdaCore's newsletter, *GNAT Pro Insider*, Ada Core Technologies was founded in 1994 by three faculty in the Computer Science department at New York University (NYU). Using the GNU compilation system (GCC) and licensing under the GNU GPL, these faculty developed the GNU NYU Ada Translator (GNAT). From their initial research project leading to the development of GNAT, the faculty worked closely with the GNU free software community to integrate free software code and licensing. In 1996, two postdoctoral computer scientists who had worked in the NYU program founded the French branch of the company, which was eventually renamed AdaCore. In the decades since, AdaCore's computer scientists developed GNAT from a compiler and debugger to a comprehensive toolset that firms can use for development in environments that require high levels of security. The firm also offers product and service expertise in the SPARK computer language and supporting development tools, fully compatible with Ada. SPARK is a verification technology that allows high-security military and civilian programs to detect defects in critical software systems and thus maintain confidence in their operations (accessed July 15, 2016. http://www.adacore.com/newsletter).

AdaCore thus offers commercial software solutions that help firms to build, verify, and maintain complex software systems. It employs the Ada programming language, designed to maximize safety and reliability in "systems that can't fail, from a security point of view," according to one Adacore executive in a 2010 interview. Another Adacore executive emphasized that by creating fail-safe systems, Ada promotes both safety and security (personal communication 2017). For example, Ada is largely used in sectors involving highly sensitive information that require software to be very robust and to last for a long time. These sectors encompass commercial and defense aerospace, including avionics where software code is integrated into different parts of planes; Ada is also used in rail transport, air traffic control, financial services, and medical devices. The customer list posted on Adacore's website includes a wide range of firms in sectors requiring high security, such as General Electric, General Dynamics, Lockheed Martin, Raytheon, the Ministry of Defense in the Netherlands, NATO, the U.S. Army, and the U.S. Air Force (accessed July 20, 2016. http://www.adacore.com/customers/list/). An Adacore executive (interview 2010) emphasized that such businesses invest extensively in their train, plane, banking, and other systems. These firms are thus primarily concerned about the quality, longevity, and security of the software.

AdaCore's business model involves a combination of software technology and support services from the engineers who build the technology. It is the main maintainer of GNAT Pro, a development environment for the Ada software that includes professional grade tools. This toolset is very large, so firms can review it to choose the tools that best fit their needs. AdaCore specializes in providing clients with support from experts in Ada programming; these experts advise the clients' development teams as they implement the technology within their particular organizational environment. As mentioned above, AdaCore also provides the verification technology SPARK Pro, so that its customers can detect potential defects in their complex software systems and correct them.

In addition to these professional grade software and services, AdaCore remains involved with the Ada free software community, primarily by offering different versions of GNAT and SPARK designed for community use. For example, the Technology Comparison Chart on AdaCore's website delineates the differences between three distinct versions of GNAT and SPARK (accessed July 20, 2016. http://libre.adacore.com/comparisonchart/). The professional versions described above, GNAT Pro and SPARK Pro, are available by subscription through AdaCore and include what AdaCore calls "frontline support," as well as access to pre-releases and the complete toolset. By contrast, the GNAT/SPARK GPL Edition is available for free download from the AdaCore website. It is licensed under the GNU GPL, and intended for free software developers and students. This community-oriented version of the software does not include access to pre-releases or support services from AdaCore. As a third option, the GNAT/SPARK Academic Program is designed for use in educational settings that comply with the terms of the GNU GPL. It is available by joining the GNAT Academic Program (GAP), designed to foster the use of Ada in academic settings. According to the GAP webpage, there are over 200 educational institutions in 35 countries where professors are using GNAT to teach Ada; the countries with six or more educational institutions engaging in such programs include Brazil, Canada, France, Germany, Italy, Poland, Spain, Switzerland, the United Kingdom, and the U.S. (accessed July 18, 2016. http://libre.adacore.com/academia/).

AdaCore has thus developed a strong, diverse network of connections in a range of organizations and communities involved with free software, making it a highly visible actor in business, developer, and free software community circles. These business and community relationships, as well as AdaCore's consistent focus on the GNAT technology and services, have supported the firm's reputation and continued development. On its website, AdaCore lists a range of free software organizations with which it collaborates to promote the development of free software, and particularly Ada. These include the International Organization for Standardization (ISO)'s group on Ada, which develops standards related to the Ada language. AdaCore supports organizations such as the Special Interest Group on Ada (SIGAda), part of the Association for Computing Machinery (ACM), that seeks to promote the scientific, technical, and organizational development of Ada. Within the business community, AdaCore is involved with System@tic Paris-Region (ICT CLUSTER), described on AdaCore's website as a coalition of 480 firms "in the field of software-dominant systems with a strong social dimension" in the Paris region (accessed July 19, 2016. http://www.adacore.com/company/community).

From the beginning, AdaCore executives understood the importance of explaining the nature and significance of free software to a wide range of audiences, from individual users to the general public, governments, and corporations. To foster such work, AdaCore supported free software organizations such as the FSF, April, and the Eclipse Foundation. Indeed, during the initial period of April's development, AdaCore recognized its potential contributions to this educational work and became its first corporate member.

In an interview in 2009 an AdaCore executive explained why April's work was so important to the firm. He noted that since AdaCore managers needed to focus their attention on developing the software and offering services, they relied on April to educate the public about the value of free software. In April's early years, when Couchet talked to this Adacore executive about expanding April to take on more organizing work, the executive encouraged this effort. He emphasized that "free software communities really need people who are dedicated" to promoting and defending free software (Adacore executive, interview 2009). Big industries like oil and pharmaceuticals have lobbyists to defend their positions. Adacore "believed in the cause" of free software and viewed it as important to have people "defending it...there need to be advocates" (Adacore executive, interview 2009). In fact, this executive (interview 2009) viewed such political work as "a full-time job." AdaCore executives did not become directly involved with this kind of political advocacy, since that would divert resources from their focus on working with their customers. April was thus engaged in critical work that helped to create the broader conditions for AdaCore to succeed in its business endeavors. This Adacore executive (interview 2009) stated, "It makes more sense, from a human, business, also from an organizational standpoint" for April to do this public education work. In turn, Adacore offered public support for April as one of its official corporate members. Adacore played a distinct, yet complementary role, by developing the technology, providing support to its clients, and building its customer base.

April thus focused on political advocacy to build a global free software community of resistance. This quintessentially political work complemented the work of software development and customer service offered by free software firms like AdaCore. Over time, the "full-time job" of organizing to defend free software became increasingly contentious as April continued its efforts. In what Couchet (interview 2010) described as the second phase of April's organizing work after 2001, April developed a multipronged strategy. It shifted the focus of its public education work, highlighting threats to free software from corporate strategies to protect their interests by reforming copyright law. Simultaneously, April united with other European free software activists to pressure the French government and the European Union to oppose these legal measures, thus extending and strengthening the global free software community of resistance.

Building the Global Community of Resistance: Struggles over Intellectual Property

As discussed in Chapter 2, Richard Stallman and the FSF used copyright law as the legal foundation to constitute free software as an alternative form of property. Definitions and applications of copyright law thus hold critical legal implications for free software. Without copyleft licenses, free software would not exist. Equally important, as discussed above, free software communities do much of their work over the Internet. Unfettered access to the Internet is crucial for the myriad processes of international collaboration that make it possible to develop free software itself, as well as free software communities. Free software activists across the globe thus paid close attention when copyright law became the focus of corporate efforts to protect proprietary interests, primarily in the film and music industries. April activists monitored such efforts in the U.S., which later spread to the European arena.

Indeed, a key dynamic of the dominant form of neoliberal globalization involved corporate and government strategies to create conditions for capital to enter markets around the world, including the emerging markets involved with the exchange of commodities in digital form via the Internet. Developments in the U.S. paved the way for broader international struggles. Boyle (2008) noted that in the mid-1990s, the U.S. Patent and Trademark Office issued a Green Paper and a White Paper outlining guidelines on intellectual property, which provided the legal foundations for that policy over the coming decades. In these guidelines, policy makers in the Clinton administration identified intellectual property's distinct sharable, reproducible qualities as a major threat to corporate proprietary control. They were primarily concerned about protecting the domestic business and export potential of digital content providers in music and film; the policy makers viewed these interests as threatened by the prospect of users illicitly copying their products and distributing them over the Internet (Benkler 2006). They thus recommended treating intellectual property similarly to other kinds of physical, non-digital property, in an effort to protect proprietary interests. Boyle (2008, 56) emphasized the significance of these early policy assumptions, stating that "[w]hen you set up the property rules in some new space, you determine much about the history that follows. Property rules have a huge effect on power relationships and bargaining positions."

In the 1990s, the U.S. government and corporations struggled to shape the political and economic conditions for producing and exchanging digital commodities. They waged these struggles, however, in the context of free software proponents' contributions to those conditions in the previous decade. As discussed with respect to the GNU GPL and copyleft, the availability of free software as a community-based form of property provided a foundation for developers in firms and communities to create a diverse range of software programs. They thus employed this form of property to carve out positions in the market and to build communities. They drew upon the freedom discourse in this process, as a narrative of power and knowledge rooted in the four freedoms to use, study, share, and improve the software.

This discourse conflicted with the proprietary discourse of neoliberal globalization, based on divergent assumptions that capital had the right to enter markets around the world and maximize profits. U.S. government guidelines for intellectual property law followed this proprietary discourse. As the Clinton administration crafted that policy in the 1990s, Boyle (2008, 56) argued that "[w]hat was being set up here was a vision of economy and culture, a frame of mind about how the world of cultural exchange operates, and eventually a blueprint for our systems of communication." The vision that Boyle described was the strategy to extend the proprietary discourse to the field of intellectual property. Such efforts built on earlier attempts in the 1980s, when the U.S. Federal Communications Commission (FCC) sought to expand U.S. telecommunications policy to regulate emerging forms of digital trade and communication made possible by the convergence of telecommunications and computer systems (Schoonmaker 2002).

Setting the Stage to Control Intellectual Property: The Digital Millennium Copyright Act

In this historical context, struggles arose in the late 1990s between proponents of the proprietary and freedom discourses over how to regulate intellectual property. These struggles had significant implications for free software, since they established key conditions for software development and use. The digital form of emerging cultural products made it easy to copy and share those products, from music and software CDs to DVDs of films. In response, corporations in the music and film industries mobilized to protect their interests. In the U.S., they supported the Digital Millennium Copyright Act (DMCA), which was passed in 1998 after three years of contentious political struggles. As will be discussed further below, similar struggles arose in countries around the world, as governments sought to implement policy changes so that their domestic laws complied with the requirements of two new World Intellectual Property Organization (WIPO) Copyright Treaties ratified in 1996 (Benkler 2006). In the U.S., corporate proponents of the DMCA supported their positions by articulating what Boyle (2008, 60) called the "story[of] the Internet Threat." This Internet Threat position resonated with the proprietary discourse, since it viewed the technological potential to copy and share on a global scale as a danger to corporate profits, particularly in the film and music sectors. Proponents of this position advocated greater controls over users who sought to copy and share files, including surveillance of those users' activities. They argued that such controls would create the conditions for creativity and innovation to thrive, since firms in those industries would be protected.

Major companies and industry associations in music and film viewed copyright as a legal vehicle to institute these controls. They proposed such controls as a necessary way to counteract what they considered to be the problematic implications of a key "fair use" provision in U.S. copyright law. Boyle (2008, 66) characterized fair use as "limitations on the exclusive rights of the copyright holder – uses that were never within the copyright holder's power to prohibit." Fair use provisions were thus rooted in the assumption that property rights of copyright holders were not absolute. These provisions were "a conditional grant of a limited and temporary monopoly" (Boyle 2008, 66). Hence, Boyle (2008) argued that in the U.S., fair use offered a vital protection for other constitutionally protected freedoms such as free speech. He referred to these "exceptions, limitations, and defenses to proprietary rights" as the "holes in the cheese of intellectual property," emphasizing that these holes were as important as the cheese itself (Boyle 2008, 67).

Boyle (2008) thus identified the importance of understanding the limitations on intellectual property law, since those were the places where freedoms were protected in a context where firms attempted to exert proprietary control. In the U.S., such struggles between proponents of the proprietary and freedom discourses arose over the DMCA. Content companies in the music and film industries wanted to secure the safety of their copyrighted property. They argued that the digital form of their property, combined with the Internet as a global communications infrastructure to exchange digital files, made their property vulnerable to users who would access it without paying for it and perhaps share it with others. They wanted to strengthen copyright law to punish those users. They went a crucial step further, however, seeking to extend copyright law to make it illegal to circumvent measures designed to protect the product by denying access to it or limiting what users could do once they had accessed it. Such "anticircumvention" measures included encryption and other digital rights management (DRM) provisions that limited whether files could be played on a particular machine, whether they could be copied, and more. The major change introduced with the DMCA was that it became *illegal to circumvent copyright protection systems*, even if users accessed the copyrighted digital content for purposes considered fair use under existing copyright law. As Boyle (2008, 95) argued, "in passing the DMCA, Congress had created a new intellectual property right inside copyright law itself." This new intellectual property right granted copyright owners "exclusive rights but *without* some of those limitations [of fair use]" (Boyle 2008, 96, emphasis in original). Practices of fair use, which had always been central to copyright law, were thus disrupted in the increasingly important sector of digital content.

This new right over intellectual property favored the interests of content providers in the music and film sectors. Simultaneously, however, the DMCA created problems for a second set of corporate interests, including hardware manufacturers, software firms, and telecommunications companies such as Internet Service Providers (ISPs). Corporations in these latter sectors pressured the U.S. government to mitigate the DMCA's negative effects on their business operations. For example, ISPs secured a qualified immunity for any cases of copyright infringement that occurred using their networks (Boyle 2008). They could thus not be held liable if users of their networks engaged in illegal activities that violated copyright. In contrast with these protections for ISPs and other telecommunications firms, software and computer firms did not lobby as strongly to protect their interests from the changes introduced by the DMCA. Benkler (2006, 414) thus described the DMCA as "an almost unqualified victory for Hollywood" over Silicon Valley.

Free software proponents were gravely concerned about the DMCA. Groups like the FSF and the Electronic Frontier Foundation (EFF) called attention to the dangers it posed for free software users, developers, and communities. As will be discussed further in the next chapter, the DMCA has had significant implications for free software communities since its passage. Benkler (2006, 413) highlighted the importance of these implications, arguing that "[n]o piece of legislation more clearly represents the battle over the institutional ecology of the digital environment than the...DMCA." Furthermore, he illuminated the costs of such legislation for new producers of digital culture that seek to remix and share parts of movies, music, and photography, building upon these earlier sources of cultural material to create new cultural products. Benkler (2006, 418) argued,

> [p]reserving the capacity of industrial cultural producers to maintain a hermetic seal on the use of materials to which they own copyright can be bought only at the cost of disabling the newly emerging modes of cultural production from quoting and directly building upon much of the culture of the last century.

Benkler (2006) did not identify the implications for free software specifically in this argument; however, the costs he warned about include threats to the legality of free software, as well as to the ability for free software communities to do their work. By seeking to institute the proprietary discourse over digital content, the DMCA threatened free software as a global community.

European Struggles over Intellectual Property and Free Software

In May 2001, three years after the DMCA was passed in the U.S., similar struggles over intellectual property rights emerged in Europe. The French free software community faced pressures from neoliberal globalization when the European Union Copyright Directive (EUCD) was published (CANDIDATS.FR 2007). As had happened in the U.S., transnational corporations from the music and film industries sought to protect the rights to their digital content by imposing restrictions on users of that content, as well as on the process of accessing and sharing that content over the Internet. These firms promoted the EUCD as a policy vehicle toward those ends. Similar to the DMCA, proponents of the EUCD sought to bring European policy into compliance with provisions of the

WIPO Copyright Treaty ratified in 1996. Moreover, like the DMCA, the EUCD exemplified the proprietary discourse, framing access to the Internet and software in terms of protecting the proprietary interests of corporations that have a legal right to defend their investments.

The publication of the EUCD sparked a second phase of political struggle to build the French free software community as part of a broader global community of resistance. April activists viewed the EUCD as a major threat to their work and mobilized to oppose it. They focused on developing their relationship with other free software activists across Europe, as well as emphasizing this broader struggle to defend free software in their local public education efforts. In the process, they provided local resistance to a global effort to assert the dominance of propriety ownership over digital content, which had key implications for software and the broader digital commons.

At this critical juncture, April activists thus shifted into a new terrain and scale of organizing. They extended their struggles to the broader European level by collaborating with individuals and associations from other countries, supporting the development of the global free software community of resistance. Furthermore, in addition to working to educate people about free software, they fought to pressure the French government and the European Union to protect the legal conditions to use it. Couchet (interview 2010) described this turning point: "It was necessary to act. This was really our first big project. We sent e-mails, we told people there were negative impacts for free software. [...] We did activities to get everyone to promote free software but also activities to defend it." The activists thus recognized the importance of simultaneously pursuing the interrelated goals of promoting and defending free software. They shifted their perspective, creating a moment of transition in the development of a global community of resistance. Under the political conditions in Europe and the U.S., where powerful corporate interests were promoting legal changes that jeopardized the prospects for using free software, defending users' rights to access it was crucial.

Hence, during this period, April activists transformed and clarified their role in French software politics, as well as in software politics across Europe. They engaged in a process of constructing and diffusing the freedom discourse as a narrative of power and knowledge within the French and larger European contexts. Within this discourse, they employed a language of struggle to emphasize the importance of defending free software as a new form of property against legislative efforts that would, in effect, mandate proprietary software. From 2001 to 2005, they targeted the European legal arena, sustaining the struggle against the EUCD as well as software patents (Karonović 2008, 2010).

By the end of that period, in early December 2005, activists escalated their struggles to promote the freedom discourse in the face of neoliberal pressures. They responded to a watershed moment, when French legislators proposed the bill "Copyright and Related Rights in the Information Society" (DADVSI). Proponents of DADVSI sought to institute the proprietary discourse by reforming French copyright law. They designed it to implement the principles of the EUCD in the French context, while also considerably extending them. The proposal of DADVSI thus brought the conflicts between the proprietary and freedom discourses to a head, creating a terrain of struggle where April drew upon its network of relationships with the broader European community of resistance to strengthen its organizing within France.

At a discussion forum in Paris a few days after the DADVSI bill was introduced, the French and broader European "militants of code" (Couture and Proulx 2008) collaborated in their struggle against the proprietary discourse. April and EUCD.INFO participated in this forum on "Copyright in the Digital Era." In his presentation at the forum, Christophe Espern, one of the cofounders of EUCD.INFO, highlighted the effects of the DADVSI bill for the rights of artists, composers, and producers (Espern 2005). The bill provided juridical protection for devices that monitored and traced Internet use. Such protections posed serious implications for artists and other producers of cultural content, as well as for consumers of that content. If passed, the DADVSI bill threatened to criminalize many commonplace activities, such as downloading music and copying CDs.

Particularly important for April and other free software activists, the DADVSI bill threatened to undermine the activities of free software users and developers. By protecting monitoring and tracking devices based upon a logic of secrecy, DADVSI effectively denied users the right to choose free software. In fact, such tracking devices made it impossible to use free software systems based upon a logic of transparency and freedom to share among users. For example, the DADVSI bill made it illegal to play DVDs with software not authorized by the DVD producer, or to use software that made it possible to circumvent copy protection. Similar to concerns over the DMCA, this "anticircumvention" measure was especially worrisome to free software proponents. They knew that this measure could apply to a wide range of popular software programs, including operating systems that could potentially be modified to circumvent copy protection even if they were not initially designed to do so. Any developer of such a software system might thus be targeted as liable for copyright infringement. Hence, DADVSI identified everyone who bypassed a monitoring or tracking device as infringing copyright. Those who made files available for downloading illegally would be subject to fines of up to €150, while those who simply engaged in illegal downloads would be subject to fines of €38. Producers and distributors of software that allowed such practices would face the stiffest penalties, including up to three years in prison or a fine of €300,000. DADVSI supporters thus sought to institutionalize the proprietary discourse by imposing DRM on all software users and to criminalize both the production and use of software programs that allowed users to circumvent copy protections (Espern 2005; Paul 2005; Bangeman 2006a,b).

In his presentation at the forum, Espern (2005) highlighted the conflict between the ways that the freedom and proprietary discourses understood the rights involved with consuming commodities in digital form. From the perspective of the freedom discourse, he explained, "when you buy a CD, you have every right to copy it. With these technical mechanisms [in the DADVSI bill], you cannot do this. It poses a problem in terms of innovation, in terms of free trade." For individual users, these problems were rooted in the fact that the monitoring and tracking software made it not only technically impossible, but illegal, for them to use free software to search out solutions to their problems with software programs. Their freedom to choose whatever form of software they wanted was restricted to protect corporations' proprietary interests. For small firms, it made them "hesitant to innovate...hesitant to compete with the big firms and try to destabilize them" (Espern 2005). Such firms were wary of competing with large companies that employed teams of lawyers who could initiate legal action against competitors on the grounds of violating DADVSI.

Hence, the DADVSI bill was extremely controversial. It sparked opposition from groups that rarely agreed on issues of software politics, including the FSF and the Business Software Alliance (BSA). The BSA's members included major U.S. software firms like Microsoft, Apple, Intel, HP, and IBM. The BSA generally worked to promote copyright protection and combat what it viewed as problems of software piracy. In the case of DADVSI, however, the measures intended to protect copyright had serious implications for proprietary software companies whose systems could be judged as contributing to copyright violation (Paul 2005).

Specific amendments to the DADVSI bill were especially problematic for free software proponents. The authors of these amendments sought to impose unprecedented forms of DRM. The amendments required suppliers of electronics equipment or software to include technical measures to prevent users from copying and redistributing digital content or software programs. Free software users and developers would thus be presumed guilty of violating the law, since their software would not include such provisions (Espern 2005). The FSF viewed this as an effort by French media corporations to force free software developers to adopt proprietary licenses. These corporations enjoyed the support of the French *Societé des Auteurs, Compositeurs et Editeurs de Musique* (SACEM), or Society of Authors, Composers and Producers of Music, which played a similar role in France as the Recording Industry Association of America (RIAA) in the U.S. A SACEM representative stated that the organization supported an amendment to the DADVSI bill that, if passed, would allow them "'to sue free software authors who will keep on publishing source code'" (FSF France 2005). A representative from the French Ministry of Culture added that free software authors would be required to change their licenses.

Days after DADVSI was published in December 2005, free software activists from France and other parts of Europe extended their combined struggle against these efforts to criminalize their community form of property. The free software community of resistance participated fully when EUCD.INFO launched a campaign, "No to the DADVSI bill." EUCD.INFO and April collaborated to argue that DADVSI favored transnational corporations and virtually ignored developers and users of free software, Internet users in general, librarians, artists, and consumer associations. In organizing against DADVSI, these activists stressed the importance of including this broader range of interests in discussions about the bill. They initiated a campaign to gather signatures on a petition demanding that these groups be allowed to participate in a substantive discussion of the bill's implications. By August 2006, the activists had gathered 173,628 individual signatures. Moreover, almost 1,000 organizations signed the petition, including 230 businesses whose activities were threatened by the bill (EUCD.INFO 2005; Espern 2005).

Despite these efforts, French lawmakers signed the DADVSI bill into law on August 3, 2006 (April 2009). Like their counterparts in the U.S. who organized against the DMCA, French and other European free software activists were thus unsuccessful at stopping what they viewed as harmful legislation from becoming law. April activists continued their organizing work over the years, however, employing the freedom discourse to fight for software freedom as it applied to policy issues such as software patents, copyright, and conditions for Internet access. They learned from their defeats and continued to develop the global free software community of resistance.

For decades, April activists built this community of resistance by defending software freedom in the face of neoliberal pressures to promote proprietary interests. In the process, they struggled over software as a vital productive force in informational capitalism. Free software activists' battles to prioritize free software challenged corporate control over proprietary software, in the process of constructing political conditions for the integration of software in economic, political, social, and cultural life. Almost 10 years after the DADVSI defeat and 20 years after April was founded, Frédéric Couchet continued as Executive Director. Reflecting back on April's history of work in a 2016 interview, Couchet emphasized that April consistently sought to do "public affairs activism," raising awareness about free software among the general public and encouraging them to give priority to using free software as a "cornerstone for a free society" (Couchet, interview 2016).

This public affairs activism involved educational work to empower individual users to grasp the significance of free software and to make

choices to use it to the greatest extent possible, even if they also continued to use proprietary hardware and software systems. Hence, during
the third phase of April's work after 2010, activists focused on educating
consumers about the implications of their choices about which software
systems to use. From a free software perspective, April activists promoted the rights of consumers to use whatever software they chose to
access content on their devices. As discussed above, DRM systems restricted these choices by making devices incompatible with free software.
Moreover, the activists wanted consumers to be aware of the subtle ways
that the digital technologies they used every day employed DRM systems
that affected their freedoms. For example, when consumers activated the
GPS tracking devices on their cell phones or tablets, or agreed to have
location data sent to applications such as weather and social media, they
made it possible to collect data that could eventually be accessed by corporations and governments. In a 2014 interview, Cerise Angier, an April
staff member, noted that the general culture of consuming digital technologies encouraged consumers to be passive users of these technologies,
rather than asserting control over them. As will be discussed further
in the next chapter, in 2013, the dangers of this more passive kind of
consumer approach were highlighted by Edward Snowden's revelations
about U.S. government surveillance. Angier (interview 2014) described
these revelations as "a shock for us all," since the activists had not realized the full extent of that surveillance. Hence, Snowden's revelations
changed the conditions for April's work, illuminating the potential impact of surveillance on the lives of consumers and citizens.

Promoting the empowerment of individual consumers of digital technologies was thus an important aspect of April's work during this third
phase of organizing. If successful, this work had the potential to involve
consumers in the global free software community of resistance. Couchet
(interview 2016) emphasized, however, that individual empowerment
was not enough. Thus, April activists worked simultaneously on what
Couchet called the individual and political levels, since the political level
was where they could make more institutional changes.

April and other free software advocates faced powerful corporate interests, including lobbying campaigns by Microsoft and Apple with extensive financial backing. For example, in a press release on its website in
December 2015, April reported that Microsoft signed a 13 million Euro
agreement with the French Ministry of Education. Under the agreement,
Microsoft would provide software and services to schools across France.
The agreement allowed Microsoft to provide its services to schools
for free, while other firms had been required to bill for such services.
Microsoft thus gained special access to French students and teachers,
who would be trained in using Microsoft systems such as the Microsoft
Cloud ecosystem and e-learning platform. In the process of becoming
familiar with these systems, the students and teachers could potentially

become ongoing Microsoft customers (Chausson 2016). April and 21 other organizations signed a statement condemning the agreement for "present[ing] proprietary software and closed formats to students as indispensable tools, thus advocating dependence as a model. This will strengthen the U.S. company's dominant position to the detriment of free software and open formats" (accessed June 27, 2017. http://www.april.org/en/partnership-microsoft-unworthy-values-french-national-education-advocates).

These organizations thus struggled to resist Microsoft's strategy to extend proprietary control over software through the French schools.

Couchet's (interview 2016) emphasis on the importance of working on both the individual and political levels resonates with Vaccari, Chadwick, and O'Loughlin's (2015) conception of multidimensional political engagement. These authors distinguish discursive forms of political engagement, where people talk about public affairs in both formal and informal settings, from partisan forms where they work explicitly to influence or support particular political candidates or parties. Furthermore, civic forms of political engagement focus on community efforts to collaborate in solving common problems (Vaccari, Chadwick and O'Loughlin 2015).

In fact, April's efforts to raise awareness about free software among French citizens and politicians combined discursive, partisan, and civic forms of political engagement. Much of their work was multidimensional, since most of their partisan work to influence politicians took discursive forms. For example, April activists often explained the importance of free software and advocated for particular policies that would promote its development and use. For April activists, this was quintessentially civic work as well, since they viewed free software as central to broader societal freedoms that affected the common good.

After two decades of such efforts, Couchet (interview 2016) noted that these multidimensional forms of political engagement were affecting the political climate around free software. French politicians slowly became more knowledgable about free software itself, as well as about its broader social significance. As a result, politicians from a broader range of political parties began to express support for free software. In the past, Socialists and other progressive politicians had been the main proponents of such positions. In April 2016, however, in what Couchet (interview 2016) viewed as a significant shift, French Senator Joëlle Garriaud-Maylam, of the right wing Republican party, proposed an amendment to promote free software and open formats (accessed July 3, 2017. http://www.senat.fr/amendements/2015-2016/535/Amdt_393.html). This was the first time that a right wing politician had proposed such an amendment. Members of this party had supported measures giving priority to free software in the past; however, they had never taken the initiative to present one. Senator Garriaud-Maylam's proposal of this amendment built upon her earlier question to the French government in 2014. At that time, she submitted a formal question in writing, challenging the Ministry of Defense's partnership with Microsoft while emphasizing the benefits of free software (accessed July 3, 2017. https://april.org/question-ecrite-de-joelle-garriaud-maylam-sur-laccord-open-bar-microsoftdefense).

Based upon these kinds of changes in the political sphere, Couchet (interview 2016) perceived a historical dynamic at work. He identified a long-term process of change, moving toward the use of free software as the wave of the future. While this dynamic of transformation was "a question of time," Couchet (interview 2016) described April's work as fomenting this wave. By continuing to contribute to the rise of this wave, April pushed for this historical movement toward free software to arrive as soon as possible.

Software Politics in the French "Digital Republic"

In late 2014, April engaged in a major effort to promote this movement toward the fuller use of free software in France. The activists responded to French Prime Minister Manuel Valls' call for citizens to participate in developing legislation that eventually became the Digital Republic bill. Over a six-month period, the government encouraged citizens to engage in an online consultation to develop the bill. Citizens were invited to submit proposals to be included in the bill, as well as to comment and vote on the proposals of others. In September 2015, the government launched a three-week online consultation on the Digital Republic bill, promoting citizen involvement in crafting the legislation before it was submitted to the *Conseil d'Etat*, the French Supreme Administrative Court. Toward this end, the government created a website with detailed information about the bill, including English translations of many of the bill's main features. I will refer to this as the Digital Republic website. This website provided a platform where anyone who was interested could learn about the bill, submit a proposal, vote to support, or leave comments about existing proposals.

The French government encouraged citizen participation by outlining some clear guidelines for how the participation process would be organized, as well as incentives for helping to choose which proposals would be taken most seriously. It committed itself to respond to the suggestions that were the most popular among participants in the commentary process on the Digital Republic bill. The government promised that the proponents of the three most popular proposals would have the opportunity to meet with Minister of State for Digital Affairs Axelle Lemaire to explain their ideas more fully. This process of digital politics was thus rooted in efforts to promote dialogue between citizens and the government, as well as among citizens themselves, concerning policy questions of how to integrate digital technologies into French political and social life. It was a case of multidimensional political engagement (Vaccari, Chadwick and O'Loughlin 2015), combining discursive conversations about civic questions concerning the contemporary role of digital technologies, as well as partisan activities designed to influence the government's policy decisions regarding those questions.

The public consultation period opened on September 26 and extended until October 18 of 2015. This period was long enough for citizens to register their opinions several times if they chose. Once the consultation period was complete, the government posted the results for the 10 proposals that received the most votes on the Digital Republic website. These results included the total number of votes received; an explanation of the proposal by its sponsor; arguments for and against the proposal made by participants in the consultation, including a tally of people who posted that they agreed with the arguments; and a response by the government. According to the Digital Republic website, 21,411 contributors participated in this process, casting 147,709 votes pertaining to 8,501 amendments, proposals, and arguments (accessed February 7, 2016. https://www.republique-numerique.fr/consultation/projet-de-loi-numerique/ranking/reponses-du-gouvernement/opinions).

April was a key contributor to that process. Indeed, the activists organized themselves to submit and sponsor two proposals that won strong support from citizens who provided feedback on the Digital Republic website. As will be detailed below, April's proposals came in third and seventh place among the top 10 proposals by the end of the consultation period. The activists, and the citizens offering their feedback, engaged in discursive processes of political engagement (Vaccari, Chadwick and O'Loughlin 2015). The French public radio service *Radio France Internationale (RFI)* quoted Prime Minister Valls' statement about this innovative political process: "'[w]e are opening a new page in the history of our democracy because this is the first time in our country and in Europe that a draft law has been opened up to contributions by citizens'" (accessed July 3, 2017. http://www.english.rfi.fr/culture/20150927-france-opens-online-consultation-draft-digital-republic-law). Political engagement in the process of developing the Digital Republic bill was thus multidimensional, merging discursive and civic forms as participants collaborated in the effort to address a common societal concern about the role of digital technologies in contemporary social life. Such engagement was not partisan in the sense that it promoted the interests of a particular candidate or party; however, it did involve responding to an effort by the government to evoke citizen feedback.

The French government's use of an online format in this process of eliciting citizen participation resonated with Vaccari's (2013, vii) work on what he called "digital politics," where "the internet has become a crucial platform for political interaction between citizens and the parties and candidates that court them." In calling for citizen participation in shaping the Digital Republic bill, and especially by employing the Internet as a vehicle for citizen involvement, the French government engaged in the kind of digital politics that Vaccari (2013) identified. This French case of digital politics goes further than Vaccari's (2013) conception, however, by promoting a particular understanding of the importance of digital technologies in contemporary society. Indeed, the French government raised substantive questions about how these technologies should be integrated into French policy measures. I thus employ a perspective on digital politics that integrates Vaccari's (2013) emphasis on the *process* of citizen interaction via the Internet with an analysis of the *substantive content* of political discourse over the role of digital technologies in contemporary political and social life.

April activists viewed the Digital Republic bill as an opportunity to extend its public education work about the importance of free software. They approached these broader processes of digital politics as a terrain of struggle over software politics. Other participants in the public consultation about the Digital Republic shared April's concerns about free software. In fact, participants from France and other parts of the world expressed strong support for free software, Internet neutrality, and the digital commons. Free software proponents thus seized the Digital Republic bill as an opportunity to engage in more traditional forms of "offline" political action, as well as "online" forms. The open nature of the process of developing the bill resonated clearly with the values of free software communities to invite sharing and collaboration in the development of the software, as well as the community itself.

In a 2016 interview, Pierre Baudin, an April staff member, highlighted the importance of values of freedom in the process of developing the Digital Republic bill. He noted that questions involved with the Digital Republic bill were often

> technical, it's sometimes very complex, but in the end it's just about freedoms. It's not so complicated. Freedom of speech is freedom of speech, whether it be in the digital sphere or just in the streets or talking with friends. It's the same freedom of speech we're defending.
> (Baudin, interview 2016)

Baudin (interview 2016) thus emphasized that from the perspective of April activists, what was most important in their work on the Digital Republic bill, as in their history of work on free software, was to focus on defending values of software freedom and their connection to broader societal freedoms.

Participants in the online consultation process for the Digital Republic bill shared this emphasis on freedom. Of the 10 proposals receiving the most votes, four were explicitly related to free software. An additional

3 of the top 10 proposals were focused on net neutrality; as will be discussed further in the following chapter, these questions of net neutrality were also integrally related to free software.

Among the four top proposals explicitly related to free software, Jonathan Crequer's proposal to use free software and GNU/Linux in schools and universities garnered the most votes. Crequer was a free software supporter who submitted his proposal as a private citizen. His proposal was the second most popular among all of the proposals offered, with 2,666 votes. In Crequer's explanation of the proposal on the Digital Republic website, he noted that Microsoft had long been aware of the importance of having young people learn to use its software. Use of certain software in schools creates an environment where young users become familiar and comfortable with those programs. Crequer's proposal sought an alternative to conditioning students to use proprietary systems, by promoting the use of free software. According to the proposal, encouraging students to use free software in their school projects would provide better protection of personal data, as well as fostering practices of sharing and transparency. Once the voting was complete, the French government posted a response to the proposal on the Digital Republic website, stating that it fit well with an article of a law on higher education and research passed in 2013. This law gave priority to the use of free software in higher education (accessed February 2, 2016. https://www.republique-numerique.fr/projects/projet-de-loi-numerique/consultation/consultation/opinions/section-2-service-public-de-la-donnee-1/utiliser-les-logiciels-libres-gnu-linux-dans-les-ecoles-et-les-universites).

On a more general level, Crequer's proposal resonated with the government's expression of support for the use of free software, particularly in a 2012 document issued by Prime Minister Ayrault calling for the state to promote the use of free software in public information systems (Direction Interministerielle des Systemes d'Information et de Communication (DISIC) 2012).

The government's response to two other Digital Republic proposals sponsored by April, however, revealed significant limits to its support for free software.

For example, April proposed to prioritize free software and open document formats in local and national public service. Similar to the Brazilian policy strategy discussed in the last chapter, this proposal sought to mobilize the government's substantial use of software in public agencies to promote the broader procurement of free software. Since the government was a major user of software, giving priority to free software systems would strengthen the market and extend the customer base for those systems. This proposal garnered substantial public support, coming in third place in the participant feedback on the Digital Republic bill, with 2,327 votes. In its explanation of the proposal on the Digital Republic website, April noted that free software and open formats shared the same goals of ensuring that users retain control over their data, in addition to promoting possibilities to share and redistribute data that are central to technological independence (accessed February 5, 2016. https://www.republique-numerique.fr/projects/projet-de-loi-numerique/consultation/consultation/opinions/section-3-loyaute-des-plateformes/donner-la-priorite-aux-logiciels-libres-et-aux-formats-ouverts-dans-le-service-public-national-et-local).

Despite the apparent fit between April's proposal and French government goals to promote the use of free software in public information systems, the government raised objections in its response to the proposal on the Digital Republic website. With regard to April's proposal to prioritize free software and open formats in local and national public service, the government framed its concerns in constitutional terms. It stated that it was necessary for that proposal to articulate with the principle of free administration of territorial communities in article 72 of the French constitution. It cautioned that April's proposal could undermine this principle and impose unduly heavy burdens on communities, especially if the use of new free software systems required retraining of their personnel. The government thus did not support this proposal, viewing it as potentially undermining the freedom of public agencies to choose to continue using proprietary systems. In addition to raising this concern, however, the government emphasized its general support for free software. It noted changes in laws regarding public education that foresaw that the decision about choices of resources should take free software and open document formats into account, if they were available. In a similar vein, the government highlighted an article in the same law that called for public service and higher education to provide digital pedagogical resources, and in particular, to give priority to free software (accessed January 25, 2016. https://www.republique-numerique.fr/projects/projet-de-loi-numerique/consultation/consultation/opinions/section-3-loyaute-des-plateformes/donner-la-priorite-aux-logiciels-libres-et-aux-formats-ouverts-dans-le-service-public-national-et-local).

April's second proposal to the Digital Republic bill raised further controversial issues concerning government support for free software. The proposal stated that "software source code is an administrative document that can be shared with the public" (accessed January 25, 2016. https://www.republique-numerique.fr/projects/projet-de-loi-numerique/consultation/consultation/opinions/section-1-ouverture-des-donnees-publiques-1/le-code-source-d-un-logiciel-est-un-document-administratif-communicable). It was ranked seventh in terms of citizen response on the Digital Republic website, garnering 1,857 votes. According to April's website describing key elements of the bill, April designed this proposal to uphold the jurisdiction of the Committee for Access to Administrative Documents (CADA) "without creating new obligations for administrations" (accessed January 25, 2016. http://www.april.org/en/

french-digital-republic-public-consultation-towards-citizens-first-software-society/). An explanatory memo about the Digital Republic bill noted that CADA was established in 1978 to oversee citizens' rights to access such documents, and its purview had been extended through amendments (accessed January 25, 2016. https://www.republique-numerique.fr/pages/digital-republic-bill-rationale). April highlighted the importance of this proposal, noting that the Public Finance General Directorate (DGFiP) had not complied with CADA's request to provide the source code for the software for income tax calculations (accessed January 26, 2016. http://www.april.org/en/french-digital-republic-public-consultation-towards-citizens-first-software-society).

In its explanation of the proposal on the Digital Republic website, April stated that government operations are regulated by laws that are increasingly complex. Public administrators are already using software to interpret these laws and will rely on such programs increasingly in the future. In the process, these administrators use algorithms to define the application of the law in cases such as the calculation of taxes or social security benefits. Such algorithms are written by experts; however, they may end up being applied in different ways than their creators had originally conceived. In these circumstances, only the experts in particular fields understand the specialized ways that these algorithms are actually applied in practice. Access to the source code of these kinds of software programs provides transparency for citizens, as well as government administrators, to understand the processes being used for fiscal and other applications. Such transparency would make it easier for citizens or administrators to question these processes if they noticed problems; it would allow more control over the way that the law was interpreted, facilitating decisions about the best way to apply it (accessed February 1, 2016. https://www.republique-numerique.fr/projects/projet-de-loi-numerique/consultation/consultation/opinions/section-1-ouverture-des-donnees-publiques-1/le-code-source-d-un-logiciel-est-un-document-administratif-communicable).

Similar to its response to April's first proposal to the Digital Republic bill, the French government responded to this proposal by raising legal concerns. In its response to the proposal on the Digital Republic website, it disagreed that legislative alterations were needed to affirm that software source code be considered an administrative document to be shared with the public. It cited CADA's ruling in January 2015 to support its position. CADA ruled that since software source code contains instructions to be executed by a computer, then the files constituting the source code are products of the general management of public finances within the context of its mission of public service. Under such circumstances, those source code files take on the importance of administrative documents and are free to be reused and shared. In addition, article 2 of the Digital Republic bill creates a right of access to the rules for the treatment of algorithms used in public administration, when their processing affects individual decisions.

Free software proponents supported a fourth proposal to the Digital Republic bill, sponsored by an individual citizen with a handle evoking Star Wars, Obi Wan Kenobi. Obi Wan proposed to end the forced sale of software with computer hardware, what is often called bundling. This proposal came in 10th place in terms of numbers of votes, with 1,754 supporters. In his explanation of the proposal, Obi Wan emphasized that in the digital age, it is important for citizens to have the freedom to choose their operating systems. Free software allows for such freedom, providing the opportunity for computer users to break their dependence on proprietary software companies. From this perspective, Microsoft's practices of bundling the Windows operating system with personal computers undermine competition. Obi Wan argued that consumers deserve to know the price of materials, and particularly the price of the licenses, before they buy. They should be free not to buy things that they do not want. Thus, if consumers want to use the Windows operating system, they can pay for it separately rather than having it bundled automatically with hardware systems. Such an arrangement would allow for transparency in pricing, since software and hardware would be sold separately, with clear prices for each (accessed February 5, 2016. https://www.republique-numerique.fr/projects/projet-de-loi-numerique/ consultation/consultation/opinions/section-3-loyaute-des-plateformes/ interdiction-de-la-vente-liee-ordinateur-systeme-d-exploitation).

Similar to the other proposals by free software supporters, the French government raised legal objections to this proposal in its response on the Digital Republic website. It argued that the proposal conflicted with the European Union's Code of Consumption, which categorized a ban on bundled sales of software and hardware as an unfair practice. Under this Code, it was not possible to prohibit such sales in a general way. Such regulations fell under the purview of the European directive concerning unfair trade practices.

Throughout the public consultation period, citizens and other interested parties contributed to the process of adding new articles and amendments to the Digital Republic bill. Once the public consultation period ended in October 2015, the draft law was approved by the government cabinet and forwarded to the National Assembly; at the Assembly, it was examined at the committee level in mid-December. In January 2016, it went to the full National Assembly before going to the Senate that spring.

The Digital Republic bill thus continued to be a terrain of struggle over software politics. Proponents of free software engaged in debates with the government as part of the process of promoting the digital commons where all citizens would have access to software programs and a range of different kinds of data. Baudin (interview 2016) was one of the

April staff members engaged in this process and attending the parliamentary hearings about the Digital Republic bill. He noted that as the government sought to resist the proposal to treat software source code as an administrative document that can be shared with the public, it introduced an exception to allow denial of such a request if providing access to the source code would endanger an administration's information system. Free software proponents objected to this exception, arguing that French law already allowed for exceptions to be made if questions of national security were at stake. If an organization could make a case that providing access to software source code as an administrative document would endanger national security, they thus had legal grounds to deny access to the code under those conditions.

Baudin (interview 2016) emphasized that adding exceptions such as the one advocated by the government would have weakened the Digital Republic bill, since it would not offer clear criteria for a judge to decide when it would be legitimate to deny access to software source code. Nonetheless, this exception was passed in the Senate. In the end, free software advocates won a victory on the general issue of defining software source code as an administrative document that can be shared with the public, when the National Assembly passed this amendment in January 2016. Despite this general victory, however, the French government succeeded in including the exception for administrations that could show that providing such access would endanger their information systems.

Political struggles intensified in debates over the amendment explicitly designed to promote the use of free software. There was an extensive debate about whether to support April's proposal to give priority to free software in the public sector, as described in April's press release about the proceedings on its website (accessed July 5, 2016. http://www.april. org/marathon-en-faveur-du-logiciel-libre-mais-le-manque-dambition-encore-prevalu). Supporters of the proposal argued that it would provide a strong legal foundation to support the use of free software, even though it did not absolutely require its use. A provision requiring organizations to give priority to free software would mean that organizations needed to consider whether there were free software systems available that met their needs.

As Baudin explained (interview 2016), April activists viewed free software as giving organizational administrations power "over their systems, to give them independence for procurement" so they would not depend on proprietary firms. If free software systems were not available, organizations would be free to choose proprietary systems. If free software was available, however, and the organization did not choose to use it, there would be a legal basis to challenge that decision. Free software proponents would thus have legal grounds to contest decisions not to give priority to free software. Judges would be able to evaluate whether organizations had considered free software options, and whether such options were in fact available, before making their decisions about which programs to employ (Baudin interview 2016).

On the other side of the debate, other members of parliament argued that it was preferable to promote the use of free software by simply encouraging its use. They viewed the proposal to give priority to free software as creating problems for competition. Moreover, they critiqued the idea of requiring the government to prioritize one technology over another.

The debate in the National Assembly and the Senate thus focused on whether it was better to encourage the use of free software or to give it priority. As Baudin (interview 2016) described, first in the National Assembly and then in the Senate, there were "long and rich debates" grounded in a general acceptance of the importance of promoting the use of free software. From witnessing these debates, Baudin sensed that there was a real movement toward the acceptance of the importance and benefits of free software. He noted, "[s]ometimes those promoting encouragement might as well have been saying to give priority" (Baudin interview 2016). These debates thus centered on the details of which word – encouragement or priority – would most fully support the generally accepted goal of promoting free software. There were no voices speaking up against the use of free software itself or the broader policy goal of fostering its adoption. On the whole, proponents of the idea of encouragement, including Minister for Digital Affairs Lemaire, viewed it as a good compromise position between free software proponents like April and those who questioned whether giving priority might hinder competition and technological choice. In the end, parliamentary delegates sided with the government to reject the amendment seeking to give priority to free software in the public sector. Instead, they passed an amendment to simply encourage the use of free software.

April activists, as well as other free software proponents, viewed this as a halfway measure that failed to give a sound legal foundation to promote the use of free software. Couchet (interview 2016) noted that encouragement is not particularly effective, since there are no clear criteria to judge whether organizations are complying with it. As noted above, if organizations are required to give priority to free software but instead choose proprietary systems, "you have to explain why, you have to start a process to switch to free software as soon as possible" (Couchet interview 2016). As a policy guideline, giving priority means that there is a process for software procurement where organizations research the programs that are available and have criteria for choosing between them. As the process of developing the Digital Republic bill continued, before the bill became enacted into law, April sought to include a decree to delineate how the law would be put into practice. They viewed the most well-balanced and effective laws as those including such decrees (Couchet interview 2016).

From the perspective of April activists, the process of developing the Digital Republic bill was fraught. Citizen response to the proposals involving free software revealed substantial public interest and support for April's goals of promoting and defending free software. In response, however, the government raised objections that slowed the movement toward those goals. Struggles over whether to prioritize the use of free software revealed both the progress toward those goals, as well as the challenges to what April activists viewed as the most effective strategy for implementing them.

The activists highlighted key ways that the development of the Digital Republic bill revealed the contradictory nature of citizen engagement in France. The French government articulated one perspective, emphasizing the historic value of encouraging input from citizens into the policy making process. It thus presented the bill as a way of employing digital communication to usher in new forms of citizen participation in the democratic process. In response, April staff member Baudin critiqued the government position. He argued that the government liked to say that the Digital Republic bill was a "co-written law, written with the citizens"; however, the government was not obligated to follow the results of the consultation process. He stated, "'don't come and say you have written [the Digital Republic bill] with us when you have pushed aside eighty percent [of the consultation feedback]'" (Baudin interview 2016). Indeed, the government chose not to follow much of the feedback it got from citizens during the consultation process. As noted above, it raised a range of objections to many of the proposals, and particularly to the key measure to prioritize the use of free software in public procurement. Moreover, Couchet (interview 2016) offered another interpretation of the Digital Republic bill and its implications for citizen engagement. Since France does not have a system of direct democracy where citizens write their own laws, Couchet (interview 2016) emphasized that "[i]t was just a consultation. [The government] cannot say it was a co-written law. But that was not the goal, in fact. The goal was to get input."

In the context of these contradictory conditions and possibilities for citizen engagement, April activists continued their work. They viewed the Digital Republic bill as another opportunity to shape the political conditions for the development and deployment of free software. They viewed the above conflicts over the Digital Republic bill as one part of their decades-long struggle to promote and defend free software. By organizing around the bill and the other phases of work discussed above, April activists built their local French free software community as part of a broader global community of resistance.

Conclusion: The Global Community of Resistance as Globalization from Below

The French free software case poses lessons to understand the prospects for building a global community of resistance that constitutes an alternative form of globalization from below. April activists made a major contribution to constructing such an alternative. They began by collaborating with the FSF to build a free software community in France. They drew upon the freedom discourse to formulate their mission as promoting and defending free software. April's collaboration with the FSF highlights how globalization may involve "powerful imaginaries enabling aspirations to transboundary political practice" (Sassen 2005, 75), even when the actors are rooted in a particular local context. This was the case for Couchet and the other activists that founded April. The FSF's work caught their imaginations and provided a model for what was possible; however, April activists put those ideas into practice in unique ways adapted to the French context. They articulated the freedom discourse to illuminate the interests at stake in both promoting and defending free software. They employed that discourse to build a global community of resistance linked to free software advocates in the U.S. and other parts of Europe. This community constituted an alternative form of globalization from below that explicitly resisted the dynamics of neoliberalism, where corporations and governments sought to extend the market for proprietary software.

European struggles resonated with free software proponents' efforts to oppose the DMCA in the U.S. April activists thus waged local struggles in France that connected them to free software activists across Europe, as well as in the U.S. These activists defended free software as a community-based form of property that contributes to the digital commons. They engaged in a process that Sassen (2005, 55) described as "localized entities becom[ing] microenvironments with global span." Through this process, French activists became conscious of "the recurrence of these types of actions in locality after locality, thereby contributing to the reshaping of these global networks for communication into global zones for interactivity" (Sassen 2005, 55). They experienced this process as they forged international alliances to fight for software freedom.

French software politics thus provide lessons to understand activist strategies to create a global community of resistance. By building this community, activists constructed an alternative form of globalization from below. The process of forging this global community involved transboundary political practice. Activists in France and across Europe, as well as in the U.S., articulated a common freedom discourse. They united in their commitment to promote and defend free software. They engaged in a process of political struggle to create the conditions for developers and users to access, create, and share free software.

April's decades of organizing reveal the importance of flexibly evolving, tenacious political action. The development of the French free software community contributes to the global development of a digital commons, grounded in free software that users and developers from around the world can access. As discussed in Chapter 2, free access to computer networks and the Internet are equally important foundations for the digital commons. Despite the successes of organizing global communities of resistance, corporations and governments persist in their efforts to promote and institutionalize a neoliberal regime. Such efforts require activists to continually span the local and the global in creative, transformative ways. Activists are organizing some of the most vital of these struggles over freedom to access the Internet.

6 Internet Politics

Organizing for Net Neutrality and Civil Liberties

Like software, the Internet is a battleground. In the context of neoliberal globalization, activists, corporations, and governments wage struggles over Internet politics that affect the foundations for the digital commons. Similar to April's struggles over the conditions for software use discussed in the last chapter, net neutrality activists battle over conditions for accessing the Internet. Indeed, both software and Internet politics affect these vital productive forces of informational capitalism. They shape the terms for software and Internet access and development, as privatized commodities subject to corporate control or digital commons open to global communities of producers and users.

Net neutrality activists organized to protect and defend users' freedoms to access the Internet on terms of their own choosing. They fought over two terrains of Internet politics, both of which were linked with global free software communities.

On the first terrain of struggle, activists defended the Internet as part of the existing infrastructure of the digital commons. They contested the technological, legal/political, and discursive conditions to access and control the existing telecommunications infrastructure. These clashes emerged in the 1990s, as activists organized to maintain and defend an open, neutral, and decentralized Internet. Since that time, activists have continued to develop and apply the freedom discourse to protect net neutrality, understood as equal access to the Internet for all users. In the process, they created a global community of resistance explicitly focused on net neutrality. I examine three cases of such activism, where participants played pivotal roles in Internet politics in the U.S., France and more broadly in Europe, and Brazil. These cases exemplify struggles over Internet politics in different parts of the world.

The first case is the Electronic Frontier Foundation (EFF) launched in 1990 to work on civil liberties issues raised by computer and information technologies in the U.S. EFF cofounder John Perry Barlow rearticulated the freedom discourse in 1996, by defending Internet users' digital civil liberties from what he viewed as the colonizing interests of governments that sought to control cyberspace. By synthesizing the defense of freedom and sovereignty, Barlow articulated what I call the freedom/

sovereignty discourse. EFF put this freedom/sovereignty discourse into practice by pursuing impact litigation work on key cases that influence policy and the law on privacy and free expression on the Internet. EFF opposed illegal surveillance and sought to promote the legal, technical, and cultural conditions to create alternatives to it.

Second, the French group *La Quadrature du Net* (LQDN) also focused its work on the fight for net neutrality. In English, its name translates as Squaring the Net, a metaphor that alludes to the impossibility of having an Internet that is "squared" or limited by restrictions on the free exchange of information by all of its users. LQDN activists built strong relationships with several European activist groups, thus contributing to the emergence of the global net neutrality community of resistance. After the terrorist attacks in Paris in November 2015 and the declaration of a state of emergency by the French government, they increasingly concentrated their efforts on resisting surveillance.

Finally, since 2003, the Brazilian government engaged in two key strategies to promote digital inclusion, designed to democratize conditions for accessing the Internet, computers, software, and databases. First, Minister of Culture Gilberto Gil supported the development of the Creative Commons community in Brazil, both through his own work as a musician and through cultural policy. In the process, he collaborated with EFF's John Perry Barlow to contribute to the development of the freedom/sovereignty discourse and the global expansion of Creative Commons. Second, President Lula introduced a program for electronic government designed to promote digital inclusion by providing new forms of political participation. Citizens used this tool to participate in developing Brazil's *Marco Civil da Internet,* commonly referred to as Brazil's Internet Constitution, or the Civil Rights Framework for the Internet. In the wake of the 2013 revelations by Edward Snowden, President Dilma Rousseff signed the Marco Civil into law in April 2014. Struggles over civil liberties and net neutrality emerged in the course of developing the Marco Civil. These struggles were shaped by the context of conflicts over Rousseff's presidency that eventually led to her impeachment in August 2016.

Debates over how to implement the Marco Civil continued after Rousseff's impeachment, as net neutrality advocates fought to equalize the terms for Internet access in Brazil and contributed to the development of the global net neutrality community of resistance.

These diverse efforts made key contributions to the broader struggle to create the political and discursive conditions to control the existing telecommunications infrastructure vital to the use of the Internet. Equally important, however, other groups organized around a second terrain of struggle over Internet politics. Indeed, the extent of surveillance over the existing telecommunications infrastructure sparked these groups to develop strategies to both evade that surveillance and create alternative telecommunications infrastructures of their own. Building upon the work of free software proponents who created their own programs, licenses, and forms of community organization, these activists developed alternative technologies to access the Internet.

Through this process of evading surveillance and developing an alternative telecommunications infrastructure, participants in the second terrain of struggle worked to make the Internet a vital part of what Bollier (2008, 9) called the commons as a "parallel social order." Such strategies resonated with Bollier's (2008, 20) argument that commoners can "[t]ranscend a rigged game by migrating to a commons of [their] own making." They were rooted in a more utopian or anarchistic view of the commons, where commoners collaborated in a process of critiquing the problems with existing structures, and in response, building and creating commons-based alternatives within the structure of the old system.

To explore how activists pursued these strategies, I examine a project to evade surveillance designed by the French activist group Framasoft. Framasoft is a nonprofit popular education network dedicated to developing a Free, Decentralized, Ethical Internet built on Solidarity. It developed a project called DeGoogling the Internet, offering resources about alternative ways to consume digital services to evade surveillance of personal data. Moreover, I explore the FreedomBox project, whose participants designed and distributed a personal web server that users carry with them. FreedomBox offers alternatives to the existing telecommunications network by providing tools for consumers and citizens to create their own community-controlled networks. Consumers can use FreedomBox to control their personal data and thus resist surveillance on multiple levels.

The Internet, Surveillance, and the Digital Commons

Edward Snowden highlighted the importance of both of these terrains of struggle in his 2016 keynote speech at LibrePlanet, a major annual free software conference sponsored by the Free Software Foundation (FSF). Speaking via videostream from exile in Russia, he emphasized the interdependence between free software and Internet freedom. The audience gave him a rousing standing ovation for several minutes. This warm reception indicated the extent to which free software proponents appreciated the importance of Snowden's 2013 revelations about National Security Agency (NSA) surveillance. In response, Snowden (2016) noted that he was always a bit surprised when people thanked him for making those revelations. He said that for him, LibrePlanet was an "extraordinary event," because it gave him the opportunity to thank the free software community for creating programs that he trusted. He emphasized that his revelations would not have been possible without free software, since he had relied on it as the only secure way to do his work (Snowden 2016).

Snowden (2016) discussed two major ways that free software and an open Internet were interdependent. In the process, he highlighted the importance of the first terrain of political struggle to defend an open Internet, both for free software supporters and for other participants in the digital commons.

First, the software used to conduct surveillance over the Internet was incompatible with free software. As Lyon (2014, 3) detailed, the software used to gather data for surveillance was based on complex algorithms designed to "allow users' data to be systematically extracted or disclosed, analyzed, and turned into what the data collectors and others, such as the NSA, hope will be actionable data." Implementation of this software generally yielded "Big Data," constituting extremely large, complex data sets that posed challenges of processing and storage. Furthermore, it is virtually impossible to protect the privacy of the information stored as Big Data. Such software, and the Big Data it collected, was antithetical to free software. Certainly, the software used to gather Big Data did not allow its users the freedom to run any program they chose, or to make changes to those programs and share them with others in the community.

Second, users who wanted to choose free software and to enjoy free access to the Internet shared a mutual reliance on the telecommunications network. Snowden (2016) argued that one of the most significant lessons arising from his 2013 revelations was the importance of controlling the telecommunications network. Lack of control over this network made users vulnerable to surveillance. Such surveillance compromised the civil liberties of all Internet users, since they were all potential targets and none had been asked for their consent.

The threats to freedom by these surveillance activities underscore the key role of the Internet in creating the digital commons. As discussed in Chapter 2, the Internet provides the technological infrastructure that allows commons participants to engage in myriad forms of interaction and collaboration. As such, the Internet comprises what Castells (2009, 415) calls "a space of communication autonomy that constitutes the foundation of the new public space of the Information Age." Due to its centrality to communications in the digital commons, as Castells (2009, 414) argues, struggles to protect and defend a free Internet are "perhaps the most decisive social movements of our age." The Internet is the communications hub of the digital commons, where a diverse range of social actors exchanges ideas, makes plans, and produces and consumes a plethora of products and services. This communications hub is governed by legal discourses that are widely contested in an ongoing process of construction. It is endangered by threats to limit net neutrality. The Internet is a vital part of what Bollier (2008, 7) describes as "[a]n infrastructure of software, legal rights, practical expertise, and social ethics [that] had to be imagined, built and defended" in order to create the commons. Hence, Bollier (2008, 301) argues that "[w]ithout net neutrality, citizens could very well be stifled in their ability to participate on their own terms, in their own voices."

The Internet thus plays a central role in processes of participation and collaboration among citizens in the ongoing construction of the digital commons. Individuals and groups engaged in both of the above terrains of struggle contribute to the ongoing development of the Internet as the communications infrastructure for the digital commons. As Chadwick (2006, 3) suggests, "the Net is itself a source of institutional innovation...the ways in which the Internet organizes and reorganizes systems of communication renders it an institutional form in its own right." This statement highlights the importance of the Internet as a social institution. It implies, however, that the Internet somehow initiated these actions of institutional development, rather than identifying the particular social actors involved. In this chapter, I explore how key actors engaged in Internet politics contribute to broader processes of constructing the Internet as a social institution. Their strategies were vital parts of institutional changes in the Internet that shaped conditions for the exercise of civil liberties in the digital sphere, as well as for the development of the digital commons.

Snowden's 2013 revelations about NSA surveillance highlighted these implications of the Internet as a social institution, largely by identifying how the surveillance processes worked. Under an order from the Foreign Intelligence Surveillance Court (FISC), the NSA mandated that the Verizon telecommunications company provides the NSA and the FBI with metadata on phone calls by millions of Verizon subscribers. These metadata, or data about data, did not include the content of the messages themselves. Nonetheless, they included a range of key information such as the contact's identity and IP address; they also detailed users' communications over the telecommunications network, such as the times, origins, destinations, and durations of their phone calls, electronic mail, and instant messages. Once the NSA had collected users' metadata, it stored these data for up to a year (Lyon 2014).

Such data collection compromised users' freedoms, since they had no idea that their communications were being monitored. Consumers logging in to social media or other Internet sites, or providing access to their location information to applications on their cell phones, were not choosing to provide metadata about their location or their online activities to the government. This lack of user knowledge and consent was central to processes of surveillance. For example, Lyon (2014) identified key surveillance trends highlighted by the Snowden revelations. One trend was to "rende[r] ordinary everyday lives increasingly transparent to large organizations...[while] organizations engaged in surveillance are increasingly invisible to those whose data are garnered and used" (Lyon 2014, 4). There was thus a tension between the hypervisibility of ordinary daily activity and the invisibility of state or corporate surveillance activities that constituted the institutional structures and practices of surveillance. I refer to this as the visibility paradox, since the hypervisibility of citizens depended upon the invisibility of state and corporate structures of surveillance. For example, in the case of the NSA surveillance, it was collecting data on the communications of telecommunications users who had no idea that their activities were being monitored. Users were making choices about their communications, assuming that when they provided information to a company like Verizon or to an application on their phone, it would not be collected and stored by the government. This clandestine process of government monitoring also involved a second surveillance trend that Lyon (2014, 4) called "the expanding securitization of daily life," that "prompts the use of extended surveillance, from neighborhoods and travel arrangements to large sporting and entertainment events." Haggerty and Gazso (2005) identified a similar trend in forms of surveillance instituted to bolster security in response to terrorist threats after September 11. They emphasized that "it is increasingly difficult to differentiate a surveillance practice dedicated to 'security' from its many other applications, as surveillance regimes instituted and justified for one purpose now rapidly assume other uses" (Haggerty and Gazso 2005, 170).

These trends in the ways that surveillance is practiced are connected to other trends in the ways that data are collected and analyzed. The technical processes of collecting Big Data are increasingly automated, making it easier and cheaper to store and process immense amounts of data. Lyon (2014, 6) notes a trend toward "adaptation," where data analysts treat the data originally collected for one purpose as easily transferrable to use for other purposes. In the process, surveillance carried out by corporations and governments is increasingly integrated. This is what happened in some cases of the NSA surveillance, where data that Verizon collected about phone calls were treated as though they had national security implications. These adaptive processes are part of another trend toward what Lyon (2014, 4, emphasis in original) calls preemptive or anticipatory data collection, where bulk data are collected from a wide range of sources "*before* determining the full range of their actual and potential uses." Moreover, this anticipatory trend involves "mobilizing algorithms and analytics not only to understand a past sequence of events but also to predict and intervene *before* behaviors, events, and processes are set" (Lyon 2014, 4, emphasis in original).

What appear to be technical considerations about how data are collected, stored, and processed are thus inextricably linked to broader political questions about how surveillance is practiced. Modes of surveillance affect civil liberties, particularly the right to privacy. There is an extensive, ongoing collection of data about consumers and citizens by a wide range of institutions, including virtually all bureaucratic organizations that require information about the individuals that work within them or consume their services. Through this process of data collection, the myriad forms of data about individuals in this range of institutions constitute what Haggerty and Gazso (2005, 172) call a "'data double:' the electronic, visual or documentary trace of ourselves that we leave behind in our encounters with modern institutions."

This process of data collection, and the ongoing constitution of data doubles for citizens in contemporary society give rise to tensions. Government surveillance efforts to promote national security often clash with advocacy groups seeking to protect privacy from government intrusion. These tensions extend to corporate collection of data on consumer activities, from searches for products online to purchases of a wide range of products and services. Consumers may appreciate what Lessig (2008, 132) calls "Little Brother" activities by corporations like Amazon that offer a range of suggestions about potential purchases based on consumers' past history as well as the purchases of others who bought similar items. Simultaneously, however, consumers increasingly operate within what Andrejevic (2007) calls "digital enclosures." In the process, consumers and citizens are involved in a virtually constant process of data collection, through a combination of their own conscious choices to provide data about themselves and invisible corporate and government practices. Bureaucratic organizations ask consumers, workers, and citizens for data about themselves in a range of forms. In many cases, individuals do not have a choice about whether to provide this data, if they want to be hired for a job, get a driver's license, receive health care in various forms, and more. All of that data can be combined in ways that the individuals providing it did not originally intend, if organizations coordinate to assemble that data in specific ways for specific purposes. As Lyon (2014, 7) argues, "the price of our freedom in both political and consumer contexts is our shaping or conditioning by algorithms."

Haggerty and Gazso (2005) highlight this convergence between the technical, political, economic, and cultural dimensions of surveillance of consumers and citizens. They build upon Haggerty and Ericson's (2000) earlier work on the "surveillant assemblage," theorizing it as a "proliferating, decentralized and uncoordinated regime of visibility" (Haggerty and Gazso 2005, 172). The concept of the surveillant assemblage captures the shifting, unpredictable ways that surveillance systems work in practice. There is always the possibility of a totalitarian state apparatus coordinating the massive amounts of Big Data being collected. The overarching nature of surveillance is more fractured, however, than a totalitarian model would suggest. There are so many different organizations collecting data, through such a range of distinct practices and systems, that surveillance practices constitute a patchwork assemblage rather than a totalitarian monolith. Haggerty and Gazso (2005, 173, emphasis in original) argue that the surveillant assemblage is not a single physical entity or system, but the sum total of the surveillance capacity that can be trained on a location or population. As such, it is less a 'thing' than it is a *potentiality* that can be actualized to varying degrees depending on what and how observational regimes are combined and aligned.

There is thus an ongoing potential to engage in a wide range of forms and practices of surveillance, including centralized, controlled activities by large government or corporate bureaucracies. This potential for centralized surveillance, integrating the data doubles of individuals from a range of formerly fractured, decentralized surveillance subsystems, raises the greatest concerns for net neutrality and digital civil liberties activists. As highlighted by Snowden's (2016) LibrePlanet speech, free software proponents share these concerns. Free software and net neutrality activists employ the freedom discourse to resist surveillance as a threat to the freedoms of Internet and software users, as well as to the general citizenry. Activists engaged in the first terrain of struggle over Internet politics seek to defend users' freedom to access and share information as they choose, as a key part of organizing to protect an open, decentralized Internet.

First Terrain of Struggle: Defending Digital Civil Liberties and an Open, Decentralized Internet

In this defense of Internet users' freedoms, activists built upon the freedom discourse and developed it in novel ways. Internet activists emerged as a global community of resistance akin to the free software communities discussed above, responding to local conditions while simultaneously contributing to broader global projects. Their local actions were not coordinated at a global level in advance. Nonetheless, however, they shared a commitment to the principles of freedom to access and share information as a common good rather than as private property. As we have seen, this commitment to the freedom discourse was central to developing the digital commons. Furthermore, these activists built upon and developed this freedom discourse in similar ways, integrating values of sovereignty and resistance to control by corporations or governments engaged in surveillance.

As in the case of the global free software community of resistance, net neutrality activists were dispersed around the world. Local actors shared common principles and strategies, thus contributing to the development of a global community. Both free software and net neutrality communities were recursive publics in Kelty's (2008) sense, striving to maintain the conditions for their own existence. Beyond this recursivity, however, their local actions simultaneously required a commitment to global projects of creating conditions to freely access and share software and information over the Internet. These global projects were central to developing the digital commons. Through their local organizing and international resonance with the commons project, these global communities of resistance constituted alternative forms of globalization from below.

Freedom/Sovereignty Discourse, Impact Litigation: Electronic Frontier Foundation

In 1990, John Perry Barlow and Mitch Kapor cofounded the EFF, which has worked primarily to protect civil liberties in the context of the increasing use of computer and information technologies. The EFF defended these digital civil liberties by choosing legal cases with the potential to impact the development of law and policy for free speech and the right to privacy for Internet users. In the process, the EFF contributed to the development of the freedom discourse, adapting it to the context of digital civil liberties on the Internet.

Barlow drew upon a unique set of skills and experiences to develop the freedom discourse. He had a multifaceted career as a cattle rancher, a lyricist for the Grateful Dead and a Fellow at Harvard's Berkman Center for Internet and Society. In 1996, Barlow employed his writing skills to craft a "Declaration of the Independence of Cyberspace," which remains posted on the EFF website. In this Declaration, Barlow contributed to the freedom discourse by articulating EFF's goal of promoting and defending users' freedoms to use the Internet in any way they chose, particularly by protecting those freedoms from government control. He referred to Cyberspace as "the new home of Mind," a separate realm from what he called "[g]overnments of the Industrial World... weary giants of flesh and steel" (www.eff.org/cyberspace-independence). According to Chadwick (2006), this Declaration exemplified a cyber-libertarian perspective on the Internet. This perspective was reflected in key themes in Barlow's version of the freedom discourse, such as the idea that Cyberspace was a separate realm, independent from the pre-existing system of economic and social relationships. Toward this end, Barlow's Declaration asserted that "legal concepts of property, expression, identity, movement, and context do not apply to us" (www.eff.org/cyberspace-independence). He thus rearticulated key themes of the freedom discourse as committed to alternatives to private property and the development of a digital commons.

At the same time, however, Barlow staked out a political position to resist what he viewed as policy changes that threatened the interests of participants in Cyberspace. In the process, he articulated a second key theme that resonated with the principles of the freedom discourse. He defended free access and sharing of information as a common good, opposing efforts to restrict access to information in the interests of private property. In the Declaration, he targeted laws such as the Tele-communications Reform Act in the U.S. that he described as "trying to ward off the virus of liberty by erecting guard posts at the frontiers of Cyberspace" (www.eff.org/cyberspace-independence). He critiqued such laws as "increasingly hostile and colonial measures [that] place us in the same position as those previous lovers of freedom and self-determination who had to reject the authorities of distant, uninformed powers" (www.eff.org/cyberspace-independence). In response to these laws, Barlow articulated an intriguing blend of the freedom and sovereignty discourses. He argued that "[w]e must declare our virtual selves immune to your sovereignty, even as we continue to consent to your rule over our bodies. We will spread ourselves across the Planet so that no one can arrest our thoughts" (www.eff.org/cyberspace-independence).

Barlow thus framed his political defense of Internet users' digital civil liberties as a form of struggle for sovereignty from governments, viewed as colonial powers seeking to control cyberspace.

In the process, he rearticulated the freedom discourse by integrating the defense of freedom and sovereignty. I will refer to this as the freedom/sovereignty discourse. This discourse resonated with the approach of Brazilian digital civil liberties advocates, as will be discussed further below.

In the decades since its founding, the EFF put the freedom/sovereignty discourse into practice, primarily through impact litigation work on key cases affecting digital civil liberties of Internet users. One of EFF's earliest cases had profound legal implications for the application of the U.S. First Amendment right to free speech to the example of software code. This case involved the defense of Daniel Bernstein, a computer science student who created an encryption software program that he wanted to publish on the Internet. The U.S. government had placed software encryption programs on its Munitions List, legally classifying them as weapons. Like flamethrowers and bombs, such weapons were regulated to protect national security; it was illegal to export them without permission from the U.S. State Department. Bernstein's desire to share the text of his program on the Internet was legally defined as exporting it. The government prevented him from posting his encryption system online without registering as an arms dealer; government officials also stated that if he applied for permission to be classified as an arms dealer, they would not grant such permission. In 1995, Bernstein worked with EFF, which organized a legal team to sue the U.S. government over its classification of Bernstein's software encryption system as munitions. In 1999, after a protracted court battle, the presiding judge issued a landmark ruling. For the first time, a court ruled that software code was legally classified as speech; code was thus protected by the First Amendment. As a result of this ruling, regulations restricting export of encryption programs were judged as violating those First Amendment rights by limiting free speech. This ruling gave rise to changes in the export restrictions on encryption software, allowing companies to use encryption to protect credit card numbers and other personal information when consumers buy products online (Coleman 2013; Electronic Frontier Foundation 2014a).

Since the passage of the Digital Millennium Copyright Act (DMCA) of 1998, the EFF has engaged in sustained work to oppose it on a number of levels. Its approach resonates with Benkler's (2006, 418) argument that laws like the DMCA "represent a choice to tilt the institutional ecology in favor of industrial production and distribution of cultural packaged goods, at the expense of commons-based relations of sharing information, knowledge and culture." As discussed in the last chapter, the DMCA was an effort to protect the proprietary interests of the film and music industry by making it illegal to produce or disseminate the range of technologies, devices, or services that allow users to circumvent measures designed to control access to copyrighted works.

The EFF targeted such anticircumvention provisions as threats to the civil liberties of users to freely engage with digital technology. From the EFF's perspective, the DMCA's anticircumvention provisions were a form of government interference in users' activities, designed to promote proprietary interests at the expense of citizens and consumers. In July 2016, the EFF filed a lawsuit that challenged these anticircumvention provisions; they simultaneously challenged "anti-trafficking provisions" in Section 1201 of the DMCA that threatened to impose extensive financial penalties and potential prison sentences on users of technology who violated them. In a discussion of the lawsuit on the EFF's website, it noted that this section of the law hinders ordinary citizens' access to and use of copyrighted materials. Beyond these limitations, Section 1201 challenges citizens' rights to speak freely about such materials. For example, these restrictions extend to copyrighted software that is integrated into an increasing array of objects that people rely on in their daily activities, from refrigerators to cars. Under Section 1201, consumers' efforts to engage in a number of activities would potentially be considered criminal, such as trying to fix a car or other object that contained copyrighted software, to convert videos to make it possible to play them on a variety of platforms, or to create tools that would enable themselves or others to access the copyrighted materials.

The discussion of the lawsuit on EFF's website cites Kit Walsh, their staff attorney, discussing the implications of Section 1201 for freedom of speech. Walsh stated,

> [t]he creative process requires building on what has come before, and the First Amendment preserves our right to transform creative works to express a new message, and to research and talk about the computer code that controls so much of our world.
> (https://www.eff.org/press/releases/eff-lawsuit-takes-dmca-section-1201-research-and-technology-restrictions-violate, accessed September 14, 2016)

As discussed in Chapter 1, software has become ubiquitous in the daily lives of consumers and citizens, often in ways of which we are unaware. A consumer who attempted to repair a refrigerator or a car that included copyrighted software could thus be in violation of Section 1201, even if that consumer had no idea that their efforts to fix a commodity that belonged to them might be illegal.

The EFF's work against the DMCA in 2016 built upon a history of such work since the DMCA's initial passage in 1998. Over this sustained period of time, the EFF worked to resist the DMCA's effects on citizens' digital civil liberties to enjoy protection from any government actions that could impede their freedom of speech. The EFF viewed the DMCA as protecting corporate interests in maintaining control over their ability to make profits from their products that included digital technologies, and particularly those where consumers might choose to fix or adapt those products to their needs. The EFF's work thus resonated with Castells' (2009, 414) argument that "the commons of the communication revolution are being expropriated to expand for-profit entertainment and to commodify personal freedom."

The House Committee on Commerce expressed similar concerns about the DMCA's implications for digital civil liberties when it issued the *Report on the Digital Millennium Copyright Act of 1998*. In this Report, the Committee highlighted concerns about protecting users' abilities to access copyrighted works in ways considered lawful under U.S. copyright law. As discussed in Chapter 3, copyright law protected users' rights to what it called "fair use." These fair use practices were linked to civil liberties, since citizens should have the freedom from government interference in their access to information as well as their speech. Such practices were changing with the increasing use of digital technologies to promote new forms of electronic commerce. The Committee on Commerce was studying these emerging forms of electronic commerce and their effects on the U.S. economy. It identified the promotion of electronic commerce as integrally linked to the protection of intellectual property rights, since

> [a] thriving electronic marketplace provides new and powerful ways for the creators of intellectual property to make their works available to legitimate consumers in the digital environment. And a plentiful supply of intellectual property – whether in the form of software, music, movies, literature, or other works – drives the demand for a more flexible and efficient electronic marketplace.
> (U.S. House Committee on Commerce 1998, 23)

It noted that a range of groups in both the private and public sectors had organized to oppose the DMCA, such as "libraries, institutions of higher learning, consumer electronics and computer product manufacturers, and others with a vital stake in the growth of electronic commerce and the Internet" (U.S. House Committee on Commerce 1998, 22).

In response to those concerns, the Committee on Commerce sought to "more precisely define the relationship between intellectual property and electronic commerce" (U.S. House Committee on Commerce 1998, 23). Such a definition involved considering the ways that technologies would be used in electronic commerce, as well as assessing the implications of those technological applications. As discussed in Chapter 3, historically, copyright law defined conditions under which users could access copyrighted works without the authorization of copyright owners. Such uses balanced the interests of copyright owners and users of copyrighted works, and generally included "conduct deemed to be in the greater public interest" (U.S. House Committee on Commerce 1998, 24). The Committee on Commerce's report on the DMCA argued that such provisions generally had neutral effects on the technology involved, since they did not explicitly regulate commercial transactions involving information technology.

By contrast, however, 62 law professors challenged this "neutrality" in a letter to Congress in September 1997. They called the anticircumvention provisions of the DMCA an "'unprecedented departure into the zone of what might be called paracopyright – an uncharted new domain of legislative provisions designed to strengthen copyright protection by regulating conduct which traditionally has fallen outside the regulatory sphere of intellectual property law'" (quoted in U.S. House Committee on Commerce 1998, 24–25). The Committee on Commerce responded to these concerns by acknowledging the potential problems with the uncharted "paracopyright zone." Simultaneously, however, it emphasized the distinctive nature of digital media and its implications for the rights of copyright owners due to the ease of copying and redistributing digital files.

The EFF raised similar critiques of the DMCA's lack of neutrality and encroachment on citizens' digital civil liberties. To pursue these concerns, it took on an impact litigation case with vital implications for academic research, particularly in the encryption field. In 2001, it represented a team of computer scientists from Princeton, Rice, and Xerox, led by Princeton professor Edward Felten. The scientists had responded to a call for researchers to study new digital watermarking technologies that the industry was considering implementing to protect digital music files. The call was issued in 2000 by a multi-industry group called the Secure Digital Music Initiative (SDMI). These digital watermarking technologies were designed to add a subtle sound into musical recordings that would serve as a copyright with information telling users not to copy the piece.

In response to SDMI's call, Felten and his colleagues studied the digital watermarks and discovered that they were easy to circumvent. By using relatively simple techniques, anyone with a rudimentary background in the signal processing field would be able to circumvent the watermarks.

Felten and his colleagues analyzed their results in a paper; they identified the workings of the digital watermarking technologies, noted their weaknesses, and proposed alternatives to strengthen the systems. They thus followed a common method employed in the field of computer security research. Equally important, their research appeared to qualify for the Committee on Commerce's provision exempting encryption research from the DMCA's anticircumvention provisions. Their paper was accepted for publication in a journal, as well as for presentation at an academic conference (Felten 2002; Electronic Frontier Foundation 2014b).

Felten (2002, 289) provided what he called a "view from the trenches" to highlight his experience with the DMCA as being aimed to "suppress criticism." He discussed the DMCA's bans on acts of circumvention, where users attempt to get around the technologies designed to limit access to copyrighted works. Such technologies include Digital Rights Management (DRM) techniques such as copy controls that prohibit users from copying the contents of CDs or converting them to MP3 format. Moreover, content scramble systems (CSS) employ encryption algorithms to prohibit users from playing the discs unless they have a licensed key. The DVD Copy Control Association licenses such keys, which are installed in the majority of DVD players sold in the U.S. (Perzanowski, 2007). As Perzanowski (2007, 2) characterized the DMCA, it was "designed to ensure compliance with the digital locks adopted by copyright holders by prohibiting their removal or bypass and banning tools that would enable removal or bypass." In addition to banning these acts of circumvention, the DMCA thus imposes a second type of restrictions on the technologies that make circumvention possible. Perzanowski (2007) emphasizes that while it is theoretically possible to imagine techniques that would control access while allowing copying, conversely, it would be possible to control copying while allowing access. In practice, however, copyright owners employ both kinds of technologies simultaneously, thus restricting both access and copying. They use the DMCA to restrict users' abilities to engage in both of these activities as well.

This second type of restrictions on technologies that make it possible to circumvent copyright has key implications for scientific research. Felten (2002, 289) aptly described such restrictions as "banning the tool that one might use to commit that act [of circumvention]." When Felten and his colleagues wrote their paper about the digital watermarking technologies, they experienced the power of corporate interests to protect themselves from what they perceived as violations of the DMCA.

In 2001, the Recording Industry of America (RIAA) wrote a letter to Felten and his colleagues, threatening to sue them under the DMCA. The RIAA claimed that the scientific paper was "a circumvention technology because it discussed the weaknesses of the copy protection technologies" (Felten 2002, 292). Felten (2002) noted that he spent a month engaged in intensive conversations with lawyers who warned him that he would be breaking the law by publishing his paper. Felten received multiple threats from a variety of people, some of whom were associated with the RIAA and others with other organizations. Simultaneously, the conference organizers and their employers were also threatened with the possibility of being sued if they participated in a process of making the paper public. In order to avoid the prospect of such a range of people being targeted for violating the DMCA, Felten and his colleagues withdrew their paper. The RIAA responded by formally taking back its threat; however, the researchers still faced threats from other parties (Felten 2002).

After this series of events, Felten and his colleagues engaged in discussion with another set of conference organizers who were interested in using the case to publicly resist the DMCA. The researchers and the organizers devised a resistance strategy, filing suit asking the court to rule that it would be legal to publish their paper. They sought a ruling that would support the researchers' rights to free speech under the First Amendment. They argued that they had a right to state, present, and publish the results of their academic research. They also asked the court to consider the question of whether or not the paper violated the DMCA. The defendants responded to the suit by allowing publication of the paper, so the case did not end up going to court (Felten 2002).

The Felten case highlights a number of problems with the DMCA that continue to resonate over a decade later. Even though the DMCA is purportedly designed to protect copyright holders from infringement, in this case, the researchers were threatened with infringement simply by attempting to publish their scientific work. They had not developed a system to break through copyright measures and violate the holders' rights; they were trying to understand the flaws in the system in order to improve it. Of equal importance, the Felten case reveals that firms are threatening to sue under the DMCA even if they are not themselves the copyright holders. In other words, firms used the DMCA as a pretext to protect their interests, even if they were not the copyright holders. Furthermore, these firms alleged that the researchers had violated the DMCA, even though they had not infringed the copyright. The RIAA had asked them to study the digital watermarks, so the researchers were engaged in this process at the request of the company. The case thus shows the extremely broad application of the DMCA as restricting any tools that make it possible to circumvent copyright protections, including academic research that simply studies the workings of those tools. Felten (2002, 293) emphasized the chilling effects of this broad application of the DMCA, arguing,

> [t]he real damage occurs when people decide that they do not want to work in a particular area; they decide not to study some important problem; they decide that computer security or copy protection is just too risky of an area in which to do research.

Due to these effects on academic research, as well as other ways that citizens may exercise their civil liberties when engaging with digital technologies, the EFF has continued its work against the anticircumvention and anti-trafficking provisions of the DMCA. On its website, it compiled resources with information about this impact litigation work, including the Felten case (accessed August 5, 2016. https://w2.eff.org/IP/DMCA/Felten_v_RIAA/faq_felten.html; www.eff.org/cases/felten-et-al-v-riaa-et-al).

The EFF's work on the DMCA is connected to its broader efforts to promote civil liberties of Internet users. Until 2014, the EFF noted the shifting conditions in the telecommunications market, with the growth of firms with quasi-monopolistic power over Internet infrastructure. As McSherry discussed in a 2014 blog post on the EFF's website, the EFF was concerned about this consolidation of Internet access providers, and their efforts to raise their profits by charging some of their users higher fees for special Internet access. The EFF began to view the Federal Communications Commission (FCC) as a potentially valuable institutional actor to enforce fundamental rules protecting net neutrality. For example, the FCC could prohibit Internet Service Providers (ISPs) from discriminating between applications, blocking users, or charging fees to allow special access to the Internet (accessed August 5, 2016. www.eff.org/deeplinks/2014/06/fcc-and-net-neutrality-way-forward). In April 2014, the FCC considered a new draft rule that would allow ISPs to charge more for a "fast lane" that offered higher-quality services than were available to other users. Simultaneously, the FCC considered a second option that would protect net neutrality by reclassifying broadband Internet service as a telecommunications service. Citizens and political officials debated these two approaches, and President Obama declared his support for the net neutrality approach in the fall of 2014. Furthermore, 4 million citizens wrote public comments to the FCC to contribute to its process of deliberation about how to approach net neutrality (Sheehan 2016).

In March 2015, the FCC (2015, 14) issued a new order recommending what it called "Sustainable Open Internet Rules." This order was based on a court ruling that the FCC had "legal authority to adopt open Internet protections" under Section 706 and Title II of the Communications Act of 1934 (FCC 2015, 14). The FCC (2015) thus supported major net neutrality principles, such as prohibiting ISPs from offering lower-quality Internet access by allowing some customers to pay higher prices to prioritize their Internet traffic. Once the FCC issued its order, EFF staff attorney Kit Walsh analyzed its features and implications in a piece on the EFF's website (accessed August 12, 2016. www.eff.org/deeplinks/2015/03/todays-net-neutrality-order-win-few-blemishes). Through these efforts, the EFF continued its work to educate and mobilize the public around questions of net neutrality.

A corporate coalition of telecommunications, cable, and wireless industry associations, including AT&T and CenturyLink, challenged the FCC's Open Internet Rules. They filed a petition with the U.S. Court of Appeals for the D.C. Circuit, characterizing the FCC's reclassification of Internet access as a telecommunications service as unlawful (United States Telecom Association et al., 2015). ISPs argued that the FCC should not have authority over the Internet, and that grounding its regulation of the Internet in the Communications Act of 1934 would threaten its investment and discourage innovation. In a similar vein, wireless carriers argued that they provided distinct, shared types of services and that they should be exempt from rules designed to prevent discrimination and blocking of Internet traffic by particular users (Selyukh 2016).

The appeals court ruled against the petition, fully supporting the FCC's Open Internet Rules. The corporate opponents of net neutrality vowed to continue their fight by appealing all the way to the Supreme Court (Selyurkh 2016). For example, on AT&T's Public Policy Blog, it published a statement by its General Counsel David McAtee in response to the appeals court ruling: "We have always expected this issue to be decided by the Supreme Court, and we look forward to participating in that appeal" (accessed August 5, 2016. www.attpublicpolicy. com/broadband-classification/att-statement-on-u-s-court-of-appeals-net-neutrality-decision/).

Struggles over net neutrality, and the FCC's role in providing ground rules to protect it, thus continued. The November 2016 election of Donald Trump to be U.S. President posed new challenges for activists engaged in these struggles over net neutrality and digital civil liberties. Donald Trump appointed Ajit Pai, an outspoken opponent of net neutrality and former lawyer for Verizon, as Chairman of the FCC. This appointment raises questions about impending conflicts in that arena. EFF researcher Kerry Sheehan (2016) compiled a comprehensive list of statements on net neutrality by Donald Trump and his advisors, all of which were critical of net neutrality and supportive of an approach more favorable to corporate interests.

In response to these shifting conditions, the EFF expanded its work on digital civil liberties with an increased focus on surveillance. It issued a plan for the first 100 days of the Trump administration to continue EFF's work as what EFF researchers Maass and Reitman (2017) called "an independent defense force" for civil liberties, "to ensure that government is held accountable and in check." Anticipating ongoing innovation in surveillance technologies, the EFF planned to continue its impact litigation work, with particular emphasis on questions of surveillance in communities that might be the focus of such surveillance. It created the Electronic Frontier Alliance (EFA), a grassroots network of community groups. These groups conducted workshops to train activists to combat surveillance by integrating the use of encryption into their communications practices. Concerned that government intelligence agencies like the National Security Administration might extend their surveillance practices, the EFA sought to "enabl[e] and cultivat[e] alliances with local communities and neighbors responding to underlying social issues from state violence and climate change to domestic violence and the rights of refugees" (Buttar 2016).

The EFF's renewed emphasis on surveillance resonated with work done in France and more broadly in Europe. As French and European activists organized to protect net neutrality, they increasingly found it important to focus on resisting surveillance. These complementary struggles to defend digital civil liberties against surveillance practices reveal the development of a global net neutrality community of resistance that spanned the U.S. and Europe.

Defending Net Neutrality, Resisting Surveillance: La Quadrature du Net

As discussed in the beginning of the chapter, LQDN, or Squaring the Net, focuses its organizing on net neutrality. On its website, LQDN defines net neutrality as

> a founding principle of the Internet which guarantees that [telecommunications] operators remain mere transmitters of information and do not discriminate between different users, their communications or content accessed. It ensures that all users, whatever their resources, access the same and whole network.
>
> (https://www.laquadrature.net/en/Net_neutrality)

In organizing to protect net neutrality, LQDN seeks to protect the decentralized architecture of the Internet that makes it possible for all users to connect and share information with each other. This architecture was based on the principle of technological neutrality as central to freedom and civil liberties, since it offers equal access to all and thus protects against discriminatory actions. It addresses efforts by telecommunications and other corporations, as well as national governments, to support business models that limit users' access to the Internet. Such models include a range of measures, such as blocking users' access to particular forms of content, services, or applications. They might also implement restrictions that limit users' freedoms to communicate in particular ways, including sharing or publishing certain kinds of information; equally problematically, they might restrict users' abilities to communicate by limiting their ability to receive messages from or send messages to certain users (www.laquadrature.net/en/Net_neutrality).

In 2008, a group of activists founded LQDN. They had originally worked with April, the free software association highlighted in the last chapter. These activists decided to expand their organizing work from defending free software into the related sphere of Internet politics. They grasped the importance of a free and decentralized Internet for the ongoing development of free software programs, as well as free software communities. They applied the freedom discourse to these questions of Internet freedom. In the process, they highlighted the importance for all citizens to have equal access to the Internet in order to be able to exercise their right to freedom of speech and access to information in the digital sphere. In fact, their motto translates into English as "Internet and freedoms."

Since its founding, LQDN's work on net neutrality has been multifaceted. The activists engaged in a range of projects, all designed to raise awareness and provide strategies for citizens to work for net neutrality in different ways. They contributed to the development of a global net neutrality community of resistance by building alliances with activists in other parts of Europe.

For example, in 2009, they issued a memorandum on "Protecting Net Neutrality in Europe." They identified major social and economic benefits of a regulatory approach based on net neutrality, as well as challenges to that approach that they targeted for organizing. In defining net neutrality, they noted that the creator of the World Wide Web, Tim Berners-Lee, emphasized the importance of users being free to connect with anyone they chose, using any application. Since the invention of the World Wide Web in 1989, as the numbers of users increased around the globe, maintaining conditions for net neutrality required investing in expanded bandwidth, growing the network to accommodate growing numbers of users.

In 2011, LQDN joined with other Internet advocacy groups to launch the Respect my Net online platform. On this site, European Internet users could submit examples of when Internet access providers violated their freedom to access the Internet. The platform thus allowed such violations to be catalogued and tracked. The website https://respectmynet. eu/ offered users a way to submit details of their case, including their country, the name of the ISP or other operator providing their Internet service, the nature of the contract they had with the provider, and whether the Internet connection was provided over a mobile or fixed line. The site also offered statistics about confirmed reports of net neutrality violations, organized according to the countries where the violations occurred and the operators who had engaged in the violations. It was one way that LQDN and other Internet advocacy groups sought to involve users in their work. Through the Respect my Net platform, users participated in monitoring the activities and counteracting the lobbying pressure from major ISPs like Deutsche Telekom, Vodafone, and Telefonica, as well as Internet firms like Facebook and Google.

In the fall of 2013, struggles arose over the European Union Commission's legislation that proposed to abandon the principle of net neutrality called the European Regulation on the Single Market of Telecommunication; this legislation was often referred to as the Telecom Single Market Regulation. In January 2014, LQDN joined four other nongovernmental organizations in a coalition to create the SaveTheInternetEU campaign. This was a sister campaign to an earlier SavetheInternet campaign focused on struggles in the U.S., active since 2006. LQDN partnered with Access Now and European Digital Rights, both based in Brussels; Digitale Gesellschaft e.V, based in Germany; and Initiative für Netzfreiheit, based in Austria. They issued a joint press release, posted in English on LQDN's website, warning that the "Regulation would allow Internet companies to arbitrarily interfere with Internet traffic, prioritising the services of cash rich online companies to the detriment of innovation and free speech" (accessed August 6, 2016. www.laquadrature.net/en/savetheinterneteu-act-now-for-net-neutrality). They noted that the draft Regulation included loopholes on what were called "specialized services," as well as policing and surveillance activities by ISPs. They argued, "[o]f biggest concern is the fact that big telecoms operators are being offered the chance to impose old, inefficient, expensive and outdated telephony business models on the currently efficient and cost-effective internet" (accessed August 6, 2016. www.laquadrature.net/en/savetheinterneteu-act-now-for-net-neutrality). They urged citizens to provide comments on the Regulation in an effort to influence the process of its development.

By launching SaveTheInternetEU, LQDN and its collaborator organizations strengthened and extended the global net neutrality community of resistance in Europe. In the initial stage of organizing, Austrian volunteers developed tools to facilitate citizen participation, from sending faxes to European Members of Parliament (MEPs) to making phone calls and sending emails. In an online article on the website of the German digital rights organization Epicenter.Works, SaveTheInternetEU activist Thomas Lohninger (2016) described how these efforts helped to create the conditions for a strong citizen response. Certainly, citizens sent more than 40,000 faxes to their MEPs right before the parliamentary elections in May 2014. In the context of such strong citizen feedback, a substantial majority of the European Parliament voted to protect net neutrality by amending the Regulation. Over the next few years, activists expanded the SaveTheInternetEU campaign to include 32 organizations from 14 countries. They continued their organizing strategy of releasing position papers on key issues to educate the public, combined with providing tools for citizens to email their countries' representatives in Brussels.

In October 2015, the European Parliament voted on net neutrality. As part of the SaveTheInternetEU campaign, Sir Tim Berners-Lee made a statement about defending net neutrality in Europe. It was posted on the website of the World Wide Web Foundation, of which Sir Tim is the founding director. He called on European Members of Parliament (MEPs) to vote for four different kinds of amendments to strengthen net neutrality in the proposed regulation. First, he recommended that MEPs vote to close the loophole for specialized services, so that telecommunications providers would not be allowed to create faster service for some customers over others. Second, he supported amendments permitting European Union member states to implement national regulations of zero rating, which will be discussed further below. Allowing national autonomy on these regulations would make it possible for governments that had already banned the practice to maintain those restrictions. Third, Sir Tim urged MEPs to vote for amendments that prohibited discrimination of different classes of users. Finally, he recommended closing the loophole that allowed ISPs to slow Internet traffic whenever they deemed that congestion was about to occur (accessed July 25, 2016. http://webfoundation.org/2015/10/net-neutrality-in-europe-a-statement-from-sir-tim-berners-lee/).

Despite these organizing efforts, the SaveTheInternetEU campaign did not achieve its main objective. It was not able to muster enough votes in the European Parliament to pass the amendments that would have clarified and strengthened the provisions on net neutrality. As Lohninger (2016) noted, there was widespread consensus, even among conservative MEPs, that the Telecom Single Market Regulation was ambiguous and contradictory. It included provisions that could be interpreted as protecting net neutrality if it was clearly enforced; however, the activists objected to the Regulation's lack of clarity, which raised the prospect that users' rights to access the Internet would not be respected.

In the wake of this setback, LQDN and their coalition of activists in SaveTheInternetEU continued to organize. They shifted focus, seeking to influence the process of enforcing the Regulation. They targeted the Body of European Regulators of Electronic Communication (BEREC), which was tasked with creating guidelines to interpret and implement the Regulation. BEREC was constituted by the national telecommunications regulators from the EU countries. On June 6, 2016, BEREC publicized the draft guidelines and opened up a six-week consultation period to consider comments by the public that ended on July 18, 2016.

The activists mobilized themselves as a global net neutrality community of resistance. They employed similar strategies used by activists in the U.S. and India. Indeed, these common political goals and strategies highlight the nature of the global net neutrality community of resistance.

In the European context, local activists in different countries coordinated their efforts. They focused on public education and citizen recruitment to pressure BEREC to create clear guidelines to protect net neutrality. The European activists offered testimony about how to put net neutrality into practice. They addressed legal questions about how to implement net neutrality within the existing legal framework; this fit with BEREC's mandate to base its judgments on a combination of technical considerations and existing regulations. Moreover, the activists provided two key tools for European citizens to express their concerns about net neutrality and thus influence BEREC's deliberations. First, after a period of declining activity on the Respect my Net site, LQDN and its partner organizations relaunched the platform in March 2016. As mentioned above, the Respect my Net platform provided citizens with tools to document violations of net neutrality. Second, SaveTheInternetEU provided a space on its website to collect comments from citizens. These combined tools made it possible to collect and deliver over 480,000 comments to BEREC by the July 18 deadline. Lohninger (2016) emphasized the historic significance of this outpouring of citizen support of net neutrality. In past consultations, BEREC had only received 100 responses. As BEREC completed its analysis of the feedback it received and prepared to adapt the guidelines to implement the Telecom Single Market Regulation, a growing range of individuals and organizations had joined SaveThe InternetEU's campaign. These included academics, nongovernmental organizations, library associations, and businesses. These diverse actors thus participated in the work of the global net neutrality community of resistance.

By August 30, 2016, BEREC had analyzed all of the feedback and come to a decision about the guidelines. This decision was a victory for LQDN and its partners in SaveTheInternetEU in their fight for net neutrality. Significantly, BEREC's final guidelines did not allow ISPs to modify users' streams of data or block them from using their cell phone to connect another device to the Internet. Of equal importance, the final guidelines prohibited telecommunications firms from selling preferential treatment of regular Internet services (Lohninger 2016).

Despite this general victory, the practice of zero rating remained unresolved by the BEREC guidelines. Zero rating is a practice where ISPs seek to attract customers by offering extremely low prices for their initial services, including commercial offers of access to so-called "free" resources like Facebook and Wikipedia. After gaining these new customers, ISPs often change their rates to make the services more expensive. Zero rating is thus a way for ISPs to charge different amounts for different kinds of data. Lohninger (2016) emphasized that the BEREC guidelines recommended reviewing rulings by national telecommunications regulators on a case by case basis, similar to the practice in the U.S.

Margaux Huard, an LQDN staff member, highlighted the complex implications of zero rating for net neutrality in a 2016 interview. She described an example from 2009, when the Wikimedia Foundation launched the Wikipedia Zero project in Africa, followed by South America. Initially, this project seemed like a way to promote the digital commons, since it involved spreading access to Wikipedia to people who had historically been disenfranchised. The German Wikimedia community observed a problem over time, however, since users in some countries were using Wikipedia to host content and share films. Because Wikipedia was free, users were tending to stay on that site rather than accessing other sites. As Huard emphasized, this situation raises a question about priorities to consider in extending Internet access to the global South. She asked, "[W]hat is most important – giving the Internet to everyone, or providing Wikipedia for everyone?" (Interview with Margaux Huard, LQDN staff member, 2016). This question is particularly vital in countries where people pay for Internet access by the minute or the hour. In such circumstances, net neutrality is especially important so that users have the chance to access all available Internet sites. Net neutrality advocates raised similar critiques of Facebook's Free Basics program, which will be discussed further below.

Through the above range of campaigns, LQDN collaborated extensively with other activist organizations to shape the broader political and legal conditions for net neutrality across Europe. In the process, they contributed to developing and strengthening the global community of resistance to address their common concerns. As discussed in the last chapter with respect to global free software communities of resistance, these activists worked within their local contexts as well as forging international alliances to expand their work across borders.

Simultaneously, LQDN continued to build upon its history of activism to defend net neutrality within France. In the fall of 2014, the French government invited LQDN to participate in the process of developing the Digital Republic bill discussed in the last chapter. LQDN staff members engaged in the first phase of meetings with other experts and government representatives to discuss the process of public consultation for the bill, as well as key themes that should be addressed. As Huard noted in an interview, the group saw the Digital Republic consultation process as an opportunity to contribute proposals to raise public awareness and understanding about net neutrality. Furthermore, they sought to pressure the government to craft a bill that included a clear, strong protection of net neutrality. In the course of those discussions, LQDN participants wrote three proposals that were among the top 10 receiving public support. Nonetheless, an unexpected turn of events led LQDN to shift away from its work on the Digital Republic bill (Interview with Margaux Huard, LQDN staff member, 2016).

The Politics of Terrorism: Shifting Focus to Surveillance

On November 13, 2015, terrorists affiliated with the Islamic State of Iraq and the Levant (ISIL) engaged in a series of coordinated attacks in Paris. French prosecutor François Molins provided a time line of the attacks to Reuters news that was published on its website (accessed July 25, 2016. www.reuters.com/article/us-france-shooting-timeline-idUSKCN0 T31BS20151114#h8KRqimXftutLeR3.97). During a football game at the Stade de France in the northern suburb of Saint Denys, three suicide bombers struck. French President François Hollande was watching the match with the German foreign minister. Other attackers engaged in mass shootings and another suicide bombing at cafes, restaurants, and the Bataclan theater, in the 10th and 11th districts of Paris. Overall, the attackers killed 129 people and wounded 352, making these attacks the deadliest in France since World War II.

These attacks brought questions of civil liberties, net neutrality, and surveillance to the forefront of French politics. On November 14, in response to the attacks, the French government declared a state of emergency. The gravity of this action was clear, since the French government had not declared a state of emergency since 1961, when army generals attempted a coup d'etat during the Algerian War. The state of emergency gave the French government, including the security forces and police, exceptional powers. These powers included searching homes without a warrant from a judge; they did not extend to searches of the homes or offices of members of parliament, journalists, or lawyers. Security forces were authorized to enforce house arrest without a trial. For example, if they viewed people as security threats, they could confine them to their house for 12 hours a day to limit their movements. The state of emergency allowed the police to prevent people from meeting with others who were viewed as security threats, even after house arrest was suspended. It also permitted the authorities to use electronic tagging technologies to track suspects under house arrest. Of particular concern to LQDN, the state of emergency made it legal to block Internet sites considered as supportive of acts of terrorism; this raised the possibility for the government to block virtually any website. Authorities prohibited protests, and the state of emergency allowed them to disband a group if they considered it as disrupting public order. The government thus had the authority to restrict people's movements, as well as to curtail public gatherings and protests. In a piece in the *Independent* describing these powers, Andrew Griffin quoted French Prime Minister Manuel Valls' explanation to Parliament that the state of emergency was "'the fast response of a democracy faced with barbarism. This is the effective legal response in the face of an ideology of chaos'" (accessed July 25, 2016. www.independent.co.uk/news/world/europe/france-state-of-emergency-declared-for-three-months-allowing-authorities-to-shut-down-websites-and-a6740886.html).

The government was only allowed to declare a state of emergency for 12 days, after which time it was required that Parliament take a vote to get an extension. Parliament repeatedly granted such extensions between the fall of 2015 and the presidential elections in April 2017.

Through these multiple extensions, the state of emergency was normalized to a certain extent. Activists viewed the perpetuation of the state of emergency as a call to action.

At the time of the November attacks, LQDN was the only nongovernmental organization based in France that focused on questions of surveillance. These activists were thus in a key position to respond to the events. In the aftermath of the attacks and the declaration of the state of emergency, LQDN staff members met with their Board to strategize their response. Within two days, they issued statements against acts of terrorism, as well as critiquing the government's response in declaring the state of emergency. In an interview in May 2016, LQDN staff member Huard emphasized the importance of issuing clear statements that provided their positions on issues, as well as an analysis of why they were either winning or losing. Such statements were vital for educating the public about the turbulent political situation, highlighting implications for civil liberties and democracy. Furthermore, Huard highlighted critical decisions the activists faced in allocating their time and energy. LQDN was in a pivotal position to organize resistance to the state of emergency, because there were no other organizations working on surveillance issues. LQDN activists thus decided to shift their attention away from work on the Digital Republic bill to focus on responding to the state of emergency.

LQDN used Twitter effectively to spread information about unfolding events and to organize people to respond. Activists tweeted links to press releases, petitions, and videos. For example, on November 20, LQDN tweeted about the parliamentary vote to extend the state of emergency. The tweet linked to a press release with further information, noting that it was "document[ing] the disaster" (my translation) (accessed August 15, 2016. www.laquadrature.net/fr/RT-prorogation-de-l-etat-d-urgence-la-quadrature-du-net-documente-le-desastre). That was retweeted 57 times and "liked" by 19 people. In the tweet that got the most response that day, LQDN asked its Twitter followers to sign a petition to create a commission for a parliamentary inquiry about the infringements on civil liberties under the surveillance laws. That tweet was retweeted by 274 people and "liked" by 77 (accessed August 15, 2016. https://twitter.com/search?q=from%3Alaquadrature%20since%3A2015-11-20%20until%3A2015-11-23&src=typd). In press releases, social media, and other public statements, LQDN critiqued the state of emergency's lack of transparency and lack of a broader discussion with civil society at large. It called for such discussions, including consideration of the effects on civil liberties and democratic institutions.

In the context of the state of emergency, struggles over Internet politics emerged in parliamentary debates over privacy and national security. In this case, the government and free software advocates were united in opposition to Amendment CL92, designed to ban strong encryption in the

Digital Republic bill. Eighteen politicians from France's conservative Republican party introduced this amendment to mandate manufacturers of cell phones, tablets, and computers to configure their systems to allow police and intelligence agencies to access the data (accessed February 20, 2016. www.assemblee-nationale.fr/14/amendements/3318/CION_LOIS/CL92.asp). According to an article by Patrick Howell O'Neill in the *Daily Dot,* many people viewed this amendment as a response to the November terrorist attacks in Paris. These debates over the Digital Republic bill were part of larger discussions over the French government's response to the Paris attacks, and particularly to the state of emergency. Debates over encryption resonated with questions about the trade-offs between liberty and security. Critics of encryption viewed it as an obstacle to the work of law enforcement who needed access to devices like cell phones as critical pieces of evidence in police investigations. They argued that law enforcement would only gain access to such devices with permission of a judge, and in the context of an investigation. Since such investigations were often time sensitive, critics of encryption viewed it as an obstacle to the timely investigation of crimes that could endanger individual lives as well as national security. On the other hand, supporters of encryption viewed it as central to online privacy, security, and civil liberties (accessed February 20, 2016. www.dailydot.com/politics/encryption-backdoors-french-parliament-legislation-paris-attacks-crypto-wars/).

For example, French Secretary of State for Digital Affairs Axelle Lemaire supported encryption, which she viewed as central to the mission of the French Data Protection Authority (CNIL). She thus voiced opposition to Amendment CL92, rejecting it on the grounds that it was contrary to the right to encryption. She compared the amendment to NSA surveillance, noting that it would endanger personal privacy. She articulated her position in the context of broader European discussions, referencing the Dutch government's position paper supporting encryption and opposing the inclusion of backdoors in digital technology products, published in January 2016. Due to Lemaire's opposition, parliamentary delegate and vice president of the Republican party Nathalie Kosciusko-Morizet withdrew Amendment CL92 after less than two weeks of discussion (Champeau 2016a, 2016b).

Actors from a wide range of political positions thus debated questions of encryption, privacy, and civil liberties in the wake of the Paris attacks. In these debates, they revisited key questions raised by John Perry Barlow in the late 1990s, but from different perspectives. When Barlow articulated the freedom/sovereignty discourse, he highlighted the importance of defending Internet users' digital civil liberties, such as the right to privacy. French participants in the above debates shared these concerns. In the context of the state of emergency, LQDN activists highlighted the threats of state surveillance to civil liberties and democratic institutions. From the other side of the political spectrum, Axelle Lemaire defended strong encryption as a way to protect personal privacy. A range of actors from divergent political positions thus sought to protect digital civil liberties in distinct ways. These positions shared Barlow's emphasis on civil liberties that formed a key foundation for the development of the global net neutrality community of resistance.

Within this broader framework of defending civil liberties, the global net neutrality community of resistance was diverse. Advocates in different national contexts developed their local strategies and communities in distinct ways. As LQDN continued its organizing in France in the context of the state of emergency, defending civil liberties against surveillance remained a touchstone for net neutrality activism. In Brazil, net neutrality advocates shared the European focus on protecting civil liberties. The Brazilian and European advocates differed, however, in their emphasis on defending sovereignty. While European net neutrality activists organized against the dangers of government surveillance, they did not articulate these concerns through specific references to sovereignty. By contrast, Brazilian net neutrality advocates employed language more similar to Barlow's 1996 declaration about the need to protect citizens from government domination of cyberspace.

As discussed above, Barlow defended the freedom of what he called the citizens of cyberspace. He encouraged them to struggle for sovereignty from governments, which he viewed as colonial powers seeking to control this exciting new realm. Barlow's commitment to the combined defense of freedom and sovereignty resonated with the 1970s sovereignty discourse of governments from the global South. In particular, the Brazilian government has pursued this defense of freedom and sovereignty in a range of ways, from the 1970s into the early decades of the twenty-first century. In the process, the Brazilian government and Brazilian net neutrality advocates contributed to the development of the freedom/sovereignty discourse, as well as to the emergence of the global net neutrality community of resistance. A diverse range of net neutrality advocates participated in this process in Brazil, largely through broader strategies to promote digital inclusion.

Promoting Net Neutrality and Digital Inclusion in Brazil

As discussed in Chapter 2, the Brazilian government played a leading role in articulating the sovereignty discourse beginning in the 1970s. From the 1970s until 1990, the Brazilian government pursued an informatics policy to promote the development of local computer and software industries. In the 1990s, the Collor administration responded to the pressures of neoliberal globalization, including a trade war with the U.S. government, by dismantling the informatics policy and opening Brazilian markets to foreign investment (Schoonmaker 2002). When Luiz Inácio Lula da Silva was elected President in 2003, he transformed that neoliberal approach to build upon the earlier informatics policy goals of promoting technological autonomy. He introduced a new focus in Brazilian information and communications policy by emphasizing the use of free software. As discussed in Chapter 4, he decided to migrate from proprietary to free software in government agencies. The Lula administration thus employed software policy to pursue larger goals of prioritizing local technological development, strengthening Brazil's position in the international division of labor, and fostering digital inclusion (Schoonmaker 2007; Shaw 2011; Takhteyev 2012). As Chan (2013, xii) noted with respect to other Latin American free software advocates in the 2000s, free software involved questions of "political sovereignty from the monopolistic power of transnational corporations in the global South." Lula thus viewed software policy as a tool to push forward broad development goals, transforming local conditions of development while strengthening Brazilian sovereignty in its relationships with foreign governments and corporations.

Cultural Projects, Creative Commons, and the Freedom/ Sovereignty Discourse

At the national level, Lula sought to foster digital inclusion, democratizing access to software and other digital technologies by social groups historically marginalized by race and class. To lead this work on digital inclusion, Lula chose Gilberto Gil as Minister of Culture in 2003. Gil was one of the leaders of *tropicalismo*, the Brazilian artistic movement that mixed distinct artistic forms in fresh ways, such as combining more traditional Brazilian and African rhythms with rock and roll. This movement thus created hybrid cultural forms through practices of remixing that were novel at the time, but have since become widely practiced in processes of sampling and sharing. Moreover, Gil and other Brazilian musicians in the *tropicalismo* movement merged art with politics. They wrote songs as a critical response to the Brazilian dictatorships in the 1960s, and were subsequently jailed and exiled.

Fitting with his interest in creating hybrid cultural forms, Gil appreciated the potential of digital technologies to contribute to this process. He was involved in projects to share artistic work through the Internet, building connections between artists and the wide range of people around the world who appreciated their work. In 1996, the same year that Barlow wrote his "Declaration of the Independence of Cyberspace," and a year after commercial use of the Internet became available in Brazil, Gil wrote a song that translated into English as "Through the Internet." In this upbeat, jazzy piece, Gil celebrated the potential of the Internet for sharing his art and connecting with his fans. He wrote about creating his own website and making a home page; he then stated,

I want to enter the network,
Promote a debate,
Come together on the Internet with
A group of fans from Connecticut.
>   (Accessed October 20, 2016. https://www.vagalume.com.
>   br/gilberto-gil/pela-internet.html, my translation)

Toward the end of the song, he wrote about wanting to use the Internet to make contact with "homes in Nepal, bars in Gabon," thus expressing a desire to extend his network of connections from the U.S. to South Asia and the west coast of Central Africa (accessed October 20, 2016. www. vagalume.com.br/gilberto-gil/pelainternet.html, my translation). This song resonated with free software and net neutrality proponents advocating the freedom to share their ideas and cultural products via cyberspace.

Through this music and other work as Brazilian Minister of Culture from 2003 until 2008, Gil contributed to the development of the freedom/ sovereignty discourse. Due to his advocacy of digital inclusion, free software, and net neutrality, his supporters sometimes affectionately referred to him as "Minister Hacker." His critics sometimes used that term as well, to emphasize their differences with his positions and imply that he was a hacker in a negative sense of undermining the stability of computer systems. In a 2004 talk at the University of São Paulo posted on the Brazilian Ministry of Culture website, Gil embraced the hacker ethic of sharing and collaboration. He discussed that ethic as rooted in the freedoms of users to run, study, redistribute, and modify free software that were legally protected by copyleft licenses such as the GNU General Public License (GPL). He argued that his commitment to software and Internet freedom was rooted in his experience with the Brazilian military dictatorship censoring his artistic work, thus emphasizing the importance of artistic sovereignty from government control. To put these values of freedom into practice, he offered a vision of Brazil becoming "a creator and developer of new programs, of new forms of licensing and creation of content, of new modes of access to content" (accessed September 9, 2016. www.cultura.gov.br/ noticias-ancine1/-/asset_publisher/QRV5ftQkjXuV/content/ministro-da-cultura-gilberto-gil-em-aula-magna-na-universidade-de-sao-paulo-usp-/11025, my translation).

Of equal importance, Gil contributed to the development of the freedom/ sovereignty discourse by putting it into practice in the emerging Creative Commons community. He highlighted Creative Commons as a key example of alternative forms of licensing that opened up new, exciting possibilities for the production and dissemination of local content, through whatever medium or purpose that users chose. He sought to strengthen possibilities for digital inclusion of groups that had historically been marginalized by class and racial inequalities. Toward this end, he developed programs to democratize access to technical resources and teachers to train Brazilians to engage in these new forms of cultural production. He stated, "we are citizens and consumers, emitters and receptors of knowledge and information, beings at the same time autonomous and connected in networks, that are the new form of collectivity" (accessed September 9, 2016. www.cultura.gov.br/noticias-ancine1/-/asset_publisher/QRV5ftQkjXuV/content/ministro-da-cultura-gilberto-gil-em-aula-magna-na-universidade-de-sao-paulo-usp-/11025, my translation).

Based upon his commitment to the work of Creative Commons, Gil supported Brazil's participation in the project. As discussed in Chapter 2, Lawrence Lessig, Hal Abelson, and Eric Eldred founded Creative Commons in 2001. The *Fundação Getulio Vargas* (FGV) Law School in Rio led the effort to develop a relationship between Brazil and Creative Commons. Gil joined this project, promoting the use of Creative Commons licenses to make Brazilian cultural products more accessible internationally.

Ronaldo Lemos, a professor at FGV Law School, was the project lead for what was then called iCommons Brazil. Once the Creative Commons license had been translated into Portuguese and adapted to fit the Brazilian context, Lemos retranslated the license into English. He provided that English translation of the Brazilian Portuguese license on the Creative Commons blog, including annotations about how and why the Brazilian iCommons participants had changed the license. In the blog discussion of August 5, 2003, iCommons participant Glenn Otis Brown presented Lemos' work to the other participants with the following message:

> The idea of this particular document is to make clear to us at Creative Commons what substantive legal aspects of the license have changed in the process of creating the first draft of the translation/adaptation. It will prove useful both in the iCommons Brazil exercise, but also as an artifact for comparing the iCommons experience in various countries.
>
> It will also serve as a great example for other iCommons countries to follow.
>
> (Accessed September 3, 2016. http://lists.ibiblio.org/pipermail/cc-br/2003-August/000019.html)

iCommons Brazil advocates thus participated in the process of developing Creative Commons as an implicit global community of resistance. Over time, they continued this process by engaging with the Creative Commons community. Pedro Mizukami and Eduardo Magrani, professors at the Centro de Tecnologia e Sociedade (CTS), or Center of Technology and Society at the FGV Law School, coordinated the project. They worked with Sérgio Branco, a researcher at the Institute of Technology and Society (ITS RIO) (accessed September 3, 2016. https://br.creativecommons.org/sobre/). CTS continues to represent Creative

Commons in Brazil, working to adapt Creative Commons licenses to the Brazilian judicial context.

Gil supported the early work on Creative Commons licenses in Brazil, both through policy as Minister of Culture and through his own artistic work. His political approach was informed by his efforts as an artist. He waged a successful legal battle to rescind the existing contracts on all of his musical pieces, under which the music companies held all rights to his work. After winning this legal struggle, he relicensed over 400 of his songs under different Creative Commons licenses. In some cases, Gil chose a license to retain all of his rights over the work; in other cases, he chose a license that gave other artists the legal freedom to incorporate the songs into remixes of their own (Rohter 2007).

Due to their mutual commitment to digital inclusion, John Perry Barlow and Gilberto Gil became friends after meeting at Tactic Media Brazil in 2003. They deliberated key questions of digital inclusion and participatory politics. In an interview with *New York Times* writer Larry Rohter (2007), Barlow stated, "'I don't think there is anyone quite like Gil anywhere in the world.'" Noting the importance of Gil's work as Minister of Culture, Barlow told Rohter (2007) that Gil is "'a spearhead. He's been thinking about I.P. [intellectual property] issues forever and clearly gets the importance of all of this. But he's also in a unique position to implement his ideas.'" By 2004, Barlow and Gil began collaborating to widen the availability of Brazilian music online. They employed Creative Commons licenses that provided legal rights for users to remix and share these cultural products.

Through their collaboration, Barlow and Gil contributed simultaneously to the development of the freedom/sovereignty discourse and the expansion of Creative Commons as an implicit global community of resistance. They developed new pathways for Brazilian artists, musicians, and creators of cultural works to contribute to a global commons of those works. They strengthened and extended the process discussed in Chapter 2, where participants in Creative Commons contributed to the development of the digital commons.

E-Democracy, the Marco Civil, and Net Neutrality

The Brazilian government engaged in a second set of strategies to promote digital inclusion by introducing new forms of political participation, as well as addressing questions of net neutrality, civil liberties, and the right to privacy. It emphasized the importance of such measures in the context of citizens' growing use of digital technologies and the Internet in their daily lives. At the same time, however, the government acknowledged major challenges for implementing these strategies for digital inclusion, due to the persistent inequalities of access to these technologies.

Toward this end, in 2009, congressional representatives in the Brazilian Chamber of Deputies designed an electronic government platform called *e-Democracia* or e-Democracy. This project was part of a broader program on electronic government initiated by Presidential decree by Brazilian President Cardoso in 2000. The Brazilian deputies designed e-Democracy to promote digital inclusion by allowing citizens to access information about government practices and services, as well as to participate politically. They piloted the program in 2009 and 2010, and then proceeded to implement it (Freitas 2016).

As Freitas (2016) noted, the Brazilian government viewed digital governance systems, or e-Democracy, as a way to promote digital inclusion by fostering new forms of political participation that could strengthen the relationship between citizens and the government. For example, Brazilian government officials developed ways for citizens to participate in parliamentary debates. Moreover, e-Democracy provided tools for citizens to collaborate in the development of bills, by making their own proposals and commenting on the full range of proposals through discussion fora. This process was similar to the French government's project of promoting citizen participation in the Digital Republic bill, discussed in the last chapter. Freitas (2016, 33) argued that the e-Democracy project created a "virtual public space for deliberation." E-Democracy provided a process for this virtual public space to operate. In this process, a member of Congress, often pressured by an organized social movement, requests that the coordinators of e-Democracy create a Virtual Legislative Community (VLC) where citizens can discuss and make recommendations about particular bills.

These efforts to promote digital inclusion were limited, however, by the enduring inequalities of access to the Internet, computers, and software in Brazil. Furthermore, government officials retained institutional control over the process. They chose which citizen contributions to consider, without providing any formal criteria about how this process should be conducted (Freitas 2016).

Despite these limitations of e-Democracy for promoting widespread political participation, citizens used this tool to register their comments about Brazil's *Marco Civil da Internet*. Commonly referred to as Brazil's Internet Constitution, or the Civil Rights Framework for the Internet, the Marco Civil had vital implications for civil liberties. Indeed, proponents of the Marco Civil presented it as a way to protect fundamental civil liberties in the context of increasing reliance upon the Internet in social, political, cultural, and economic activities. Struggles emerged during the process of developing the bill, however, that resulted in two key concessions opposed by activists for digital civil liberties. Digital rights groups opposed a mandate to collect and store data on users' connection logs. Of equal importance, they opposed practices of zero rating where ISPs appealed to customers with reduced prices for initial subscriptions that included "free" access to popular sites like Facebook. Similar to the zero rating practices discussed in the last section, Brazilian ISPs used this approach to charge customers different prices for different kinds of data.

Freitas (2016) noted that congressional representatives only integrated 9 of the 44 citizen contributions offering suggestions about how to change the proposed Marco Civil bill. These nine contributions came from organized groups, including the Collective Progressive Bloggers of Paraná, journalists from media outlets such as Globo TV Network and telecommunications firms like Oi, professors at the Federal University of ABC, and the Getúlio Vargas Foundation (FGV).

Brazilian President Dilma Rousseff signed the Marco Civil into law on April 24, 2014. Many of the provisions of the Marco Civil, however, depended on secondary regulations. These secondary regulations included data retention limits and zero rating. Implementing the Marco Civil was thus inextricably linked with struggles over how to develop regulations in these two key areas.

First, while debates developed over the Marco Civil in 2014, similar debates unfolded over a comprehensive Data Protection Bill that would establish key provisions to protect individual privacy. These debates were complementary and thus interconnected with the Marco Civil. Similar to the United States, Brazil did not have comprehensive legal restrictions on the collection, use, and disclosure of personal data (Pinho and Rodriguez 2015). According to a special report on data protection in Brazil by InternetLab, a São Paulo-based, independent research group specializing in law and technology, debates over data protection were prolonged. The special report, issued in September 2016 and available on InternetLab's website, discussed how these debates extended from 2014 into 2016 (www.internetlab.org.br/en/data-protection-special/). During this period, the Brazilian Congress and Senate considered a number of preliminary draft bills with a range of approaches to regulate the collection and processing of data about individuals. The Brazilian Constitution included general protections of the rights to privacy; however, Brazil did not have legislation detailing the nature of those rights, particularly with respect to personal data. Internet activists were primarily concerned with the implications of this lack of regulation for citizens' rights to privacy. Furthermore, the lack of such regulations raised questions about the protection of personal data that affected the economic interests of Brazilian firms. For example, over 100 countries enacted regulations on data protection that the European Union considered adequate to allow them to receive personal data from European citizens. Brazil's lack of regulation meant that it did not qualify for that list, meaning that some Brazilian companies were prevented from receiving data about European citizens.

In some cases, this lack of data protection limited Brazilian firms' opportunities to compete in the market. For instance, in 2012, Google chose Chile as the site for its first Latin American data center. Google estimated that the investment would be worth $150 million. Chile had data protection laws since 1999, creating market conditions that Google considered more secure for protecting personal data (www.internetlab. org.br/en/data-protection-special/).

Policy debates over data protection in Brazil took a dramatic turn in the context of struggles to impeach President Dilma Rousseff. On May 11, 2016, the Brazilian Senate voted to suspend Rousseff from office while they conducted an impeachment investigation. After a conflictual period fraught with debates over corruption, on August 31, 2016, the Senate voted 61:20 to remove Rousseff from office. In one of her last acts as President before her suspension in May, Rousseff submitted a draft data protection bill that had been prepared by the Ministry of Justice through a process of online public debate. Once Michel Temer became President, however, Deputies introduced different bills that had not been developed through such an extensive process of debate. Debates over data protection thus continued, and the InternetLab special report noted that a final outcome remained uncertain (www.internetlab.org.br/en/ data-protection-special/). In February 2017, the South American affiliate of the international human rights organization Article 19, which special-izes in protecting freedom of expression and information, issued a study comparing three bills under consideration by the Brazilian Congress. All of the bills sought to regulate corporate and government practices for handling personal data (www.article19.org/resources.php/resource/38616/ en/brazil:-new-study-analyses-bills-on-personal-data-regulation).

Before her suspension in May, Rousseff signed a decree that had equally important implications for the Marco Civil. This decree affected the sec-ond set of struggles over developing regulations concerning net neutral-ity and zero rating. These regulations would affect key conditions for implementing the Marco Civil. For example, decree 8771 was intended to clarify aspects of the Marco Civil that had been considered question-able or undefined. It specified conditions under which net neutrality rules did not apply to particular telecommunications services. Furthermore, it provided guidelines for telecommunications providers about how to deliver applications and structure data packages. An online Bloomberg News article described how Rousseff signed the decree on May 11, mere hours before the Senate voted to remove her from office (accessed August 20, 2016. www.bna.com/brazil-internet-decree-n57982072502/).

In a May 25 statement on its website, the South American affiliate of Article 19 praised decree 8771 as affirming the principle of net neutral-ity. Article 3 of the decree called for safeguards for unrestricted public access to the Internet in order to implement the Marco Civil's call for equal treatment of all Internet users. Article 4 of the decree stated that discrimination or degradation of Internet traffic should be considered exceptional measures. Such measures were only warranted when tele-communications providers had to give priority to providing emergency services, or when they were needed for technical reasons that affected the ability to provide Internet services or applications. The decree clarified the conditions under which administrative authorities could request access to data from users. It also required federal authorities to publish annual reports of all of the requests they made, including the numbers of users affected and the numbers of requests that were accepted and declined. The decree addressed questions of data retention, defining responsibilities of people who had access to stored data and establishing guidelines for how that access would be given (www.article19. org/resources.php/resource/38392/en/brazil:-important-step-forward-for-the-brazilian-civil-rights-framework-for-the-internet).

Decree 8771 highlighted the ways that implementing the Marco Civil was linked to debates over how to implement its guarantee of net neutrality. For example, the decree was designed to ban the practice of zero rating, due to the problems it raised for net neutrality. The South American affiliate of Article 19 analyzed these problems in a report assessing the implementation of the Marco Civil after its first six months. This report highlighted the Marco Civil's guarantee of net neutrality, so that all data would be treated equally without discriminating according to content, origin, or destination; the type of service being offered; or the kind of equipment or application being used. Some companies doing business in Brazil offered commercial services that net neutrality advocates viewed as problematic.

Conflicts over net neutrality largely hinged on whether the practice of zero rating violated the net neutrality provision of the Marco Civil. The Article 19 report noted that offering telecommunications subscribers the so-called "free" access to social media was a potential violation of net neutrality. Such a violation was significant because many Brazilian Internet users obtained their Internet access through cell phone plans that offered restricted access to some Internet sites, through 3G and 4G networks. For example, some cell phone plans included limited access to Facebook, Twitter, and Orkut, as well as use of email services such as Gmail, without providing access to other Internet sites. Telecommunications operators were thus limiting users' connections to the Internet to particular sites and services. Through these restrictions, they were not complying with the Marco Civil's net neutrality provision; they were not providing equal access to all sites (Article 19, 2015).

The practice of zero rating thus became a focal point for ongoing Brazilian struggles over net neutrality. These struggles resonated with those waged in Europe and Africa, as discussed in previous sections; moreover, they shared similar goals to struggles over zero rating in India, to be discussed in the next section.

Indeed, these distinct local actions in different parts of the world shared a common focus to defend conditions for net neutrality. They revealed the emergence of the global net neutrality community of resistance. Activists around the world pursued common aims, often without knowing each other or directly coordinating their activities. As noted above, these actions took distinct forms in particular national contexts. European net neutrality activists placed greater emphasis on protecting civil liberties from government surveillance, while Brazilian advocates highlighted the importance of defending national sovereignty. Overall, however, these net neutrality advocates in different parts of the world shared a fundamental struggle to protect citizens' freedoms to access the Internet on equal terms. Toward that end, they employed strategies to protect the existing telecommunications infrastructure vital to the use of the Internet. In the process, these actors defended net neutrality as a key condition for the digital commons. Certainly, their work laid a foundation for other net neutrality advocates to engage in a second set of struggles for Internet freedom.

Second Terrain of Struggle: Evading Surveillance, Creating Alternative Infrastructures

When Snowden revealed the NSA's surveillance activities in 2013, it became clear that those activities relied upon the telecommunications network to gather user data. Snowden (2016) thus emphasized that the lack of control over telecommunications providers, including the network path over which communications traveled, made users vulnerable to surveillance. In this context where telecommunications providers might be hostile to user freedoms, Snowden (2016) suggested two potential responses. First, users might employ intricate modes of encryption, tunneling, and mixing their communications to evade potential surveillance. In this case, they might protect their freedoms by making their communications unreadable by government or corporate actors. Second, they might devise strategies to create alternative networks, thus replacing the telecommunications providers. Community-controlled telecommunications infrastructure projects would allow them to operate in the spaces between the large networks. They could thus remain undetected.

As discussed above, the surveillant assemblage (Haggerty and Ericson 2000; Haggerty and Gazso 2005) created a context where citizens and consumers were subject to complex, shifting forms of surveillance in their everyday lives. This ubiquitous web of surveillance posed challenges for protecting civil liberties in a democracy, including the right to privacy.

Eben Moglen analyzed these practices of surveillance and sought innovative solutions to address their threats to civil liberties. Moglen had a valuable combination of skills and knowledge to craft such solutions, particularly in the context of ubiquitous Internet use. He began his career as a programmer working for IBM; in 1975, he helped develop the first email system in the U.S. Subsequently, he became a lawyer and free software advocate. Moglen worked closely with other free software proponents over many years, serving as the legal advisor to FSF until 2006. In 2005, he founded the Software Freedom Law Center (SFLC), which offers pro bono legal services to free software developers, communities, and corporations. He continues to serve as Director-Counsel and Chairman of SFLC, as well as Professor of law and legal history at Columbia University.

Perspectives on Resisting Surveillance

Moglen recognized the vital implications of Snowden's revelations for democracy and citizenship. In the fall of 2013, he gave a series of four lectures at Columbia Law School entitled "Snowden and the Future." In those talks, he highlighted the relationship between debates about privacy and the freedom of citizens in a democracy. He called upon his audience to consider ways to resist contemporary systems of surveillance. He explored the significance of what we mean by privacy, delineating the importance of three elements of privacy for a democratic society. Secrecy and anonymity allow citizens to choose the people with whom we want to discuss our ideas about contemporary events, and thus to decide whether we want to make our ideas public. Autonomy allows citizens to exercise our rights to free speech, as well as to make other life decisions, without coercion or violation of our rights to secrecy and anonymity. From this perspective, privacy is multidimensional. It affects interconnected aspects of our experiences as individuals and in relationship to others in a democracy.

Conditions for privacy and other civil liberties transformed after September 2001. Since that time, world economic and political powers developed a global consensus about the necessity of surveillance. For example, Moglen (2013a) described a conversation with a senior official in the Obama administration who noted that U.S., Chinese, and European government officials all agreed that surveillance was inevitable and should not be limited. Moglen (2013a) underscored the significance of this consensus on the necessity of surveillance as a key threat to democracy. He argued that

> [w]hat had opened by the end of the first decade of the 21st century was a gap between what the people of the world thought their rights were and what their governments had given away in return for intelligence useful only to the governments.
>
> (Moglen 2013a, 6)

This gap was central to the visibility paradox discussed above, where citizens were unaware of the extent to which corporations and governments surveilled their daily activities. With his revelations about NSA surveillance, Snowden exposed the extent of this surveillance. He illuminated the many ways that surveillance contradicted civil liberties fundamental to democracy, such as free speech and the right to privacy.

Moglen (2010) understood the nature of contemporary surveillance as largely rooted in the increasing centralization of network services on the Internet, based on a design called "server client architecture." In contrast to the original technical design of the Internet as a peer-to-peer communications system, the corporations offering network services stored user data in centralized servers, including logs of user activity. These logs were useful in facilitating the operation of the systems, making it possible to troubleshoot bugs in the software and keep track of how computers were functioning. More problematically, however, this increasing storage of user data in centralized servers created "vast repositories of hierarchically organized data about people at the edges of the network that they do not control" (Moglen 2010). Since most users do not understand how servers operate, they do not understand the implications of this arrangement. Indeed, the increasing predominance of centralized servers and data logs undermined the original peer-to-peer architecture of the Internet. Users became increasingly dependent on web servers owned by corporations, otherwise known as the "cloud." Instead of the original peer-to-peer model of the Internet, users became dependent on these centralized servers in the "cloud." They participated in a wide range of terms of service agreements that allowed corporations to store their data, as well as to mine that data for marketing purposes (Moglen 2010).

For example, as Scally (2015) notes, there is a contradiction between Google's claim that Gmail users preserve control over their intellectual property and the actual terms of its service agreement. On Google's website on terms of service, it states that "[s]ome of our Services allow you to upload, submit, store, send or receive content. You retain ownership of any intellectual property rights that you hold in that content. In short, what belongs to you stays yours" (www.google.com/intl/en/policies/terms/). At first, this statement sounds like users of Google services will be able to maintain control over their intellectual property. The next section of the agreement, however, reveals that users are allowing Google extensive control over their content. It states,

> [w]hen you upload, submit, store, send or receive content to or through our Services, you give Google (and those we work with) a worldwide license to use, host, store, reproduce, modify, create derivative works (such as those resulting from translations, adaptations or other changes we make so that your content works better with our Services), communicate, publish, publicly perform, publicly display and distribute such content.
>
> (https://www.google.com/intl/en/policies/terms/)

This statement covers such a wide range of applications of user data that it is difficult to imagine exactly what it means. The terms of service agreement continues into perpetuity, even if a user decides to stop using Google services. Through a centralized process of storing and mining user data, Google's "automated systems analyze your content (including emails) to provide you personally relevant product features, such as customized search results, tailored advertising, and spam and malware detection. This analysis occurs as the content is sent, received, and when it is stored" (www.google.com/intl/en/policies/terms/). When consumers consent to these terms of service, they thus give Google permission to continually analyze the content of all of their emails, documents, or other materials that they send or store through Google's services. They pay for these services with their data, and Google's ongoing control over that data for a multitude of possible uses.

In a similar vein, Facebook's Statement of Rights and Responsibilities informs users that "you own all of the content and information you post on Facebook, and you can control how it is shared through your <u>privacy</u> and <u>application settings</u>" (www.facebook.com/legal/terms). Similar to Google's terms of service agreement, this statement initially appears to provide users with choices about how they want to protect their privacy, and thus retain control over their data. The Statement continues, however, declaring,

> For content that is covered by intellectual property rights, like photos and videos (IP content), you specifically give us the following permission, subject to your <u>privacy</u> and <u>application settings</u>: you grant us a non-exclusive, transferable, sub-licensable, royalty-free, worldwide license to use any IP content that you post on or in connection with Facebook (IP License). This IP License ends when you delete your IP content or your account unless your content has been shared with others, and they have not deleted it.
>
> (https://www.facebook.com/legal/terms)

Facebook appears to give users more of an option to terminate the corporation's license over their content than Google's perpetual control. The last clause of the Statement, however, includes a major loophole undermining this control. If Facebook users have shared content with friends, and those friends have not deleted it, Facebook retains its license. Furthermore, Facebook's algorithms are designed to surveil its users when they are on the site, noting what users read and how long they spend reading it, as well as the web pages that they visit that include Facebook "like" buttons. As Facebook and other social media sites such as Twitter are surveilling our reading in this manner, Moglen (2013b, 5) argues that they are undermining "[t]he anonymity of reading [as] the central, fundamental guarantor of freedom of the mind." He refers to

Facebook's efforts to provide its users with options about how to control their privacy as a distraction. This distraction is designed to make users feel like they have real choices that they need to think about, instead of focusing their attention on the underlying problem of corporate surveillance of consumers' reading. He states, "[t]his is the system that we allowed to grow up so quickly that we did not understand its implications. Which is how ecological crises happen" (Moglen 2013b, 7). Moglen thus provides an intriguing perspective on the implications of the visibility paradox. Since this paradox combines the hypervisibility of citizens' lives with the invisibility of corporate and government surveillance, it reflects an ecological crisis in our digital environment.

In the wake of the Snowden revelations, Moglen (2013a) identified two main challenges to organizing people to resist contemporary systems of surveillance. First, there is a sense of hopelessness to counteract the pervasive nature of surveillance, since privacy has become quite difficult, if not impossible, to attain. Second, people seem to feel that as long as they are not doing anything wrong, they do not have a reason to be concerned about violations of privacy or other civil liberties. In response to these tendencies, Moglen (2013a, 7–8) advocates resistance:

> If we are not doing anything wrong, then we have a right to do everything we can to maintain the traditional balance between us and the power that is listening. We have a right to be obscure. We have a right to mumble. We have a right to speak languages they do not get. We have a right to meet when and where and how we please so as to evade the paddy rollers.

To resist the current surveillance system, Moglen (2013a) suggests that we can rely on two constitutional traditions. The first involves the Supreme Court ruling against surveillance on the grounds that it is unconstitutional. That depends on the decision of the justices and the workings of the institutional legal regime. The second tradition relies on collective action and is rooted in a constitutional tradition arising from resistance to slavery. Moglen (2013a, 9) argues that "[r]unning away from slavery is a group activity." He cautions that we in the U.S. have "forgotten how much of our constitutional tradition was made in the contact between people who needed to run away in order to be free and people who knew that they needed to be helping, because slavery is wrong" (Moglen 2013a, 9). This part of our constitutional tradition involves fighting to protect everyone's right to be free, because slavery is wrong, and because encroaching on freedom of speech is wrong. Moglen urges citizens to demand that their governments protect their rights to be free from spying by outsiders, and to observe the rule of law over governmental practices of surveillance over their own citizens.

Moglen (2013a, 12) calls on us to do what he calls "the most important political work of the later 21st century," to "re-imagine what a Net at peace would look like: cyberpeace." This state of cyberpeace would involve the end of surveillance that undermines citizens' freedoms. Ending such surveillance would allow us to protect a cornerstone of democracy. Certainly, ending such surveillance involves addressing both the actions of the government national security apparatus and the corporate operations that undergird it. Moglen (2013b, 2) refers to these corporate activities as violating "privacy [as] an ecological rather than a transactional substance." He argues that data mining corporations profit by presenting privacy as a transaction between a corporation and a consumer, where corporations offer services such as free email from Gmail or Yahoo in exchange for a consumer agreeing to allow the firm to read their mail. The U.S. has become the heart of the global data mining industry, due to its lenient privacy protection laws.

In contrast to the corporate view of privacy as a transaction with its customers, Moglen (2013b) views privacy as involving broader social relationships. Consumers who choose to use a free email service in exchange for allowing a firm to read their messages thus allow firms such as Google and Yahoo to receive copies of all of the messages from the people with whom they correspond. Snowden's revelations highlight how such firms share that information with the NSA. Moglen (2013b, 3) argues that these threats to privacy are prime examples of "ecological crises created by industrial overreaching," comparing these threats to other examples of industrial overreach such as climate disruption.

Strategies toward Surveillance: Resisting Facebook's Zero Rating, Degoogling, Freedombox

Moglen's (2013b) perspective on ecological crisis resonates with concerns of net neutrality activists to promote equal access to the Internet. These activists devised multiple strategies to promote such access, ranging from large-scale government policy decisions to choices available for individual users.

For example, net neutrality activists in India organized to push for government policy to address this ecological crisis. They struggled to oppose Facebook's Free Basics program. Similar to other practices of zero rating discussed above, Free Basics offers access to a range of popular Internet services such as Wikipedia, the BBC, weather and health sites, as well as Facebook itself. It was designed to operate on 2G and 3G networks, offering scaled-down versions of the services that would operate more smoothly on such networks than the original versions. Facebook founder Mark Zuckerberg characterized Free Basics as a strategy to promote Internet access for disenfranchised populations who had historically lacked it. By February 2016, Facebook stated that Free Basics had made it possible for over 19 million people in 36 countries to gain access to the Internet.

Facebook originally sought to bring the program to India in February 2015, calling it Internet.org. Indian net neutrality activists organized to pressure the Indian government, arguing that Free Basics gave an unfair advantage to some Internet services, privileging them over others. Through the practice of zero rating, Free Basics exempted the services it included from data caps that applied to other services. The Telecom Regulatory Authority of India studied the issue, releasing a white paper that ruled against Facebook. It ruled that it was illegal for any service to either offer or charge what it described as "discriminatory tariffs for data services on the basis of content" (quoted in Hempel 2016). Zuckerberg objected to the ruling, arguing that he was working to benefit millions of users who could not get online to advocate for themselves. He released a video arguing that net neutrality advocates needed to be more reasonable in their stances. He questioned, "'[A]re we a community that values people and improving people's lives above all else? Or are we a community that puts the intellectual purity of technology above people's needs?'" (quoted in Hempel 2016). The Indian case thus exemplifies struggles between activists, national governments, and corporations over net neutrality and the conditions under which citizens will gain access to the Internet.

Moving from the national to the individual level, consumers face choices about how to respond to the ecological crisis posed by the surveillant assemblage. In some significant ways, consumers with ready access to Facebook, Gmail, and other popular digital services face choices comparable to the ones confronting the Indian government. Most important, consumers must decide whether to participate in these ubiquitous services. Individual users make choices about their own activities; however, as Moglen (2013b) argued, these choices have ecological implications. The Indian government's ruling against Facebook, as a result of pressures from civil society, was a key choice in shaping the ecology of Internet use in the country as a whole. At the individual level, consumer decisions about digital services also affect the broader ecology of Internet use. Once consumers know the extent of the surveillance that is involved with these services, they have other consequential decisions to make. They face questions about whether to continue to participate in their own surveillance, as well as the complex web of surveillance practices within the surveillant assemblage.

Internet activists employed two major strategies to offer resources for consumers deciding how to respond to the surveillant assemblage.

As noted above, the first strategy involved what Snowden (2016) described as evading surveillance through modes of encryption and mixing their communications. Activists devised ways for users to encrypt or otherwise conceal their messages while continuing to use the existing telecommunications infrastructure.

In a 2014 interview, French free software activist Cerise Angier highlighted the importance of such strategies in the wake of the Snowden revelations. Angier was a staff member for April, the French free software association discussed in the last chapter. She emphasized that the Snowden revelations were shocking, since April activists had not realized the extent to which surveillance was being conducted. These activists were thus caught in the visibility paradox, confused by the invisibility of government and corporate surveillance practices. Angier noted that in the past, French media had sometimes portrayed April and other free software activists as overly "paranoid" about the potential problems posed by proprietary software systems. Such accounts downplayed the importance of the activists' efforts to defend consumers' abilities to choose the kinds of software they wanted to use and the ways they wanted to share digital files. After Snowden's revelations, Angier (interview 2014) wryly commented, "[w]e're supposed to be the paranoid ones, but we realized we were overly optimistic."

Angier observed that more people were aware of the problems with surveillance after the revelations; however, it required effort to change their practices of engaging with digital services. This was inconvenient, posing a hassle for consumers who were accustomed to engaging with those services in particular ways. Angier emphasized that as people learned to interact with technology, they were taught to be passive users who simply consumed the technology as a black box. They were not taught about how the technology worked, or how to control it themselves. They thus lacked the information required to make fully knowledgeable choices about how they wanted to engage with it (Interview with Cerise Angier 2014).

To combat these entrenched consumer practices, Angier highlighted the importance of work by another French activist community called Framasoft. Framasoft is a nonprofit popular education network dedicated to developing a Free, Decentralized, Ethical Internet built on Solidarity. Established in 2004 and based in Lyon, it has six paid staff. Framasoft contributes to the strategy of evading surveillance by developing a project called DeGoogling the Internet. On their website, they offer multiple ways to evade surveillance by changing practices of consuming digital services (https://degooglisons-internet.org/alternatives). They designed the project to approach consumers as making active choices about their relationship to technology and digital services. Toward that end, the website offers an extensive list of alternatives to systems that mine user data. The list includes links to the project websites, so that consumers can research further information and download free alternative services if they choose. For example, as alternatives to web browsers like Google Chrome, Internet Explorer, Safari, and Opera, Framasoft recommends Firefox, The Onion Router (Tor), Qupzilla, and Midori. As an alternative to email clients like Outlook and Apple Mail, Framasoft recommends Thunderbird with Enigmail, Tor Birdy, Kmail, and Sylpheed. As an alternative to online payment systems like Paypal, Google Wallet, and Apple

Pay, Framasoft recommends Bitcoin and Litecoin. As an alternative to Search engines like Google, Bing, and Yahoo, Framasoft recommends Searx, DuckDuckGo, and Disconnect, among others. Furthermore, the site includes suggestions for alternative forms of shared calendars, note-taking, collaborative writing, online surveys, presentations, partic004ipative spreadsheets, social networking, and more. This extensive col004lection of alternatives to systems that collect and mine user data gives consumers a range of practical ways to evade surveillance. By accessing the Framasoft website, consumers reconfigure their use of digital services to strengthen their privacy and control over their personal data.

As Snowden (2016) argues in his LibrePlanet address, evading sur004veillance is an important way to protect citizens' civil liberties. It is not sufficient, however, since corporate-controlled telecommunications structures continue to provide a basis to engage in extensive surveillance. To address the limitations of evasion, Moglen and his free software col004leagues designed the FreedomBox. This technology provides consumers with an alternative, community-controlled telecommunications infra004structure. As Snowden (2016) recommends, this type of infrastructure allows users to communicate in the spaces between the large networks without being detected.

The FreedomBox is a personal web server that users carry with them. Sometimes referred to as a mesh network, the FreedomBox allows users to resist centralized control over their Internet use, as well as their data. By plugging the FreedomBox into a power jack, users access their data in a variety of social networking sites, send email, or write and publish documents.

In February 2011, Moglen (2011) announced the launch of the non004profit FreedomBox Foundation in a speech at the Free and Open Source Software Developers' European Meeting (FOSDEM) in Brussels. He urged the free software developers to contribute to the project, particu004larly by creating software to run on the small, individualized web serv004ers. He posed a vision of having the boxes available around the world at affordable prices. In a month, the FreedomBox Foundation raised about $85,000 from about 1,000 contributors for its launch on Kickstarter. After the first year and a half, however, developers and technology com004mentators expressed concerns that the project was floundering. In a June 2012 *Wired* article, aptly titled "Good News for Spies and Dictators: 'FreedomBox' is in Danger of an Early Death," Lorenzo Franceschi004Bicchierai reported how developers were responding to perceived risks to the project. In June 2012, Nick Daly, one of the key FreedomBox developers, announced that their first beta release would be at the end of 2012. Daly noted that this was an intentionally ambitious goal for the initial beta release. He urged more developers to respond to this chal004lenge by becoming involved in the project (accessed January 25, 2017. www.wired.com/2012/06/freedombox/).

Creating FreedomBox was complicated. Developers had to integrate existing software for onion routing, encryption, and virtual private networks with tiny computers called "plug servers." They needed to integrate these existing technologies and software in a way that was easily accessible for general users who were not developers themselves. Furthermore, the developers needed to make it possible for the FreedomBox to operate in a decentralized way so that users could bypass the centralized telecommunications infrastructure. As a result, users could control their data and keep their personal web servers in their homes where they could be free from data mining by corporations and governments (accessed February 13, 2017. http://freedomboxfoundation.org/learn/).

Participants in the Debian free software community, discussed in Chapter 3, rose to this challenge. They created the first "Developer Preview" of FreedomBox by February 2013. This first version included full hardware support in Debian, as well as basic software tools such as cryptography and a box-to-box communication design. The first version used Tor network, free software that enables anonymous communication online. The Debian community developed subsequent versions of FreedomBox, releasing version 0.2 in March 2014 with new services such as Instant Messaging and OwnCloud. They released version 0.3 in January 2015, including the capability to route traffic for Tor network as well as a firewall. They released three more versions in 2015, as well as six different versions in 2016. In this process, the Debian community engaged in sustained work to continue to improve the features and functionality of FreedomBox. In January 2017, the Debian community released FreedomBox Plinth v0.13.1, which included new applications for collaborative editing of text documents and a Domain Name Server in the system menu. The Release Notes for each FreedomBox version are available on the Debian wiki (accessed February 20, 2017. https://wiki.debian.org/FreedomBox/ReleaseNotes#Version_0.1_.282013-02-26.29).

The FreedomBox Foundation website describes the FreedomBox as "an organizing tool for democratic activists in hostile regimes" and "an emergency communication network in times of crisis" (accessed February 20, 2017. http://freedomboxfoundation.org/learn/). Instead of having their data stored in centralized servers owned by corporations like Facebook, Google, and Apple, FreedomBox users store their data on their own web servers. They also keep logs of their Internet searches and transactions on their personal web server. Using the FreedomBox, they send encrypted voice and text communication, as well as backups of their files, to other FreedomBox users. They engage in social networking, anonymous publishing, media sharing, and microblogging. FreedomBox users have a better chance of protecting their privacy, since they own the logs of their own Internet use. If an individual, corporation, or government wants to see those logs, they need a search warrant. Choosing to use a FreedomBox is thus a key way to resist the surveillant assemblage, by employing a tool to subvert it through an alternative communications system.

Conclusion: Building the Global Net Neutrality Community of Resistance

Internet politics, including resistance to the surveillant assemblage, thus takes diverse forms. As net neutrality proponents organized to shape the conditions for accessing the Internet, they built a global community of resistance. As in the case with the free software activists discussed in the last chapter, this community of resistance constituted an alternative form of globalization from below. Moreover, net neutrality activists employed and extended the freedom discourse as a foundation for their work. Like the free software activists, they drew upon resources of political will and skill to create imaginative forms of transboundary political practice that contributed to the development of the digital commons. As part of this global community of resistance, net neutrality activists from the U.S., Brazil, France, and other parts of Europe devised multiple strategies to protect and defend Internet users' freedoms. Through these strategies, they targeted two terrains of struggle over Internet politics.

First, since the 1990s, net neutrality activists applied the freedom discourse to defend Internet users' freedoms to access the Internet on equal terms. In the process, they struggled over the conditions to access and control the existing telecommunications infrastructure. In a range of countries around the world, they engaged in local actions that shared a common focus on net neutrality. From the EFF's impact litigation work to LQDN's organizing in France and more broadly in Europe, these activists built a global net neutrality community of resistance. EFF founder John Perry Barlow articulated the freedom/sovereignty discourse, highlighting the connections between protecting Internet users' freedoms and struggles for sovereignty against government and corporate control of cyberspace. This discourse resonated with Brazilian government concerns about promoting digital inclusion and protecting citizens' privacy from government and corporate surveillance. Indeed, net neutrality activists in the U.S., France, and Brazil increasingly integrated resistance to surveillance into their campaigns defending net neutrality. They shared concerns about the threat of surveillance to citizens' civil liberties and to democratic institutions. Through this range of efforts, net neutrality activists around the world worked to control the existing telecommunications infrastructure for using the Internet. They acted as a global community of resistance. They opposed corporate and government efforts to allow firms to profit from the Internet in a range of ways, such as charging more for faster services. They supported net neutrality to democratize access to the Internet as part of the digital commons.

On the second terrain of struggle, net neutrality activists developed strategies to evade surveillance and to design alternative telecommunications infrastructures that they owned and controlled. They articulated perspectives about the contemporary nature of surveillance as undermining democratic institutions and civil liberties, including the right to privacy. They engaged in public education work, informing citizens about surveillance practices and offering resources to protect themselves from it. Activists highlighted the importance of such practices in the wake of Edward Snowden's revelations about NSA surveillance. Those revelations illuminated the pervasive nature of surveillance, which extended beyond the activists' previous expectations. The French group Framasoft developed a project on DeGoogling the Internet, providing users with resources about free software alternatives to the ways they consume digital services. From web browsers to search engines, software, and more, Framasoft offered users a wide array of choices to protect their privacy and avoid the collection of their personal data. Furthermore, the FreedomBox project created a personal web server that users can carry with them. Software developers from the Debian community participated in the project, integrating multiple forms of software to create a personal web server that was relatively simple to use. Taken together, these strategies complemented efforts to control the existing telecommunications infrastructure. Net neutrality activists thus employed a range of ways to defend equality of access to the Internet, while simultaneously defending civil liberties and democratic institutions from corporate and government surveillance. In the process, they continued to build the global net neutrality community of resistance. They forged this community as an alternative form of globalization from below.

7 Global Communities of Resistance and the Digital Commons

Since the 1970s, myriad local struggles contributed to the development of the digital commons.

In the early 1980s, free software advocates in the U.S. forged a key foundation for the digital commons. Employing U.S. copyright law, they created free software as an alternative form of property based on complex forms of community ownership, rather than strictly proprietary ownership.

The GNU General Public License (GPL) protected users' freedoms to access, modify, and share software. Through copyleft, it grounded free software in the freedom discourse. This discourse was a narrative of power and knowledge rooted in the principles of freedom to access and share information as a common good rather than as private property. By the late 1980s, Brazilian researchers worked to secure the freedom to access global computer networks. As discussed in Chapter 2, these distinct local struggles in the U.S. and Brazil laid two main foundations for the digital commons as an alternative to private property. The digital commons were grounded in free software as a new form of property as well as opening up access to global computer networks. In the early 2000s, proponents of a digital commons designed Creative Commons and Wikipedia. Through these global projects involving local participants from around the world, these proponents extended the digital commons into new areas, including art, creative work, and encyclopedic knowledge.

Free software communities made key contributions to the continued development of the digital commons. Through activities ranging from coding software to writing documentation and translating the software into different languages, free software advocates built a multitude of software systems. In Chapter 3, I explored the Debian and Drupal cases to highlight both the possibilities and challenges involved with developing free software communities as part of the digital commons. The Drupal and Debian communities both operate through processes of peer production that are simultaneously linked to market-based firms. Debian peer producers create software that the Canonical corporation markets and distributes as the Ubuntu operating system. There is a distinct division between the work done by Debian peer producers and Canonical's work in creating and distributing Ubuntu. In Drupal's case, peer producers of the Drupal web content management system coordinate their activities with Acquia as a market-based firm. This coordination occurs largely through Dries Buytaert's leadership in both Acquia and the Drupal peer community. Despite these differences in the ways the projects are structured, both Debian and Drupal software are produced through a mix of commons-based peer production and proprietary production.

Both market-based firms and commons-based peer communities participate in the development of the digital commons. In the process, the commons are linked with capitalist markets. These firms and communities contribute to the commons by producing free software.

The challenges to develop the digital commons arise not from this mix of forms of production, but from the nature of the software that is produced. Drupal is licensed under the GNU GPL. It constitutes an alternative to the proprietary software form. It is a catalytic form of property that spreads through capitalist markets by legally protecting users' freedoms to access, modify, and share the software. By contrast, Debian is open-source software, licensed so that it allows developers to include proprietary elements. The Canonical corporation changed Ubuntu's license to the GNU GPL, in response to user's concerns about limitations on their freedoms. Somewhat paradoxically, peer producers at Debian create software that includes proprietary elements, while paid workers at Canonical produce free software. It is thus the legal form of the software, defined by the license, that determines whether the software takes the catalytic property form and contributes to the digital commons.

Beyond the alternative property form of the software itself, free software communities contribute to the development of the digital commons in other ways. They develop community structures and relationships central to commons practices, spreading those practices around the world. These communities constitute alternative form of globalization from below, where local advocates across the world coordinate their work as part of broader global projects. By developing these communities to produce free software and support all of the activities that requires, they implicitly resist neoliberalism. They do not organize as political activists to explicitly oppose neoliberalism; however, they build free software and community structures that pose alternatives to the neoliberal drive to promote the expansion of global capital.

For example, in Chapter 3, I highlight the Drupal community process of fostering the development of communities in the global South. Through extensive discussion and a series of international meetings, Drupal participants supported the growth of local communities in Latin America and India. In the process, the global Drupal community implicitly resisted neoliberalism's drive to prioritize proprietary interests. The expanding communities in the global South developed organizational structures and personal relationships among the participants, as well as developing free software as an alternative to the proprietary software form. In Chapter 4, I examine how LibreOffice and The Document Foundation (TDF) participants employed the strategy of forking to preserve the freedom of their community to access, modify, and share software. The process of creating organizational structures was critical to support community growth and development.

These organizational structures laid necessary foundations for TDF to develop an implicit global community of resistance. Through software production and community development, free software proponents constituted implicit global communities of resistance to the proprietary interests of capital.

Due to the centrality of software for production in informational capitalism, it becomes a political battleground. Many corporations and governments promote proprietary interests in the software market. In Chapter 5, I explore software politics that arise as free software activists struggle with corporations and governments to shape the terms for software use. I focus on the case of free software activists in France, who built a global community of resistance with an explicit political focus. They drew upon the work of the Free Software Foundation (FSF) in the U.S. to apply the freedom discourse to the French context. They articulated this discourse as they forged alliances with other European free software activists to defend free software in the broader European arena.

Net neutrality activists engage in similar struggles to shape the terms to access the Internet. They battle corporate and government interests that seek to profit from Internet access. They oppose government and corporate efforts to engage in surveillance of citizens to collect data on a myriad range of their activities. In Chapter 6, I highlight two terrains of struggle over Internet politics. First, net neutrality activists organize to shape the conditions for access and control over the existing telecommunications infrastructure. They defend users' rights for equal access to the Internet, as well as their civil rights to be free from government and corporate surveillance. In the context of increasing webs of such surveillance in the surveillant assemblage, net neutrality activists recognize the importance of developing strategies to evade surveillance. They engage in a second terrain of struggle, offering users resources for alternative ways to access and search the Internet. These free software alternatives allow users to evade surveillance by encrypting messages and employing other privacy protections. Of equal importance, net neutrality activists worked to develop alternative telecommunications structures that they could control themselves. I highlight the example of the FreedomBox project that offers users a personal web server through a mesh network.

As in past decades, the details of conflicts over software and Internet politics will continue to shift over time. Nonetheless, the underlying dynamics of those struggles are clear. In the context of informational capitalism, software and the Internet are battlegrounds. Thus, free software and net neutrality proponents wage ongoing efforts to protect software and Internet freedom as key foundations for the digital commons. In the process, they build both implicit and explicit global communities of resistance to neoliberalism.

These communities have the potential to be transformative. They target software and the Internet as vital informational productive forces, creating conditions for structural change in informational capitalism. Coders, system administrators, web designers, and other information technology workers play key roles in creating software and Internet systems. Their role is comparable to Marx and Engels' (2017) vision of the emerging industrial working class as the force for revolutionary change in the nineteenth century.

In the contemporary context, however, consumers also play a pivotal role. As consumers, if we choose to participate in these forms of social change, we can turn the ubiquity of software and the Internet to our advantage. As Benkler (2013a, 2013b) argues, the commons consistently exist alongside, and interspersed with, proprietary markets. As we navigate our lives, we continually shift between activities that engage simultaneously with commons and markets. From a consumer's perspective, much of our work on the web involves the use of free software. We all use free software in some of our web searching, even if we are not aware of it. We are similar to the PHP developers that Larry Garfield highlighted in his address to the Drupal conference in Colombia; those developers make Drupal development possible, even if they have never met anyone in the Drupal community or explicitly worked on Drupal. Like those PHP developers, in the process of engaging with free software and the commons, we are all part of the implicit global community of resistance. If we want to consciously support the development of the digital commons, we can become more aware of this and make choices accordingly. We can use free software such as LibreOffice or participate in other free software projects. Furthermore, we can be part of the explicit global community of resistance by joining battles to defend free software and net neutrality. In myriad ways, we can join local actors from all over the world to engage in implicit and explicit global communities of resistance.

As consumers, we have critical choices to make. We can live in a state of distraction, our attention diverted by an endless stream of incoming messages. From moment to moment, we can follow the latest push notifications from a variety of corporate entities. In the process, we can allow ourselves to be tracked within the web of the surveillant assemblage. By contrast, we can choose to employ our power as consumers to engage with multiple forms of software and the Internet that constitute the digital commons. As Bollier (2008, 9) argues, we may choose to contribute to the commons as a "parallel social order," prioritizing practices of sharing and community over the proprietary practices of the market.

This kind of utopian, anarchistic approach to the commons resonates with community efforts to construct sustainable economies. As Schor and Thompson (2014, 3) argue, proponents of such economies "are taking on the task of building another kind of economy in the shadow of what increasingly looks like a declining system."

The digital commons, along with other alternative economies, exist in the shadows of the dominant capitalist economy. Similar to Marx and Engels' (2017) image of communism as a specter haunting Europe, the digital commons constitute a specter haunting informational capitalism. Whether we choose to participate or not, that specter will continue to haunt. Nonetheless, as we navigate the commons and proprietary worlds, we may choose to support the development of the commons by engaging with global communities of resistance. Due to the intertwined nature of the commons and proprietary systems, it is likely that we will continue to engage with both systems. Nonetheless, it is useful to consider potential actions we can take to promote the development of the digital commons.

In their efforts to develop alternatives to the dominant capitalist system, proponents of the digital commons share similar challenges to proponents of sustainable economy communities. Sustainable economy communities seek to transform a range of ways that we produce and consume, highlighting the implications for environmental and societal health. Free software and net neutrality communities promote alternative forms of producing software and consuming digital services through the Internet, highlighting the implications for civil liberties and democracy amidst growing surveillance.

I teach a sociology class on Sustainable Alternatives to Capitalism, where we explore the connections between these communities. In the class, we compare these communities' goals and challenges to understand what they might learn from each other. In the process, we practice the "hacker ethic" of networking, connecting, and sharing information to solve problems. We grasp the myriad ways in which we create sustainability and the digital commons through local actions and relationships, by building community organizations and consuming products ranging from food to software.

In teaching this class, I encounter many students who are well versed in the key concerns of sustainable economy communities. They have studied questions of fair trade and environmental sustainability. They have grappled with the disturbing science about climate change and the ecological implications of the ways that they consume food, clothing, and other daily goods. Many of these students have already made changes in their consumption practices and are committed to making more. At the same time, however, many of these same students lack an awareness of the importance of free software and net neutrality communities. They approach learning about these questions with a touch of reluctance. In part, they are deeply ensconced in their normalized patterns of consuming the Internet and software. As Moglen (2013b) argues, they are entwined in a complex ecology of Internet and software use that is difficult to untangle. Part of this difficulty is the lack of consumer understanding of the ways that this ecology is structured. Even when students, or other consumers, learn about the extent of surveillance involved with this ecology, they may feel hopeless about creating alternatives to it. Furthermore, many of my students have not considered the implications of their software and Internet use for net neutrality and the digital commons. They are keenly aware of the ecological crisis facing the planet, yet largely unaware of the ecological crisis facing the digital commons.

Despite these challenges, education and consciousness raising can be powerful tools. As environmental activist and writer Bill McKibben (2007, 232) argues,

> [i]t's extremely hard to imagine a world substantially different from the one we know. But our current economies are changing the physical world in horrifying ways. It's our greatest challenge – the only real question of our time – to see whether we can transform those economies enough to prevent some damage and to help us cope with what we can't prevent. To see if we can manage to mobilize the wealth of our communities to make the transition tolerable, even sweet, instead of tragic.

As my class studies the parallels between sustainable economy, free software, and net neutrality communities, students become more knowledgeable. As their knowledge of these questions grows, some also become more committed to transforming their practices of consuming software and the Internet. Their resolution to engage in socially and environmentally just consumption of a range of commodities extends to new practices in the digital sphere.

McKibben (2007) identifies the proliferation of farmers' markets around the U.S. as a key sign of the vibrant nature of local economies. He highlights the importance of growing and consuming local food for developing a web of environmentally and socially sustainable communities. He calls these "deep economies," rooted in local relationships between consumers, producers, and the planet. These deep economies are sustainable, since they foster the development of diverse forms of local production, becoming less dependent on fossil fuels for producing or transporting the products. They nourish local relationships, as producers and consumers meet and get to know each other at farmers' markets and other local community venues. Juliet Schor (2010) proposes that such communities create lifestyles that are simultaneously more socially meaningful and healthier for the planet.

As others have built upon Schor's (2010) work, they identified a range of accomplishments and challenges involved with developing what they call plenitude or new economy communities (Schor and Thompson 2014). Significantly, Holt (2014) analyzes key reasons why the sustainable economy movement has not spread more widely or effectively. He is particularly concerned about the lack of connection to mainstream communities of working-class, working-poor, and middle-class people who do not do professional or managerial work. He argues that the sustainable economy movement has been coopted as part of a broader process of cultural branding. Businesses develop products and ad campaigns to appeal to upper-middle-class consumers seeking farm to table meals, organic food, and other "sustainable" or "green" products. Values and practices of sustainability become branded and incorporated into new capitalist markets, rather than challenging dominant capitalist practices. This process of cooptation is similar to the ways that firms like IBM engage with open-source software. Such firms contribute to the development of open source as a strategy to broaden their market and appeal to particular corporate clients.

Like sustainable economy communities, free software and net neutrality communities face challenges in conveying their message to broad audiences of working, middle-class, and poor people. As we have seen in the above chapters, there is a rich array of free software and net neutrality communities around the world. Moreover, there are numerous such communities not mentioned in this book. Participants in these communities engage in myriad local activities such as coding, translating, documentation, activism, and education, as they simultaneously contribute to global projects. As the students in my classes indicate, however, there are many people who do not know about the work of these communities. Without information about these efforts, it is difficult to grasp their broader social implications for democracy, citizenship, and civil liberties in our contemporary age.

To extend and deepen the work of global free software and net neutrality communities of resistance, I propose a possible future scenario. Similar to the proliferation of farmers' markets in an array of rural and urban communities, I advocate proliferating community spaces where people can learn to change the ways that they consume software and the Internet. One example of such a project is Crypto Harlem, organized by former data journalist Matthew Mitchell. Mitchell offers Cryptoparties where black activists and other Harlem residents can learn strategies to counteract the surveillant assemblage. As Doctorow (2015) describes, these parties are an "attempt to help black people armor themselves against everyday surveillance, promoted through barbershops, hair salons, black churches and flyers in the neighborhood." Mitchell advocates a process of engaging with the community in these local spaces where people gather, rather than by publicizing the Cryptoparties on the Internet.

Certainly, this kind of outreach is key to spreading the information to a wider range of people. Like McKibben's (2007) deep economy, these Cryptoparties involve building relationships among people in local communities. They are similar to activities by many local free software communities around the world, where they do public education work to raise awareness about the possibilities of using free software. They are quintessentially pedagogical, educating people, and raising awareness as well as teaching practical strategies and skills.

Indeed, Cryptoparties resonate with Paulo Freire's (1974) pedagogy of liberation, where oppressed people engage in a process of empowerment. Through this process, oppressed people, such as the Harlem residents attending Cryptoparties, "unveil the world of oppression" (Freire 1974, 40). They learn to identify the sources of their oppression and to apply their knowledge to act. They engage in what Freire (1974, 36) calls "praxis: reflection and action upon the world in order to transform it." Equally important, for Freire (1974, 52), praxis "cannot be purely intellectual but must involve action; nor can it be limited to mere activism, but must include serious reflection." Through praxis, the oppressed thus transform the conditions of their oppression, as well as their own perceptions of the world and of themselves.

As discussed in the above chapters, April, the Electronic Frontier Foundation (EFF), *La Quadrature du Net* (LQDN) and TDF all engage in a range of public education work. In order to move this educational work forward to reach more people, we need to expand it more widely in communities beyond existing free software and net neutrality advocates. We need to develop pedagogical projects such as Crypto Harlem that are rooted in local communities, developing deep economies of social and economic relationships of the kinds that McKibben (2007) and other sustainable economy proponents advocate (Schor 2010; Schor and Thompson 2014). By engaging in Freireian (1974) processes of praxis, we can extend the pedagogy of liberation to our consumption of software and the Internet. In the process, we will create relationships, spaces, and organizational structures to expand and strengthen global communities of resistance. Those communities will continue to contribute to the development of the digital commons. Both implicit and explicit global communities of resistance constitute alternatives to neoliberal globalization, shaping the digital commons as a specter haunting informational capitalism.

References

Adams, Tracey L. and Erin I. Demaiter. "Skill, education and credentials in the new economy: The case of information technology workers." *Work, Employment and Society* 22, no. 2 (2008): 351–62.

Adler, Emanuel. *The Power of Ideology: The Quest for Technological Autonomy in Argentina and Brazil.* Berkeley: University of California Press, 1987.

Andrejevic, Mark. *iSpy: Surveillance and Power in the Interactive Era.* Lawrence, KS: University of Kansas Press, 2007.

Amadeo, Ron. "Google's iron grip on Android: Controlling open source by any means necessary." *ars technica.* Accessed July 28, 2015. http://arstechnica.com/gadgets/2013/10/googles-iron-grip-on-android-controlling-open-source-by-any-means-necessary/1/, 2013.

Arrighi, Giovanni. "Globalization, State Sovereignty, and the Endless Accumulation of Capital." In *States and Sovereignty in the Global Economy*, edited by David A. Smith, Dorothy J. Solinger, and Steven C. Topik, 53–73. London: Routledge, 1999.

Article 19. "Marco Civil da Internet: seis meses depois, em que pé que estamos?" Accessed February 2, 2017. http://artigo19.org/blog/2015/01/23/analise-marco-civil-da-internet-seis-meses-depois-em-que-pe-que-estamos/, 2015.

Azzam, Amin, David Bressler, Armando Leon, Lauren Maggio, Evans Whitaker, James Heilman, Jake Orlowitz, Valerie Swisher, Lane Rasberry, Kingsley Otoide, Fred Trotter, Will Ross, and Jack McCue. "Why medical schools should embrace Wikipedia: Final-year medical student contributions to Wikipedia articles for academic credit at one school." *Academic Medicine* 92 (2017): 194–200.

Bacon, Jono. *The Art of Community.* O'Reilly Media: Sebastapol, 2009.

Bangeman, Eric. "French Legislation Might Chase iTMS out of the Country." *Ars Technica.* Accessed July, 30, 2009. http://arstechnica.com/old/content/2006/03/6371.ars, 2006a.

———. "French Parliament Passes DRM Bill. Will Apple Bolt?" *Ars Technica.* Accessed July 29, 2009. http://arstechnica.com/old/content/2006/03/ 6428. ars, 2006b.

Bauwens, Michel. "Class and capital in peer production." *Capital & Class* 33 (2009): 121–41.

Benkler, Yochai. *The Wealth of Networks: How Social Production Transforms Markets and Freedom.* New Haven: Yale University Press, 2006.

———. "Commons and growth: The essential role of open commons in market economies." *University of Chicago Law Review* 80 (2013a): 1499–1555.

———. "Practical anarchism: Peer mutualism, market power, and the fallible state." *Politics & Society* 41 (2013b): 213–51.

———. *Nation as Network: Diaspora, Cyberspace & Citizenship*. Chicago: The University of Chicago Press, 2014.

Blum, Andrew. *Tubes: A Journey to the Center of the Internet*. New York: HarperCollins Publishers, 2012.

Bollier, David. *Viral Spiral: How the Commoners Built a Digital Republic of Their Own*. New York: The New Press, 2008.

——— and Silke Helfrich, eds., *The Wealth of the Commons: A World Beyond Market and State*. Amherst, MA: Levellers Press, 2012.

boyd, danah. *It's Complicated: The Social Lives of Networked Teens*. New Haven: Yale University Press, 2014.

Boyle, James. *The Public Domain: Enclosing the Commons of the Mind*. New Haven: Yale University Press, 2008.

Buttar, Shahid. "Grassroots digital rights alliance expands across U.S." Accessed March 24, 2017. https://eff.org/deeplinks/2016/11/grassroots-digital-rights-alliance-expands-across-us, 2016.

Campaign for a Commercial-Free Childhood. "Don't let Mattel's new "digital nanny" trade children's privacy for profit." Accessed July 27, 2017. http://commercialfreechildhood.org/action/dont-let-mattels-new-digital-nanny-trade-childrens-privacy-profit, 2017.

Candidats.fr. Accessed June 20, 2009. http://www.candidats.fr/index.php/2007/01/27/11-principe-des-mesures-techniques-, 2007.

Capek, P.G., S.P. Frank, S. Gerdt, and D. Shields. "A history of IBM's open-source involvement and strategy." *IBM Systems Journal* 44 (2005): 249–57.

Carvalho, Marcelo Sávio Revoredo Menezes. "A Trajetória da Internet no Brasil: Do Surgimento das Redes de Computadores à Instituição dos Mecanismos de Governança." Master's thesis, Universidade Federal do Rio de Janeiro (UFRJ), 2006.

Castells, Manuel. *The Rise of the Network Society*. Oxford: Blackwell, 1996.

———. *Communication Power*. New York: Oxford University Press, 2009.

Chadwick, Andrew. *Internet Politics: States, Citizens, and New Communication Technologies*. New York: Oxford University Press, 2006.

Champeau, Guillaume. "NKM demande des backdoors contre le chiffrement." *Numerama*, January 12. Accessed March 16, 2016. http://numerama.com/politique/138264-nkm-demande-des-backdoors-contre-le-chiffrement.html, 2016a.

———. "Chiffrement: le gouvernement rejette les backdoors." *Numerama*, January 13. Accessed March 16, 2016. http://numerama.com/politique/138689-chiffrement-le-gouvernement-rejette-les-backdoors.html, 2016b.

Chan, Anita Say. "Coding free software, coding free states: Free software legislation and the politics of code in Peru." *Anthropological Quarterly* 77 (2004): 531–45.

———. *Networking Peripheries: Technological Futures and the Myth of Digital Universalism*. Cambridge, MA: MIT Press, 2013.

Chausson, Cyrille. "Free software groups protest France school software deal." *Open Source Observatory*, February 15. Accessed June 27, 2017. https://joinup.ec.europa.eu/community/osor/news/free-software-groups-protest-france-school-software-deal, 2016.

CISION PR Newswire. "Mattel's nabi brand introduces first-ever connected kids room platform in tandem with Microsoft and Qualcomm – Aristotle." Accessed July 27, 2017. http://prnewswire.com/news-releases/mattels-nabi-brand-introduces-first-ever-connected-kids-room-platform-in-tandem-with-microsoft-and-qualcomm---aristotle-300385221.html, 2017.

Claburn, Thomas. "Google's secret patent portfolio predicts gPhone." *InformationWeek*, September 19. Accessed July 29, 2015. http://informationweek.com/googles-secret-patent-portfolio-predicts-gphone/d/d-id/1059389?cid=nl_iwk_daily, 2007.

Coleman, E. Gabriella. "The political agnosticism of free and open source software and the inadvertent politics of contrast." *Anthropological Quarterly* 77 (2004): 507–19.

———. *Coding Freedom: The Ethics and Aesthetics of Hacking*. Princeton: Princeton University Press, 2012.

Coombe, Rosemary J. and Andrew Herman. "Rhetorical virtues: Property, speech, and the commons on the world-wide web." *Anthropological Quarterly* 77 (2004): 559–74.

Corbet. "OpenOffice.org community members launch Document Foundation." *LWN.net*, September 28. Accessed June 10, 2013. http://lwn.net/Articles/407383/, 2010.

Couture, Stéphane and Serge Proulx. "Les Militants du Code." In *L'Action Communautaire Québécoise à l'Ère du Numérique*, edited by Stéphane Couture, Serge Proulx and Julien Rueff, 14–35. Québec: Presses de l'Université du Québec, 2008.

Currie, Morgan, Christopher Kelty and Luis Felipe Rosado Murillo. "Free software trajectories: From organized publics to formal social enterprises." *Journal of Peer Production* 3 (2013).

de Laat, Paul B. "Governance of open source software: State of the art." *Journal of Management and Governance* 11 (2007): 165–77.

Della Porto, Donatella, Massimillano Andretta, and Lorenzo Mosca. *Globalization from Below: Transnational Activists and Protest Networks*. Minneapolis: University of Minnesota Press, 2006.

Direction Interministerielle des Systemes d'Information et de Communication (DISIC). "Usage du logiciel libre dans l'administration." Paris: République Française, 2012.

Doctorow, Cory. "Harlem Cryptoparty: Crypto matters for #blacklivesmatter." Accessed July 18, 2017. http://boingboing.net/2015/12/11/harlem-cryptoparty-crypto-mat.html, 2015.

Doueihi, Milad. *La Grande Conversion Numérique*. Paris: Seuil, 2008.

Drahos, Peter and John Braithwaite. *Information Feudalism: Who Owns the Knowledge Economy?* London: Earthscan Publications, 2002.

Electronic Frontier Foundation (EFF). "A history of protecting freedom where law and technology collide." Accessed September 10. https://eff.org/about/history, 2014a.

———. "Unintended consequences: Sixteen years under the DMCA." Accessed October 12, 2016. https://eff.org/wp/unintended-consequences-16-years-under-dmca, 2014b.

Engelfriet, A. "Choosing an open source license." *IEEE Software* 27 no. 1 (2010): 48–49.

Escobar, Arturo. *Encountering Development: The Making and Unmaking of the Third World*. Princeton: Princeton University Press, 1995.

Espern, Christophe. "Le projet de loi DADVSI." Presentation at discussion forum "Le droit d'auteur à l'ére numérique." Accessed June 13, 2009. http://carrefour-numerique.cite-sciences.fr/live/dadvsi_textes.html#eucd, 2005.

EUCD.INFO. "Pétition demandant le retrait de l'ordre du jour parlementaire du projet de loi DADVSI.'" Accessed June 16, 2009. http://eucd.info/petitions/index.php?petition=2, 2005.

Evans, Peter B. "State, capital, and the transformation of dependence: The Brazilian computer case." *World Development* 14 (1986): 791–808.

———. "Declining hegemony and assertive industrialization: U.S.-Brazil conflicts in the computer industry." *International Organization* 43 (1989): 207–38.

Federal Communication Commission, "Report and Order on Remand, Declaratory Ruling, and Order," FCC 15-24. Accessed November 21, 2017. transition.fcc.gov/Daily_Releases/Daily_Business/2015/db, 2015.

Felten, Edward W. "The digital millenium copyright act and its legacy: A view from the trenches." *Journal of Law, Technology & Policy* 21 (2002): 289–93.

Fichman, Pnina and Noriko Hara. "Introduction." In *Global Wikipedia: International and Cross-Cultural Issues in Online Collaboration*, edited by Pnina Fichman and Noriko Hara, 1–5. New York: Rowman & Littlefield, 2014.

filhocf. "Agora o BrOffice chama-se LibreOffice." Posted April 5. Accessed June 5, 2013. http://broffice.org/agora_o_bro_chama_libo, 2011.

Fontana, John. "IBM takes aim at Office with free productivity apps." *Network World*, September 18. Accessed September 26, 2015. http://networkworld.com/article/2285484/software/ibm-takes-aim-at-office-with-free-productivity-apps.html, 2007.

Foucault, Michel. *The History of Sexuality. Volume I: An Introduction*. Trans. Robert Hurley. New York: Vintage Books, 1978.

Freire, Paulo. *Pedagogy of the Oppressed*. New York: The Seabury Press, 1974.

———. "Sociotechnical and Political Processes Shaping Digital Democracy in Brazil: The Case of the Project *e-Democracia*." In *Inovação, Governança Digital e Políticas Públicas: Conquistas e Desafios para a Democracia*, edited by Christiana Soares de Freitas, 31–45. Arraes Editores, 2016.

FSF France. "French Government Lobbied to Ban Free Software." Accessed July 31, 2009. http://www.fsffrance.org/news/article2005-11-25.en.html, 2005.

Fuchs, Christian. "Critique of the Political Economy of Informational Capitalism and Social Media." In *Critique, Social Media and the Information Society*, edited by Christian Fuchs and Marisol Sandoval, 51–65. New York: Routledge, 2014.

———. *Reading Marx in the Information Age: A Media and Communication Studies Perspective on Capital Volume I*. New York: Routledge, 2016.

Gamalielsson, Jonas and Björn Lundell. "Sustainability of Open Source software communities beyond a fork: How and why has the LibreOffice project evolved?" *The Journal of Systems and Software* 89 (2014): 128–45.

Gamalielsson, Jonas, Björn Lundell, Jonas Feist, Tomas Gustavsson, and Fredric Landqvist. "On organisational influences in software standards and their open source implementations." *Information and Software Technology* 67 (2015): 30–43.

Garfield, Larry. Keynote address at DrupalCon Latin America. Accessed July 31, 2017. https://youtube.com/watch?v=-lLILaIZr44, 2015.

Gay, Joshua, ed. *Free Software, Free Society: Selected Essays of Richard M. Stallman*. Boston: GNU Press, 2002.

Gençer, Mehmet and Bülent Özel. "Forking the commons: Developmental tensions and evolutionary patterns in open source software." *IFIP Advances in Information and Communication Technology* 378 (2012): 310–15.

Ghedin, Rodrigo. "Acabou a confusão: BrOffice passa a ser LibreOffice no Brasil." *Meio Bit*, March 18. Accessed June 5, 2013. http://meiobit.com/82603/broffice-libreoffice-brasil/, 2011.

González-Barahona, Jesús M. and Gregorio Robles. "Libre software in Europe." In *Open Sources 2.0: The Continuing Evolution*, edited by C. DiBona, D. Cooper and M. Stone, 161–88. Beijing: O'Reilly, 2006.

Haggerty, Kevin D. and Amber Gazso. "Seeing beyond the ruins: Surveillance as a response to terrorist threats." *The Canadian Journal of Sociology* 30 (2005): 169–87.

Haggerty, Kevin D. and Richard V. Ericson. "The surveillant assemblage." *British Journal of Sociology* 51 (2000): 605–22.

Harvey, David. "Time-Space Compression and the Postmodern Condition." In *Modernity: Critical Concepts. Volume IV after Modernity*, edited by Malcolm Waters, 98–118. London: Routledge, 1999.

———. *A Brief History of Neoliberalism*. Oxford: Oxford University Press, 2005.

Hempel, Jessi. "India Bans Facebook's Basics App to Support Net Neutrality." *Wired*, February 8. Accessed January 20, 2017. https://wired.com/2016/02/facebooks-free-basics-app-is-now-banned-in-india/, 2016.

Hess, Charlotte and Elinor Ostrom. "Introduction: An Overview of the Knowledge Commons." In *Understanding Knowledge as a Commons: From Theory to Practice*, edited by Charlotte Hess and Elinor Ostrom, 3–26. Cambridge, MA: The MIT Press, 2006.

Hillenius, Gijs. "Mayor of Munich: 'EU laptops should have LibreOffice or OpenOffice." *European Commission Joinup*, December 20, 2011. Accessed June 10, 2013. http://joinup.ec.europa.eu/news/mayor-munich-eu-laptops-should-have-libreoffice-or-openoffice, 2011.

Hillesley, Richard. "LibreOffice – A fresh page for OpenOffice." *The H Open*. Accessed July 5, 2013. http://h-online.com/open/features/LibreOffice-A-fresh-page-for-OpenOffice-1097358.html, 2010.

Hirst, Paul and Grahame Thompson. *Globalization in Question*. Malden, MA: Blackwell, 1999.

Holt, Douglas B. "Why the Sustainable Economy Movement Hasn't Scaled: Toward a Strategy that Empowers Main Street." In *Sustainable Lifestyles and the Quest for Plenitude: Case Studies of the New Economy*, edited by Juliet B. Schor and Craig J. Thompson, 202–32. New Haven: Yale University Press, 2014.

IBM Corporation. "IBM Is Committed to Linux and Open Source." Somers, NY: IBM Corporation. Accessed September 29, 2017. https://www-01.ibm.com/common/ssi/cgi-bin/ssialias?htmlfid=LXB03001USEN, 2008.

Intergovernmental Bureau for Informatics (IBI). *Latin American Regional Meeting on Transborder Data Flows*. Rome: Intergovernmental Bureau for Informatics, 1982.

Karanović, Jelena. "Sharing Publics: Democracy, Cooperation, and Free Software Advocacy in France." Ph.D. thesis, New York University, 2008.

———. "Contentious Europeanization: The paradox of becoming European through anti-patent activism." *Ethnos* 75 (2010): 3, 252–74.

Kelty, Christopher M. *Two Bits: The Cultural Significance of Free Software.* Durham and London: Duke University Press, 2008.

Landzelius, Kyra. "Introduction." In *Native on the Net: Indigenous and Diasporic Peoples in the Virtual Age,* edited by Kyra Landzelius, 1–42. London: Routledge, 2006.

Langman, Lauren. "Globalization from Below." In *The Wiley-Blackwell Encyclopedia of Globalization,* edited by George Ritzer, 864–70. Chichester, West Sussex: Wiley-Blackwell, 2012.

Lessig, Lawrence. *Free Culture: How Big Media Uses Technology and the Law to Lock Down Culture and Control Creativity.* New York: Penguin Press, 2004.

———. *Code version 2.0.* New York: Basic Books, 2006.

———. *Remix: Making Art and Commerce Thrive in the Hybrid Economy.* New York: Penguin Press, 2008.

Lethbridge, Timothy C., Jorge Díaz-Herrera, Richard J. LeBlanc Jr. and J. Barrie Thompson. "Improving software practice through education: Challenges and future trends." FOSE, 12–28. Future of Software Engineering (FOSE'07), 2007.

Lih, Andrew. *The Wikipedia Revolution: How a Bunch of Nobodies Created the World's Greatest Encyclopedia.* New York: Hyperion, 2009.

Livingstone, Randall. "Immaterial Editors: Bots and Bot Policies across Global Wikipedia." In *Global Wikipedia: International and Cross-Cultural Issues in Online Collaboration,* edited by Pnina Fichman and Noriko Hara, 7–23. New York: Rowman & Littlefield, 2014.

Lohninger, Erstellt von Thomas. "How we saved the Internet in Europe." Epicenter. Works. Accessed March 23, 2017. https://epicenter.works/content/how-we-saved-the-internet-in-europe, 2016.

Lyon, David. "Surveillance, snowden, and big data: Capacities, consequences, critique." *Big Data & Society* 1 (2014): 1–13.

Maass, Dave and Rainey Reitman. "EFF's 100-Day Plan." Accessed March 24, 2017. https://eff.org/deeplinks/2017/01/our-100-day-plan, 2017.

Madden, Joe. "How much software is in your car? From the 1977 Toronado to the Tesla P85D." *Quantitative Software Management.* Accessed July 26, 2017. http://qsm.com/blog/2015/how-much-software-your-car-1977-toronado-tesla-p85d, 2015.

Manijak, Peter. "New certification program addresses growing popularity of Drupal." *Go Certify.* Accessed January 29, 2016. http://gocertify.com/articles/new-certification-program-addresses-growing-popularity-of-drupal.html, 2014.

Markus, M. Lynne. "The governance of free/open source software projects: Monolithic, multidimensional, or configurational?" *Journal of Management and Governance* 11 (2007): 151–63.

Marx, Karl. *Grundrisse: Introduction to the Critique of Political Economy.* New York: Vintage Books, 1973.

——— and Friedrich Engels. *The Communist Manifesto.* Northampton: Pluto Press, 2017.

McKibben, Bill. *Deep Economy: The Wealth of Communities and the Durable Future*. New York: Henry Holt and Company, 2007.

McMichael, Philip. "Globalisation: Trend or Project?" In Rolan Palan, editor, *Global Political Economy: Contemporary Theories*, 100–113. London: Routledge, 2000.

———. *Development and Social Change: A Global Perspective*. Thousand Oaks, CA: Sage, 2017.

Meyer Maria, Jessica. "Why big government sites run Drupal." *Governing. com*. Accessed August 4, 2015. http://governing.com/news/technology/Why-Big-Government-Sites-Run-Drupal-.html, 2012.

Moghaddam, Roshanak Zilouchian, Bongen, Kora and Michael Twidale. "Open Source Interface Politics: Identity Acceptance, Trust, and Lobbying." *Extended Abstracts on Human Factors in Computing Systems*. New York: ACM, 2011.

Moglen, Eben. "Freedom in the cloud: Software freedom, privacy, and security for Web 2.0 and cloud computing." Speech at Internet Society's New York Branch Meeting on February 5. Accessed February 25, 2017. https://softwarefreedom.org/events/2010/isoc-ny/FreedomInTheCloud-transcript.html, 2010.

———. "Why political liberty depends on software freedom more than ever." Speech at the Free and Open Source Software Developers' European Meeting on February 5. Accessed February 25, 2017. https://softwarefreedom.org/events/2011/fosdem/moglen-fosdem-keynote.html, 2011.

———. "Snowden and the future, part II; oh, freedom." Accessed February 10, 2017. http://snowdenandthefuture.info/documents.html, 2013a.

———. "Snowden and the future, part III; the union, may it be preserved." Accessed February 10, 2017. http://snowdenandthefuture.info/documents.html, 2013b.

Moreno, Ana M., Maria-Isabel Sanchez-Segura, Fuensanta Medina-Dominguez, and Laura Carvajal. "Balancing software engineering education and industrial needs." *The Journal of Systems and Software* 85 (2012): 1607–20.

Murdock, Graham. "Producing Consumerism: Commodities, Ideologies, Practices." In *Critique, Social Media and the Information Society*, edited by Christian Fuchs and Marisol Sandoval, 125–43. New York: Routledge, 2014.

Murphy, Brian M. *The International Politics of New Information Technology*. New York: St. Martin's Press, 1986.

Noonan Nyman, Linus. *Understanding Code Forking in Open Source Software: An Examination of Code Forking, Its Effect on Open Source Software, and How It Is Viewed and Practiced by Developers*. Publications of the Hanken School of Economics. Helsinki, Finland: Hanken School of Economics, 2015.

———, Tommi Mikkonen, Juho Lindman and Martin Fougère. "Forking: The Invisible Hand of Sustainability in Open Source Software." *Proceedings of SOS 2011: Towards Sustainable Open Source*. Tampere University of Technology. Department of Software Systems. Report 19: 1–6, 2011.

———and Tommi Mikkonen. "To fork or not to fork: Fork motivations in SourceForge projects." *Open Source Systems: Grounding Research. IFIP Advances in Information and Communications Technology* 365 (2011): 259–68.

————— and Juho Lindman. "Code forking, governance, and sustainability in open source software." *Technology Innovation Management Review* 3 (2013): 7–12.

O'Mahony, Siobhán. "Nonprofit Foundations and Their Role in Community-Firm Software Collaboration." In *Perspectives on Free and Open Source Software*, edited by Joseph Feller, Brian Fitzgerald, Scott A. Hissam and Karim R. Lakhani, 393–413. Cambridge, MA: MIT Press, 2005.

Organization for Economic Cooperation and Development (OECD). *Transborder Data Flows and the Protection of Privacy*. Paris: Organization for Economic Cooperation and Development, 1979.

Parens, Bruce. "The Open Source Definition." In *Opensources: Voices from the Open Source Revolution*, edited by Chris DiBona, Sam Ockman, and Mark Stone, 171–88. Beijing: O'Reilly & Associates, Inc, 1999.

Paul, Ryan. "France's Proposed Copyright Reforms Are More Draconian Than the DMCA." *Ars Tecnica*. Accessed July 30, 2009. http://arstechnica.com/old/content/2005/12/5729.ars, 2005.

PC World. "The 100 best products of 2010." *PC World* 28 (2010): 12, 86–90, 92, 94, 96, 98, 100.

Perzanowski, Aaron K. "Evolving Standards & the Future of the DMCA Anticircumvention Rulemaking." *Journal of Internet Law* 1:1 (2007).

Phipps, Simon. "Transparency and privacy." *Wild Webmink*. Accessed September 25, 2015. http://webmink.com/essays/transparent-private/, (2011a).

—————. "OpenOffice.org and contributor agreements." *LWN.net*, May 20. Accessed September 25, 2015. https://lwn.net/Articles/443989/, (2011b).

Pillar, C. "How piracy opens doors for windows." *Los Angeles Times*, April 9, C1, C10, 2006.

Pinho, Larissa and Katitza Rodriguez. "Marco Civil Da Internet: The Devil in the Details." Electronic Frontier Foundation, *Deeplinks Blog*, February 25. Accessed January 27, 2017. https://eff.org/deeplinks/2015/02/marco-civil-devil-detail. 2015.

Portes, Alejandro. "Globalization from Below: The Rise of Transnational Communities." In *The Ends of Globalization: Bringing Society Back In*, edited by Dan Kalb, Marco van der Land, Richard Staring, Bart van Steenbergen, and Nico Wilterdink. 253–70. New York: Rowman and Littlefield, 2000.

Rahemipour, Jacqueline. "Every end is a new beginning." *The Mail Archive*. Accessed June 20, 2013. http://mail-archive.com/dev@native-lang.openoffice.org/msg04865.html, 2010.

Raymond, Eric. "A Brief History of Hackerdom." In *Opensources: Voices from the Open Source Revolution*, edited by Chris DiBona, Sam Ockman, and Mark Stone, 19–29. Beijing: O'Reilly & Associates, Inc, 1999.

Robles, Gregorio, Santiago Dueñas and Jesús M. González-Barahona. "Corporate Involvement of Libre Software: Study of Presence in Debian Code over Time." In IFIP International Federation for Information Processing, 234, *Open Source Development, Adoption and Innovation*, edited by J. Feller, Fitzgerald, B., Scacchi, W., Silitti, A., 121–32. Boston: Springer, 2007.

Robles, Gregorio, Jesús M. González-Barahona and M. Michlmayr. "Evolution of volunteer participation in libre software projects: Evidence from Debian." In *Proceedings of the First International Conference on Open Source*

Systems, edited by M. Scotto and G. Succi, 100–107. Genova: University of Genova, 2005.

Robles, Gregorio and Jesús M. González-Barahona. "A comprehensive study of software forks: Dates, reasons and outcomes." *IFIP Advances in Information and Communication Technology* 378 (2012): 1–14.

Rohter, Larry. "Gilberto Gil Hears the Future, Some Rights Reserved." *The New York Times*, March 11, 2007.

Rosencrans, Nick. "Usability Evaluation Summary Report." Office of Information Technology Usability Services, University of Minnesota, 2011.

Rousseff, H.E. Dilma. Statement at the Opening of the General Debate of the 68th Session of the United Nations General Assembly, 2013.

Sassen, Saskia. "Electronic Markets and Activist Networks: The Weight of Social Logics in Digital Formations." In *Digital Formations: IT and New Architectures in the Global Realm*, edited by Robert Latham and Saskia Sassen, 54–88. Princeton: Princeton University Press, 2005.

Sauvant, Karl P. *Trade and Foreign Direct Investment in Data Services*. Boulder, CO: Westview Press, 1984.

Scally, Derek. "De-Google your life: It's worth the hassle if you value your privacy." *Irish Times*, May 14. Accessed February 22, 2017. http://irishtimes.com/business/technology/de-googleyour-life-it-s-worth-the-hassle-if-you-value-your-privacy-1.2211355, 2015.

Schoonmaker, Sara. "Technological Dependency in Brazil: New Terms for Power and Resistance." PhD diss., Boston College, 1990.

———. "Trading on-line: Information flows in advanced capitalism." *The Information Society* 9 (1993): 39–49.

———. "Capitalism and the Code: A Critique of Baudrillard's Third-Order Simulacrum." In *Baudrillard: A Critical Reader*, edited by Douglas Kellner, 168–88. Cambridge: Basil Blackwell, 1994.

———. *High-Tech Trade Wars: USA-Brazilian Conflicts in the Global Economy*. Pittsburgh, University of Pittsburgh Press, 2002.

———. "Globalization from Below: Free software and alternatives to neoliberalism." *Development and Change* 38 (2007): 6, 999–1020.

———. "Software politics in Brazil: Toward a political economy of digital inclusion." *Information, Communication & Society* 12 (2009): 4, 548–65.

——— and Pierre-Amiel Giraud. "French software politics: Activism and the dynamics of globalization from below." *Revista Eletrônica de Sistemas de Informação* 12 (2014): 3.

Schor, Juliet B. *Plenitude: The New Economics of True Wealth*. New York: Penguin, 2010.

——— and Craig J. Thompson. "Introduction: Practicing Plenitude." In *Sustainable Lifestyles and the Quest for Plenitude: Case Studies of the New Economy*, edited by Juliet B. Schor and Craig J. Thompson, 1–25. New Haven: Yale University Press, 2014.

———and Craig J. Thompson, eds. *Sustainable Lifestyles and the Quest for Plenitude: Case Studies of the New Economy*. New Haven: Yale University Press, 2014.

Schulz, Charles-H. "Give up spoon-feeding: Use a fork instead." September 28. Accessed November 1, 2010. http://standardsandfreedom.net/index.php/2010/09/28/give-up-spoon-feeding-use-a-fork-instead/, 2010.

Schweik, Charles M. and Robert C. English, eds. *Internet Success: A Study of Open-Source Software Commons.* Cambridge, MA: MIT Press, 2012.

Scollan, Becca, Abby Byrnes, Malia Nagle, Paul Coyle, Cynthia York, and Maleka Ingram. "Drupal Usability Research Report." Interaction Design & Information Architecture, University of Baltimore, 2008.

Seidman, Stephen B. "The Role of Professional Societies in the Emergence of Software Engineering Professionalism in the United States and Canada." In IFIP International Federation for Information Processing, Volume 280, *E-Government; ICT Professionalism and Competences; Service Science,* edited by Antonino Mazzeo, Roberto Bellini, and Gianmario Motta; 59–67. Boston: Springer, 2008.

Selyukh, Alina. "U.S. Appeals Court Upholds Net Neutrality Rules in Full." *The Two-Way: Breaking News from NPR.* Accessed July 14, 2017. http://npr.org/sections/thetwo-way/2016/06/14/471286113/u-s-appeals-court-holds-up-net-neutrality-rules-in-full, 2016.

Sharwood, Simon. "Libre Office comes to Android." *The Register,* May 29. Accessed January 23, 2016. http://theregister.co.uk/2015/05/29/libre_office_comes_to_android/, 2015.

Shaw, Aaron. "Insurgent expertise: The politics of free/livre and open source software in Brazil." *Journal of Information Technology and Politics* 8 no. 3 (2011): 253–72.

Sheehan, Kerry. "Trump and his advisors on net neutrality." Accessed March 24, 2017. https://eff.org/deeplinks/2016/12/trump-and-his-advisers-net-neutrality, 2016.

Sneddon, Joey. "Ubuntu 18.04 to ship with GNOME desktop, not unity." *OMG! Ubuntu!* Accessed July 30, 2017. http://omgubuntu.co.uk/2017/04/ubuntu-18-04-ship-gnome-desktop-not-unity, 2017.

Snowden, Edward. "The last lighthouse: Free software in dark times." Keynote address at LibrePlanet, Cambridge, MA, March 19–20. Accessed March 2, 2017. https://media.libreplanet.org/u/libreplanet/m/libreplanet-2016-the-last-lighthouse-3d51/, 2016.

Söderberg, Johan. *Hacking Capitalism: The Free and Open Source Software Movement,* Routledge, New York, 2008.

Spreeuwenberg, Kimberley and Thomas Poell. "Android and the political economy of the mobile Internet: A renewal of open source critique." *First Monday* 17 (2012): 7. Accessed July 28, 2015. http://firstmonday.org/ojs/index.php/fm/article/view/4050/3271.

Shiva, Vandana. *Protect or Plunder? Understanding Intellectual Property Rights.* London: Zed Books, 2001.

Steinmetz, Kevin F. *Hacked: A Radical Approach to Hacker Culture.* New York: New York University Press, 2016.

Takhteyev, Yuri. *Coding Places: Software Practice in a South American City.* Cambridge, MA: The MIT Press, 2012.

Terranova, Tiziana. "Digital Labor." In *Digital Labor: The Internet as Playground and Factory,* edited by Trebor Scholz, 33–57. New York: Routledge, 2013.

The Document Foundation. *Progress Report about 2013 Fiscal Year.* Berlin: The Document Foundation, 2013.

———. *2014 Annual Report.* Berlin: The Document Foundation, 2014.

———. *2015 Annual Report*. Berlin: The Document Foundation, 2015a.

———. *Next Decade Manifesto*. Accessed December 29. http://wiki.document-foundation.org/TDF/Next_Decade_Manifesto, 2015b.

The H Open. "Oracle wishes LibreOffice the best, but won't directly cooperate." *The H Open*, 5 October, 2010.

Tigre, Paulo Bastos. *Technology and Competition in the Brazilian Computer Industry*. New York: St. Martin's Press, 1983.

Turkle, Sherry. *Reclaiming Conversation: The Power of Talk in a Digital Age*. New York: Penguin Press, 2015.

United Nations Centre on Transnational Corporations (UNCTC). *Transnational Corporations and Transborder Data Flows and Brazil*. New York: United Nations, 1982.

United Nations Centre on Transnational Corporations (UNCTC). *Transborder Data Flows: A Technical Paper*. New York: United Nations, 1983.

United States Telecom Association, et al., "*Amicus Curiae* Brief in Support of Respondents on Behalf of Writers Guild of America, West, Inc.; Future of Music Coalition; and National Alliance for Media Arts and Culture." Accessed November 21, 2017. static.politico.com/c0/2a/2917ce7e44eba011fbf229345f6, 2015.

U.S. House Committee on Commerce. *Report on the Digital Millennium Copyright Act of 1998*. Rept. 105–551, pt. 2. 105th Congress, 2d sess., 22 July, 1998. Washington, DC: U.S. Government Printing Office, 1998.

Vaccari, Cristian. *Digital Politics in Western Democracies: A Comparative Study*. Baltimore: Johns Hopkins University Press, 2013.

Vaccari, Cristian, Andrew Chadwick, and Ben O'Loughlin. "Dual screening the political: Media events, social media, and citizen engagement." *Journal of Communication* 65 (2015): 1041–1061.

Varisco, Daniel Martin. "September 11: Participant webservation of the 'War on Terrorism.'" *American Anthropologist* 104 (2002): 934–38.

Wallerstein, Immanuel. *The Modern World System*. New York: Academic Press, 1974.

———. "States? Sovereignty? The Dilemmas of Capitalists in an Age of Transition." In *States and Sovereignty in the Global Economy,* edited by David A. Smith, Dorothy J. Solinger, and Steven C. Topik, 20–33. London: Routledge, 1999.

Walls, Colin. "Software in cars." *Embedded*. Accessed July 26, 2017. http://embedded.com/design/operating-systems/4442406/Software-in-cars, 2016.

Wang, Xiapeng, Kuzmickaja, Ilona, Stol, Klaas-Ian, Abrahamsson, Pekka, and Brian Fitzgerald. "Microblogging in open source software development: The case of Drupal and twitter." *IEEE Software* 29 (2014): 2–10.

Weber, Steven. *The Success of Open Source*. Boston: Harvard University Press, 2004.

Wigand, Rolf T., Carrie Shipley, and Dwayne Shipley. "Transborder data flow, informatics, and national policies." *Journal of Communication* 34 (1984): 153–75.

Young, Robert. "Giving It Away: How Red Hat Software Stumbled across a New Economic Model and Helped Improve an Industry." In *Opensources: Voices from the Open Source Revolution*, edited by Chris DiBona, Sam Ockman, and Mark Stone, 113–25. Beijing: O'Reilly & Associates, Inc, 1999.

Interviews

Adacore executive. Interview by author. Paris, 2009.

——. Personal communication with author, 2017.

Adacore executive. Interview by author. Paris, 2010.

——. Interview by author. Paris, 2014.

Baudin. Pierre. (Association for Promotion and Research on Free Computing (April) staff member). Interview by author. Paris, 2016.

Chastain, Anton. (Board of Directors, Association for Promotion and Research on Free Computing). Interview by author. Paris, 2010.

Couchet, Frédéric (Executive Director, Association for Promotion and Research on Free Computing). Interview by author. Paris, 2010.

——. Interview by author. Paris, 2016.

Costa, Jorge da (Brazilian Drupal community member). Interview by author. Skype from Porto Alegre, 2014.

Daalman, Marie (Belgian Drupal developer). Interview by author. Skype from Rio de Janeiro, 2014.

Hallot, Olivier. (LibreOffice Brazil community member). Interview by author. Skype from Rio de Janeiro, 2010.

Huard, Margaux. (Squaring the Net staff member). Interview by author. Paris, 2016.

Project lead, OpenOffice.org Native Language Confederation. Interview by author. Paris, 2010.

Schulz, Charles-H. Interview by author. Paris, 2010.

The Document Foundation (TDF) Board member. Interview by author. Skype from Germany, 2010.

——. Interviews by author. Skype from Germany, 2011.

——. Interview by author. Skype from Germany, 2012.

Valk, Alain (French software developer). Interview by author. Paris, 2010.

Index

Printed in the United States
by Baker & Taylor Publisher Services

Printed in the United States
by Baker & Taylor Publisher Services